FROM THE PEWS IN THE BACK

From the Pews in the Back

Young Women and Catholicism

Edited by Kate Dugan and Jennifer Owens

Foreword by Mary Ann Hinsdale

Afterword by Donna Freitas

LITURGICAL PRESS

Collegeville, Minnesota

www.litpress.org

Cover design by Ann Blattner. Photo by Monica Haller.

Pseudonyms have been used in a number of these essays.

1	2	3	4	5	6	7	8

Library of Congress Cataloging-in-Publication Data

From the pews in the back : young women and Catholicism / edited by Kate Dugan and Jennifer Owens.
       p.   cm.
   ISBN 978-0-8146-3258-1 (pbk.)
    1. Catholic women—Religious life—United States.   2. Young women—Religious life—United States. I. Dugan, Kate. II. Owens, Jennifer.

BX1407.W65F76   2009
282'.7308422—dc22

                                    2008054743

Contents

Foreword

When Harvard Divinity School students Jen Owens and Kate Dugan contacted me a few years ago to ask my advice about a book project they were mulling over I was immediately eager to hear more about it. Having taught young Catholic women in undergraduate theology and graduate ministry courses for the past twenty-five years, I am often asked, "Are young people still interested in the Catholic Church?" When the question is posed even more specifically, as in, "What are *young Catholic women* thinking about the Catholic Church today?" it gets even trickier.

Since I am no longer a "young Catholic woman" (at least by the calendar's calculation), I resolve to fend off these invitations saying, "Why not ask *them* yourselves?" But many people who ask me such questions either don't have much contact with young adults (especially not with young Catholic women), or I soon learn that what they really want is for me to tell them what can be done about the fact that their son, daughter, or grandchildren don't go to church anymore.

So, I proceed to give an anecdote or two from my teaching experience and finally end up saying something like, "Well, you know, according to the social scientists who study the 'millennial generation,' the cliché 'I'm spiritual, but not religious' captures the attitude of many young people." I tend to agree generally that young people do not seem to be as "invested" in religious institutions as were previous generations; however, I also am convinced that social scientists have tended to neglect the *female* segment of millennials and hardly anyone has been listening to younger *Catholic* women.

I confess that I have "weakened" and have twice committed my thoughts to print on the subject of what young Catholic women are looking for from the church, but in each case my attempts to answer that question always end with an insistent, mantra-like "they simply want to be heard. But no one seems to be listening!"[1] Thus, it brings me great joy to see Jen and Kate's project come to fruition in *From the Pews in the Back*, and I am honored to be asked to include a few words here. But perhaps what is most exciting is that now, young Catholic women are saying it for themselves.

The collection that Jen and Kate have assembled rings true with the countless conversations and stories I have heard from young Catholic women. As Jen and Kate note, they are simply presenting a snapshot of young female voices within U.S. Catholicism. What I find especially appealing in these reminiscences, however, is that they are giving voice to the experience of a new, post–Vatican II generation of progressive laywomen who desire to claim their rightful role in the church they call home.

These essays shine a light on an underrepresented segment of that James Joycean version of Catholicism where "here comes everybody." The women whose reflections are assembled here— single, married, lesbian, straight, Anglo, Latina, Asian-American— are most of all *real*. Yes, they are a highly educated and theologically sophisticated group. Their religious identity has been forged in honesty, unflinchingly facing both the "beauty and the beastliness" of Catholicism. I am glad that their bushel baskets have been overturned so that my generation can see the bright, shining

---

[1] Mary Ann Hinsdale, "Is Anybody Listening? Catholic College Women Talk about the Church," *The Catholic World* 233 (1990): 54–56; "What Do Young Catholic Women Want (from Their Church)?" *New Theology Review* 20 (2007): 22–32.

light of their hopes for the future of the church. Reminiscences of family meals, the songs, prayer, and poetry that make up the rich sacramental imagination of Catholicism mark these reflections. In them we also read how the challenging, prophetic words of Jesus, reaching out to those most on the margin—the excluded, the vulnerable, the invisible—strengthen these women's resolve to be Catholic role models for others, especially their own children. In every story, even the ones by women who have become angry and disenchanted, there is both a longing for and a refusal to give up the conviction that Catholicism is home.

This is a book that I would give to anyone who wonders what young Catholic women are thinking about the church today. To be sure, there will be some who will shake their heads and think, "These smart women are wasting their time," or, "They'll get over it" (some may even consider them "deluded"). I hope, however, that older, progressive Catholics of my generation will perhaps find in these younger women the courage to carry on and that young Catholics seeking a church that not only preaches justice but acts justly will be heartened to find they are not alone.

Jen Owens and Kate Dugan are certainly conscious that there is no one-size-fits-all young Catholic woman. But they have discerned well that the voices of young women living on the edge, those who constantly find themselves negotiating between frustration with the patriarchy of the church and the threat of forced spiritual eviction from their religious home deserve to be heard. I applaud the courage, hope, and passionate ambivalence of these young women.

I wager that these first-person narratives will be a powerful spiritual resource for anyone who works with young Catholic women or who just wants to understand where they are coming from. I speak particularly to the ordained (bishops, priests, and deacons) who minister to and collaborate with women such as those represented in this volume. Whether one agrees with everything these authors are saying is not the issue. Listening to them, however, is vital to understanding an important segment of "generation next."

So, if you really are interested in listening to young Catholic women, I invite you to open yourself up to the stories collected in this book. I guarantee that if you do, you will *learn* a lot, you will *laugh* a lot, and at times, perhaps simply *lament*. But my fondest hope is that these essays will serve as a springboard for much-needed intergenerational conversations about what the Spirit is doing among young Catholic women at the beginning of this third millennium.

Mary Ann Hinsdale, IHM, PhD
Boston College
February 1, 2009

Acknowledgments

The Bantu-speaking people of South Africa recognize the spirit of *ubuntu*, the sense that, as Archbishop Desmond Tutu describes, "We are people through other people. We cannot be fully human alone. We are made for interdependence." In countless ways, this project has been birthed by each of the Catholics who influenced us, encouraged us, and urged us to *be* Catholic.

We are Catholic through other Catholics.

Though we cannot thank enough people for supporting us, we mention a few in a vain attempt to express gratitude. Robert Orsi of Northwestern University was the first person to affirm that an idea hatched on the Boston subway could become a real, live book and provided ongoing support as that began to happen. Fr. Tom Rausch, SJ, of Loyola Marymount University was the first professor to encourage Jen to continue writing and has been a dialogue partner since then, graciously critiquing parts of this text throughout its development. Tim Muldoon of Boston College became a cheerleader for this project, literally since the first day we met him, and has shared his time, his energy, and the fruits of his experience with us along the way—even though we were, scandalously, never students at Boston College. Jim Nickoloff, formerly of the College of the Holy Cross and Weston Jesuit School of Theology, organized Dorchester's Spirituality in the Pub and reminded us of the importance of conversation between the margins and the center. Mary Ann Hinsdale, IHM, of Boston College invited us in for tea, recommended reading, and crafted a foreword. Kerry Egan of Iowa Wordwrights encouraged us to be proud and unapologetic throughout this project. Kerry Maloney of Harvard Divinity School advised us to tend our friendship, assuring us that the book would flow from there. Roberto Goizueta of Boston College offered Kate academic space to research this project. Susan Abraham of Harvard Divinity School carefully critiqued a draft of our manuscript, and Ryan Rivera's last minute read of the introduction helped us to assert our goals, finally. Thank you, all.

And thank you to Helena Fleig, Stephanie Almozara, and Christy Cummings, our friends, conversation partners, and fellow Catholics at Harvard. To Kate's mom, whose weekly read of *Our Sunday Visitor* helped us recruit authors. To Greg Skinner, who came to know this project as his "other wife." To Jen's brothers and sister—to David, whose openness about his experience of faith inspired Jen to write about hers, and to Dan and Janeen, whose spirit and imagination continue to bring light to Jen's life. To Jen's parents, who have instilled in her an appreciation for stories of all kinds.

Finally, to the more than one hundred young women who shared their stories of Catholic identity with us—thank you. You inspire us.

Introduction

Two years ago, we walked into the back room of an Irish pub in Dorchester, Massachusetts. The room was filled with a group of Catholics eager to discuss Catholic identity in higher education. We found seats among women who could have been our grandmothers—women who experienced the renewal of the Second Vatican Council as adults. Some left their habits at the convent, many opened doors for Catholic women in theological education, and all found themselves attending Mass in the vernacular. We also sat down among women who could have been our mothers—women who weaned themselves from the *Baltimore Catechism*, reacted to *Humanae Vitae*, and encouraged their daughters to become altar boys. Yet only a few members of that first generation of girl altar servers sat among us, and we wondered why we didn't hear more women our age talking about being Catholic.

In front of us, a woman with kind eyes and graying hair wondered aloud why young people aren't at Mass, aren't *really* acting very Catholic. To our left, a woman in her fifties looked at us and wondered where young Catholics go after they graduate from Catholic colleges. A woman who didn't catch our eyes asked, Why don't they get it? They have to be patient with the church. They need to stay and make the changes we haven't been able to make.

It's hard to find the right words when asked to speak for an entire population. So, mostly, we didn't say much. At one point,

Jen talked about the need for more engaging catechesis, but the conversation quickly returned to worried anecdotes about absent-from-the-pews young adult Catholics. We sat there quietly, listening.

After two hours of saying very little, we were anything but quiet on the subway ride home. Why, we wanted to know, is Mass attendance *the* trademark of Catholic identity? Why not include a commitment to social justice or service work? And was there a misconception in the room that because we grew up after Vatican II, we didn't grow up memorizing prayers or learning Catholic guilt?

We walked off the subway and, for the next couple months, kept wondering: What makes us say "I'm Catholic," especially when so many of our Catholic grade school friends no longer do? How do young women describe Catholic identity? How do we express our Catholicism? How would conversations like the one in Dorchester be different if young women had a significant voice? We have spent our Catholic lives learning from the experiences of Vatican II Catholics; what could these older Catholics learn from our experiences?

Our generation is the first to come of age without any experiences of pre–Vatican II Catholicism, and that makes us a bit of an anomaly to older Catholics who knew popes before John Paul II and can't imagine grade school Masses in English. Our Catholicism looks different from the Catholicism of women who grew up in the 1950s or 1960s. Nuns no longer surround us in our Catholic grade schools and we are invited to lead parts of liturgies. We grew up with first reconciliations rather than first confessions, and parish musicians played guitars, not just pipe organs. Our Catholic identity—filled with an appreciation for Catholic spirituality, supported by experiences of Mass in the vernacular, and flush with high expectations for the roles of women—is unprecedented in the history of American Catholicism.

Yet, as it did on the previous generation's women, being Catholic is having a powerful impact on our lives. Catholic social teaching is the reason many women decide to commit them-selves to lives of service. A lifelong appreciation of the depth of the Catholic tradition inspires a new generation of scholars to work for change from within the institution. Despite the church's position on gay marriage, the pull of Catholic identity keeps lesbians attending Mass. And a realization that Catholicism can be written into our DNA, ingrained in our bones, is part of why Catholic women called to priesthood have not become Episcopalians.

This collection—twenty-nine memoirs about being Catholic and young and a woman written by authors born in the 1970s and 1980s—is our attempt to explore these often conflicting, sometimes complementary, realities.

We both grew up in Catholic families, came of age in Catholic communities, and graduated from Catholic universities.

We met as students at Harvard Divinity School, where neither of us had ever felt so *Catholic*. Studying at a largely Protes-tant divinity school taught us that young Catholic women have unique perspectives on religious identity. We encountered an unspoken assumption that religious expression should be quiet, subdued, interior. In contrast, our religious lives were shaped by parading through our hometowns as we prayed the Stations of the Cross and by receiving birthday gifts of Catholic trinkets—statues filled with holy water, crucifixes, rosaries, illustrated copies of *The Lives of the Saints*. Hearing classmates profess an Emersonian personal consciousness or describe their Bud-dhist quest toward Enlightenment was startling in contrast to our own experiences of memorizing Vatican-proclaimed moral dictums as teenagers. At a time when it is hip to write your own spirituality, we can recite Mass parts and the rote prayers of our childhood without skipping a beat. And perhaps most jar-ring, at Harvard we studied with women who will be ordained leaders in United Church of Christ, Presbyterian, and Lutheran congregations, acutely aware of just how closed the door to ordination is to us.

Reflecting on our first year at Harvard, we realized our Catholicism made us distinct, in both our pluralist academic environment and in our Catholic community. Our religious practices seemed quaint and old-fashioned to our peers; the exclusion of women from the collar, archaic. We were astonished to realize we were somewhat foreigners in a predominantly Protestant landscape. And, yet, as young women with unique perspectives on being Catholic, we also felt like foreigners among the Catholics in Dorchester.

So we started asking other young Catholic women how they talk, think, and write about being Catholic. In February 2007, we started a blog, www.fromthepewsintheback.com, and began inviting women born in the 1970s and 1980s to write and send us stories about their Catholic identity. We designed a poster and sent it to college campuses, parishes, and intentional communities across the country. We printed playbills and carried them around in our backpacks, handing them to any woman who outed herself as under thirty-six and Catholic. We e-mailed any young woman we thought might be interested in writing about being Catholic, and anyone we imagined might know someone who would be interested. We contacted previously published authors who we hoped might write for this collection.

Two months later, we had received just over one hundred memoirs by women from around the country. The majority of the memoirs we received came from women who have, at some point, struggled to be Catholic and hold political or social positions against which Catholicism teaches—moms who have been on birth control, female seminarians who believe in women's ordination, lesbians who don't believe their lifestyle ought to be condemned.

Many of the young women in this collection push boundaries of the Vatican's definition of Catholic identity, and do so with profound respect. These women are high school teachers and campus ministers, HIV/AIDS patient caregivers and lawyers, students and sisters, grant writers and journalists. These authors live committed lives, and they bring that same commitment to exploring and defining Catholic identity. We are forward-thinking women of faith whose reflections on our experiences of life are filled with hope, and we challenge our church to think carefully about how it can be even more faithful to Jesus' radically inclusive message.

◆

Several Vatican II Catholics have researched our generation with devotion, working to understand how we express our Catholic identity. And to these, our teachers, we are grateful. Yet, with this collection, we are excited that young women are the authors—we do not speak through the filter of a researcher or a statistician, but from our experiences of being Catholic. By creating a place for ourselves in the conversation about young adult Catholic identity, we are shaping the story of our experiences within the wider Catholic tradition.

In *Speaking of Faith*, religion commentator Krista Tippett describes the power of "narrative theology"—the first person attempt to describe religious identity and ideas. There is, she writes, "a profound difference between hearing someone say this is *the* truth, and hearing someone say this is *my* truth." Throughout this collection, women's identities bump up against Catholic identities—and we explore the collisions and messiness. We speak honestly and carefully from our own perspectives, of our own truths, creating our own narrative theologies.

As editors, our individual experiences are rooted in our Catholic communities. So much so that even in our late twenties, we can still recite the rote prayers we learned as children—Guardian Angel; Bless Us, O Lord; Our Father; Hail Mary; Glory Be; the Nicene Creed. These prayers gave rhythm to our Catholic upbringings. We bowed our heads to them before meals and held hands to them each Sunday. We mouthed them quickly before tests and track meets. Their rhythms continue to have a grounding effect on our transient, twenty-something lives. Hearing them echo off the lips of a congregation at Mass and reciting them alongside loved ones reminds us just how Catholic we are. Reflecting the power of these prayers in Catholic identity, we open each of the five chapters with a popular rote prayer.

Because this project is both personal and public for us, we have interwoven our own stories of Catholic identity. At several places in our introductions, we switch from this joint voice to Jen's or to Kate's individual one. While this project has been a life-giving partnership, our experiences of Catholicism are different, and the occasional shifts in voice throughout give us the chance to weave the chapter's theme and prayer into our own Catholic experiences.

The first chapter, "Growing Up Catholic," explores the powerful pushes and pulls of being raised Catholic. In their often-cited study, *Young Adult Catholics: Religion in the Culture of Choice*, sociologist Dean Hoge and his team conclude that there is a "Catholic glue," a firm, yet somewhat indefinable, imprint of Catholicism that keeps young adults saying, "I am Catholic." Three-quarters of the Hoge sample report that being Catholic is "special" and they cannot imagine themselves in another tradition, but only 31 percent go to Mass weekly. Even if young Catholics don't attend Mass regularly and don't participate in the weekly life of a parish, young adults baptized as children are still quite likely to say, "I am Catholic." The question lingers after reading Hoge: why are young Catholics working creatively to carve out a space in the tradition? For the authors in this chapter, the answer appears to be rooted in growing up Catholic.

The young women in chapter 2, "Faith in Action," explore the relationship between being Catholic and crafting lives committed to service and social justice. Thousands of young Catholic women spend their spring breaks doing service projects around the country and around the world. After college, many of these women commit to a year or two of service and social justice work in programs like the Colorado Vincentian Volunteers, the Jesuit Volunteer Corps, or the St. Joseph Workers.

Jesuit priest and Catholic theologian Thomas Rausch, after years of observing the students in his classroom, worries that our generation's emphasis on service and social justice work threatens to reduce being religious into leading ethical lives. Rausch, in *Being Catholic in a Culture of Choice*, describes a need for the majority of young Catholics to more intimately understand the relationship between social justice and Catholic identity. The women in this chapter understand that need. For many, a passion for serving others and striving for justice is fertile ground for growing healthy and dynamic Catholic identities. After being reminded of the power of a Catholicism that is lived for the poor, Kate Barch Heaton writes, "The knowledge that I *can* live courageously for God, sharing my home and comforts with friends rich and poor—this knowledge sustains me." This linking of social justice and Catholic identity keeps us saying, "Yes, I'm Catholic."

Our third chapter is broadly titled, "Being a Catholic Woman." The need for this chapter grew out of a theme we noticed in many memoirs—a tension between being Catholic and being a woman in the twenty-first century United States. Several women in this chapter are what we are calling conscientized Catholics. We're aware of the church's shortcomings and are in the midst of discerning how to work from within the church and our Catholic identity to address them. On the whole, we are more informed about the tradition than most members of our generation, having attended Catholic universities or attained advanced degrees in theology. Within the context of the Catholic Church, we are going through the process of what liberation educator Paulo Friere describes as conscientization, a process of reflection, awareness, and action. We are reflecting on their own experiences of exclusion from the hierarchy, like Meagan Yogi does with her childhood realization that she cannot be a priest. We are becoming aware of oppression as Margaret Scanlon does in asking why the Virgin Mary is regularly held up as her model for being a Catholic woman. And we are starting to make change in the church like Deborah Heimel who works, in small ways, to have conversations about homosexuality in the church. All the while, the women in this chapter claim Catholicism as their own.

In the fourth chapter of this collection, "Vocation," young women describe their journeys of understanding how they are called to live. Vocation can be a tricky thing for young Catholic women. In our lives outside the church, we have more career opportunities than Catholic women before us—and we expect that same expanse of opportunity in our church lives. As the women in this collection illustrate, our generation grew up playing Mass in the homes we were raised in, exploring an expansive variety of ways to pray in Catholic school, and traveling around the country doing service work. We seek active roles in our faith communities. Many of us attend seminary with laymen and priests-in-training, ever aware that we are unable to answer calls to ordained priesthood. So we find creative ways to live out our vocations. Laywomen study to become Catholic theologians, a twenty-something English major discovers a calling in caring for HIV/AIDS patients, a feminist uses her Catholic life to change unjust structures, and an artist finds that her call to write connects her to God.

Chapter 5 is called "Spiritual Identity" because the memoirs in this section challenge the assumption that so many young Americans are drawing a thick line between being "spiritual" and "religious." Certainly, many of us, including many Catholics, do. Even so, the Hoge study suggests that when young Catholics look for more in their spiritual lives, we actually tend to look within the Catholic tradition to find ways of being spiritual—to Thomas Merton's contemplative practices, to biblical stories of faith, to Jesus' real presence in the Eucharist. There is something inescapable about Catholic ritual that becomes a part of us. Our identities are bound up in Catholic spirituality. We sit in the pews in the back during Mass, our babies laugh and talk and fuss from the crying room, our eyes scan the crowd for potential friends or partners. We explore other traditions, and they expand our understanding of Catholicism. Being Catholic is not a side note to these women's identities—the women in this chapter are in the midst of figuring out how to be *both* spiritual and Catholic.

◆

During a high school trip to confession, Emily Jendzejec waited in line behind her lifelong best friend, Natalie. As Emily prepared to tell the priest her sins, "Natalie opened the door and with her head hung low, made her way to the altar to do her penance, flashing that same annoyed grin only a best friend can understand."

Emily giggled after a frustrating experience with the sacrament of reconciliation, all the while fully participating. This is the spirit of Catholicism alive in these memoirs—young women who wink and cross their fingers at parts of the tradition, while they stake a firm claim in their Catholic identity. Here are twenty-nine women who acknowledge the pushes and pulls of being Catholic in this generation, and who do so for at least twenty-nine different reasons. No two stories in the pages that follow are the same, though some common themes emerge.

We find these stories engrossing—some make us laugh, some make us pause, and after reading others, our eyes well up. But perhaps what we find most powerful in this project is the emerging sense of solidarity. We feel a sense of community that comes from knowing that other young women are talking about and thinking about and figuring out how to be Catholic and young and a woman. And we find kinship here.

Inspired by this kinship, we bring together the voices of twenty-nine women who further the dialogue about what it means to be Catholic—and their perspectives are only the beginning. The breadth and depth of the experiences of young Catholic women offer a wellspring of faith-filled wisdom. We invite Catholics of all backgrounds, perspectives, and histories to join us in a dialogue that Catholic women lead and the full Catholic community facilitates. And we invite men and women from many faith communities to join us. We do not know where these women's voices will lead, yet we are filled with hope that this collection will expand, cultivate, and challenge a conversation about shifting religious identities. Welcome.

Growing Up Catholic

Angel of God, my guardian dear,
To whom God's love commits me here,
Ever this day be at my side,
To light, to guard, to rule, and guide.
Amen.

A distinct Catholic birthmark is an inescapable part of the identities of the women in this chapter. We had guardian angels and rosaries at bedtime. And Catholic school uniforms that required creativity as we squeaked out our individuality. We knelt during Sunday morning Mass, and we have ex-nuns for moms, ex-priests for dads. We celebrated Folk Masses, crowned the Virgin Mary in May, and made first reconciliation.

We are undeniably Catholic, by birthright.

For as long as I (Jen) can remember, Sunday Mass has been a regular part of my family's routine. If I ever doubt that I should study theology, my mom reminds me how much I loved going to Mass when I was small. She describes how I would try to sing along, standing as best I could atop that wooden pew, my arms outstretched, waving and clapping in time with the cantor's; how I would bow my head with the rest of the congregation as they recited communal prayers, my own lips moving with the rhythm

1

of theirs, not quite shaping the same words but sensing that something holy was happening in these people coming together and wanting to be a part of it.

*I have fond memories of Masses at St. Irenaeus. The nubbiness of the ratty brown carpet over the cold linoleum in the parish hall where we had children's Mass, how privileged I felt to sit with my brother so close to where the priest gave the homily. The almost overwhelming smell of incense that seeped into our clothes during Lent; how it made those dresses and skirts I so resented having to wear each Sunday slightly more tolerable. The procession of candles and the pilgrims who carried them on Holy Thursday; how small I felt walking out of the church amid all those flickering lights. What it was like to be a part of the chorus of voices—*Jesus, remember me when you come into your kingdom—*echoing through our neighborhood as we made our way to reverence the Eucharist before Good Friday. I was only beginning to understand what it meant, knowing that it was bigger than me, than my family, than our community. Something in all of that made it transcendent.*

Mass was a part of my family's routine, but it was more than that too. It was a holy deep breath that readied us to plunge back into our day-to-day lives.

Nelle Carty's family inhaled that holy deep breath most evenings at their dinner table. With her family each night, Nelle learned how to pray and how to enjoy family time. At that table she also learned that her dad used to be a priest and her mom a nun before they started the Carty family. Watching her parents devote themselves to both family and Catholicism inspires Nelle—she realizes that being Catholic "will always remain an integral part of who I am."

Angela Batie can relate. Her former-nun-turned-mom always knew a lot more about eucharistic theology than she did about the social cues of 1980s moms. Together, they stumbled through everything from skating parties to First Communion. Growing up with her mom, Angela is realizing, formed her Catholicism; her mom, Angela writes, gave "me Catholicism just as much as she [gave] me thick hair and the strange shape of my instep."

Like Nelle and Angela, part of Sr. Julie Vieira's Catholicism feels genetic, like it has been passed on through bloodlines as much as any other way. As a daughter of a faith-filled guitar player, she spent countless rehearsals for Folk Mass running through church pews, exploring holy sites, tiptoeing into the sacristy. This appreciation for the sacred infuses the way she looks at the world—now, holiness is all around her, not only in church.

Growing up in my (Kate's) family implied Catholicism—we lived a block away from the Catholic grade school and a half block from the church. I was eighteen and in college before I realized most kids don't grow up with a guardian angel watching out for their souls, lots of families skip religious observations while on vacation, and not everyone tries to understand what the priest is saying when he turns off the microphone during the Benediction.

Eileen Campbell's family shared that sense of implicit Catholicism. Her grandma was born in Knock, Ireland, in the year the Virgin appeared there. Pictures of JFK and Bobby hung next to pictures of the pope on the walls of her grandparents' home. Even as Eileen has repeatedly tried not to be Catholic, being Catholic is, she surrenders, "in my blood and bones and sinews and inner world, despite what seemed like my best efforts to keep it out."

In many ways, these women are describing the "Catholic glue" that Hoge and his team observed in young adult Catholics— and it certainly sticks for Sarah Keller. She fondly remembers the drama of her "first real date," both of them dressed in their Catholic school uniforms and eleven-and-a-half-year-old Sarah convinced they'd marry. And that drama seems appropriate— after all, we had angels watching over us and we learned math and transubstantiation in the same room. Of course we'd marry our first kiss.

Elizabeth Duclos-Orsello's glue looks different—it is mired in the yawning gap she feels between being Catholic and being feminist. Ever since her confirmation, Elizabeth has been looking for creative ways to hold these two pieces of her identity together. Growing up under the wing of her mother's activist Catholicism and her father's former priesthood has kept that process dynamic.

This chapter is full of memories like these—formative ones that help us make sense of why we continue to claim Catholicism as our own.

The Communion Dress

Angela Batie

The information packet sent to parents in preparation for First Communion stressed that dresses did not have to be fancy. Simple and pretty would suffice. The parish was trying to shift the focus of the special day from frilly dresses to the actual sacrament. My mother's greatest error was believing it. To be fair, it wasn't her fault that she didn't know better. In the decades when her sisters and friends were raising children, my mother was Sister Helen in a Benedictine convent.

By the time she had me, she was twenty years older than the other mothers, hardly privy to their inside information—birthday party locations (the Tacoma Soccer Club, of course), the correct bicycle brand (Huffy), and the de rigueur in plaid uniforms (the jumper with the bib top that could be removed upon entering sixth grade). My mother was a working mother at the Catholic hospital, my parties were in the backyard, and my uniform was a throwback to 1951, the one-piece shapeless v-neck version. Mom might have had a better grasp of eucharistic theology than any of the other mothers, but she wasn't quite sure how to dress her daughter for the occasion.

Most of the time, my mother and I stumbled through these things together, like two sleuths without all the clues. And we *were* able to make just enough sense of the social mores to stave off complete disaster. The times we missed the mark were close misses, a general approximation of the right answer: a Trapper Keeper in the wrong color, pet mice instead of kittens. The communion dress might have been a close miss too if the stakes had not been so high. Even here, Mom got quite a few things right—the veil, haloed by small, synthetic white flowers, and lace-trimmed ankle socks with white patent leather shoes whose heels click-clicked when they bounced against the linoleum in our kitchen.

But the dress was one mistake after another. We found it—my rainbow dress—at the Kids' Exchange, a consignment store we frequented. It wasn't a rainbow of primary colors, but it was most certainly a shocking palate of pastel pinks, purples, greens, blues, and yellows in a vertical striped pattern. It even had a snappy white jacket, making the whole ensemble one of the prettiest outfits I had seen in my life. As I stepped out onto the front porch of our house, Mom stood beaming at me and Dad took out the camera, his Protestant baptism and skepticism about the divinity of Jesus not dampening his pride. My little sister shyly fingered the delicate lace at the hem, gazing reverently at the thin fabric. In all honesty, I was crazy about that dress. I felt beautiful.

Until I got to the church.

The first person I saw was Natalie. Her dress was shiny and satiny—all white, all Nordstrom. All I knew of Nordstrom was that there was a piano on the first floor with a small man playing it and that we didn't go in there. Sarah, who was similar to Natalie in all things, had a similar dress. I was accustomed to being the odd one out in our tenuous threesome, so my sense of mild disorientation was not unfamiliar. But then I saw Anna, and her dress was all white with a bell-shaped skirt. I could almost hear it ring as it swooshed back and forth. I started to worry.

The final straw was Jane, who was usually as socially clumsy as I was, but whose mother was a seamstress. Her dress had a full skirt with bits of tulle underneath and was adorned with layer upon layer of lace trim and pearly beads. Her short sleeves were full and puffy, she had thick white tights under her gown—and the gloves! She even had lace, wrist-length gloves, just like a lady. I took notice and looked every direction on the church steps, realizing that I was adrift in a gleaming sea of white, my rainbow like a bold stroke upon a blank canvas. I saw my mom gazing at the crowd. Her face looked like it did the time we hit a baby deer with our car at Mount Saint Helen. I saw my dad, hand on my mom's shoulder, his camera now dangling from his wrist, abandoned; documenting this moment no longer seemed such a good idea.

Natalie's unruly kinks and Sarah's sporty ponytail had both been coaxed and persuaded into gentle waves that, though they looked soft, didn't budge beneath the thick veneer of Aqua Net. Even *their* mothers couldn't have done that, a fact they confirmed when they boasted about the family friend who had come by the house to do their hair and paint their nails. I touched my practical, stick-straight bowl cut and was disappointed that it hadn't spontaneously curled without my knowledge.

Somewhere between the final bell on Friday and the Saturday morning eucharistic celebration my friends had become fluffed and meringued, and the parish hall looked more like a glossy sheet torn from a grocery checkout bridal magazine than the place where I had eaten maple bars after Mass so many times before. They looked the part even more than my sister and I did when we were make-believe brides pacing evenly down the garden path in our backyard, roses from Mom's garden clutched in our grasp. No one had said anything about getting married today.

We gathered in the foyer in the rear of the church, forming two lines like dominoes, each bride walking alongside one of our male counterparts. A man I had never seen before dodged to and fro down the aisle with a big camera, but I knew that you weren't allowed to walk around during the procession, and the priest wasn't even stopping him! My friends (or so I thought—I couldn't really recognize them from behind any more) stepped forward one-by-one into this suddenly unfamiliar sanctuary, picture-perfect brides of Christ pacing delicately forward. My cheeks felt hot and my stomach felt like it was pulsing, threatening to pop right out of my belly button, the same way it felt the time I was scolded for talking during silent reading. My shiny new shoes were bolted to the worn carpet.

This wasn't what I thought I was getting into.

I had been practicing for First Communion at the Catholic hospital, where Mom and I carried out secret communion ceremonies. I "helped" Mom at work by staying underfoot as she prepared the chalice and paten for Sunday morning Mass, laying out carefully ironed linens, each with a tiny red embroidered cross front and center. In the privacy of the sacristy, Mom (the priest) would reverently administer the sacrament (host, unconsecrated) to my piously outstretched hands. The twinkle in her eye was the only hint that we were frauds.

She was the first lay chaplain to be hired by that hospital, a position that eventually led to her promotion as the pastoral care director for the whole Franciscan healthcare system in our area. The colleagues I met as she went about her work were all distinguished by "Father" or "Sister." I tried to imagine my mother with the same white-brimmed veil as the nuns, but all that I could envision was Mom in the blue velour bathrobe that she wore while watching the Seahawks with me lodged under her arm, my forehead on her shoulder. Even the patients didn't quite know what to make of a lay chaplain, and when she was pregnant with me they addressed her as "Sister" in spite of her seven-months-pregnant physique.

Tales of her ministry at the hospital were never privy to my sister's and my probing. She shielded us from the grief, illness, and death she witnessed daily. The only time she talked with me about her work in any detail, I was a high school student filled with aspirations to be a math teacher or lawyer. I asked how her day was when she stepped into the living room, a question of formality rather than curiosity. Her thick tone alerted me that her answer would be anything but rote. She sat down next to me and described a chapel service that morning. One of the women interns, a Protestant minister, preached a beautiful sermon, she told me. Mom described her poise, her wit, her wisdom. As I listened, she told me, confessionally, that she had started to cry at the end of the sermon, but not because its content moved her. "I realized that you would never be able to do that in our church." She took off her glasses and rubbed a lens with the crumpled tissue in her hand.

Her observation seemed strange at the time. I had never considered that I would want to preach, much less that it would be painful to be prohibited from doing so. That moment stewed and simmered for years, though, and carved a space in me where I became receptive to the ways God was drawing me into a vocation to serve the church. Mom saw something in me that I couldn't identify for myself until much later, when the roundabout road of discernment led me first to a lay service program, then to a part-time job in ministry, and finally to Yale Divinity School.

Now, when she tells curious acquaintances about my graduation and my new job as a campus minister, they often speculate that I'm following in her footsteps. It isn't that I have mimicked her choice of profession, though. It was the way she lived that cultivated a place where the seeds of vocation could take root and sprout. My sister and I didn't fully understand what she did from nine to five, but we received the ministry that took place in our household, the way she presided over our conversations and was priest to our confessions. She treated *us* like vessels of the altar, reverently and gently. We would turn to her words of encouragement as though they were Scripture. Her affirmations, like pieces of psalms, her insights gospel. In life's dire circumstances, we clung to those words like rosary beads.

She bestowed one of these verses while we stood at the Sea-Tac airport at 4:30 in the morning, waiting for my flight to graduate school. Dad circled the airport in the family car to evade parking regulations while Mom walked in with me, neither of us quite ready to let go. I asked her, voice wavering, why it was so hard to say goodbye. She bit her lips and opened her teary eyes wide, "Love makes you want to be with your beloved."

The security officer pounced and shuffled her away, and I was left alone, her words making it hard to swallow.

Years later, awakening to feminism and desperate for guidance, I asked my mother why she had stayed in the church. There was no pause. "Because it's home," was all she said. I realized that this home of hers was, unexpectedly, home for me too. She had given me Catholicism just as much as she had given me my thick hair or the strange shape of my instep. It's my inheritance, a home with a roof that leaks sometimes, and a basement that smells musty, but that has strong beams and stands against the wind. She is unapologetic about it, even when I wrestle with some of the issues that loom over the church, particularly when I open ordination invitations from my classmates. She doesn't see my future as one of heartbreak and struggle, but one full of promise, deeply enriching and meaningful.

We laugh, now, about my First Communion wardrobe fiasco, and I am mischievously proud of the dress I wore that day in second grade. From the back of the sanctuary I had paused and scanned the congregation for my parents, finding their heads turned expectantly in the roped-off pews at the front of the church. As my mother's gaze locked on mine, I finally found the familiar in that suddenly foreign place. The photographer and these strange children walking alongside receded from view until it was just Mom and me in the sacristy of the hospital chapel.

And just like that, the thumping in my stomach became excitement and my bolted-down shoes released their grip on the floor. Even the rainbow First Communion dress couldn't interfere with God that day. I fidgeted quietly through the service until the big moment, then walked toward the altar just as we had practiced. My family stood slightly behind me when I stepped toward the priest, hands outstretched and eager to receive what was given. An unfamiliar warmth settled in the place where I figured my heart was. In those moments, I understood why we were supposed to kneel after Communion. I understood that I was participating in something greater than myself. As I retreated to the pew, I saw my classmates bathed in the light from the stained-glass windows, a rainbow of colors—honeyed oranges, Lenten purples, passion reds—tinting their white dresses and dancing in their curls.

After a year of service with the Holy Cross Associates, Angela Batie earned her Master of Divinity from Yale Divinity School. She now works as a campus minister at St. Louis University.

Small Rebellions, Small Surrenders

Eileen Campbell

As far back as I can remember, my experience of being Catholic has been full of tiny, undramatic, barely noticeable rebellions. My first open rebellion failed—the one where I informed my parents, at age eight, after what must have felt like years of frustration, that I had decided to leave Our Lady of the Cape and become a Unitarian. After that, I hid my protests, priding myself on mouthing the words to prayers at Mass instead of speaking them; or, on braver days, refusing to move my lips at all; referring in a low grumble to the weekly CCD classes as "Cape Cod Dump." Later, in high school, driving to the evening Mass and instead of going inside, shivering in the car reading Kerouac by flashlight. "What was the homily about?" my parents would ask when I returned home. "Jesus," I'd snap as I ran upstairs and slammed my bedroom door.

I don't think it occurred to my parents that they might have a kid who wouldn't want to be Catholic. They were both raised in Irish-Catholic families in Irish-Catholic neighborhoods in New York City. My mother's grandmother was born in Knock, Ireland, the year that the Virgin Mary appeared there. I inherited an appreciation for the miraculous from her side of the family. My father's father was born in Donegal, Ireland; he and his brothers joined the informal ranks of what would later be called the Irish Republican Army. The political dimension of being Irish

Catholic I inherited from him, along with a slew of rebel songs. My parents went to Catholic schools. Cousins and siblings became nuns and monks. A picture of the pope and portraits of JFK and Bobby hung in my grandparents' living rooms. Being Catholic was the air my family breathed.

I staged a second rebellion as a teenager. I told my parents that I was practically an adult, and, seeing as we lived in a democracy, they couldn't force me to be Catholic any longer. They made it clear that I would attend Mass or find another place to live, but they did strike a deal. If I went through with the two-year preparation for confirmation, I could decide between being confirmed or leaving the church. I reluctantly agreed, and dutifully, if smugly, attended the classes, sniggering occasionally in the face of the impossible and the miraculous that Catholics are asked to accept as truth. "What is your problem with the virgin birth?" my confirmation teacher asked once, in response to one of my outbursts. "Well, come on," I replied with a snort. Who was she kidding?

As confirmation approached, the instructors impressed upon us the weight of the decision we were about to make. We would become adults in the community, they told us. Were we ready? I didn't think so. I felt only the weight of the tradition bearing down on me, suffocating me, demanding that I turn off my brain. I simply assumed that the rest of my fellow students weren't listening, or didn't care. How else was it possible that I didn't know anyone with doubts like mine? How were they all so blindly obedient and unquestioning?

After completing the two years of preparatory classes, I decided to tell my parents that I had made up my mind to call it quits with Catholicism. I sat with my father in the front seat of my parents' Toyota, parked just outside his parents' retirement home in upstate New York. Somehow, it seemed like the right time to fess up. "I've decided not to get confirmed," I nervously blurted out. It is possible that I just added it to a more innocuous statement, something like, "Yes, it really *is* amazing that Grandpa makes ten pounds of mashed potatoes every time we're here and, by the way, I'm not getting confirmed." I suspected my father would be sympathetic. After all, this was the man who had raised me in the rebellious folk tradition of Pete Seeger, Peter, Paul, and Mary, and Tom Paxton, and who had always reminded me, in Joseph Campbell's words, to "follow your bliss."

"It's not for me," I told him. I couldn't find God within the confines of the church, and I wanted to be honest about who I was. That's when he told me, in not so many words, that he and my mother had been bluffing all along, and that I had better figure out a way to reconcile with the church before my confirmation date. Besides, did I want to break my grandmother's heart? Astonished, I played what seemed like my last card. I warned him, "If you ask me to do this, I'll be standing up in front of the entire congregation and lying to them, not to mention to the priest and the bishop, and our entire extended family."

"Okay," he replied. It was a compromise he could live with, one that wouldn't kill my grandmother on the spot.

Looking back, more than a decade later, I am relieved I decided not to break my grandmother's heart. But at the time, it felt like a choice between staying true to myself and surrendering to the mandates of a communal identity. My conflict with my parents over my Catholicism was perhaps a microcosm of that larger struggle to be both Catholic and a modern American.

I can't identify a specific turning point when I started thinking about Catholicism differently. Instead, like my small, unsuccessful rebellions as a kid, the rest of my life as a Catholic has involved small moments that have brought me closer to a reconciliation with where I came from: a moment of conflict during college when I realized that my family's values were not universal; a transcendent flash in Jerusalem, looking out over the City of David as dusk fell, when I acknowledged how much the Christian story means to me; or, last summer, at a family reunion in Donegal, when I joined my grandfather's former parish at a graveyard Mass. There, standing on my great-grandparents' grave, looking out at the green-brown hills while the priest recited the Our

Father in Gaelic, I felt that praising is also powerfully connected to rootedness—to family and tradition, and also to the earth.

Turning back toward Catholicism has been not so much a process of letting it in as discovering that it is already there—in my blood and bones and sinews and inner world, despite what seemed like my best efforts to keep it out. These small epiphanies have been moments of powerful surrender. Like surrendering to a power greater than myself, they have shown me the value of subsuming a piece of my individuality to a larger whole. This does not make me feel small, but expansive. It is the feeling that, as Augustine writes, "I cannot grasp the totality of what I am."

And yet, this process of surrender is not uncomplicated. The Catholic Church as an institution holds firmly to policies of exclusion toward women and gays that I find abhorrent and irreconcilable with the radically inclusive message of the gospels. That I tentatively call myself Catholic now does not mean that I have reconciled those things with the rest of what it means to be Catholic. Instead, I have sought out different models of being within the Catholic Church, people like Dorothy Day, Gustavo Gutiérrez, and South African Bishop Kevin Dowling, who embody Catholicism's long-standing dedication to justice and to the poor. Dowling runs an HIV/AIDS hospice and treatment center in Freedom Park, a shantytown where 50 percent of the mothers test HIV positive. He was the first African bishop to call on the church to lift the ban on condoms, arguing that in the context of HIV/AIDS, condoms prevent the transmission of death. His rebellions have not yet exiled him from church leadership; in the meantime, he calls himself a member of the "loyal resistance." After meeting Bishop Kevin through my own work on HIV/AIDS, I recognized that those elements that inspire and sustain Dowling in his work—his deep reverence for the beauty and dignity of every human person, his hope and generosity in the face of overwhelming despair, his commitment to justice and an authentic ethic of life—also emanate from our shared tradition. And if he is a member of the "loyal resistance," this is a label I would be proud to claim.

I don't seek answers now in the same way that I did as a teenager—I have more room for contradiction, for the push and pull of living in two worlds, two times, and two histories. And while I continue to seek and find the sacred in unexpected places, I now see the value in trying to find God in the particular, in the stories and rituals that were handed down to me. I speak now during Mass, not so much with the conviction of belief, but with an appreciation for the mystery of faith. *Lord, I am not worthy to receive you, but only say the word and I shall be healed.*

I also acknowledge that those aspects of my tradition that sometimes alienate me also challenge me to go deeper, to reckon creatively with the space between the church's vision and the world as I see it. I realize that I am not so strong or modern that I do not need a community of faith. And, as I've gotten older, my family has let me in on their own doubts and struggles with Catholicism, which has opened up for me a whole new sphere of being in the church. Yes, doubt can exist. No one tells you that, though, when you need it most. They just say, "Do it for Grandma," and ask you to swallow it whole.

Claiming my tradition became easier once I discovered that the Catholic Church is big enough to let me exist in the gray zones, where the loyal resisters have always struggled to live and breathe. And that's where I'm looking for my imperfect place within the tradition. While my eight-year-old self felt like it would be possible to convert, my twenty-eight-year-old self doesn't really think that's possible anymore.

Eileen Campbell recently completed her Master of Divinity at Harvard Divinity School. She is a grassroots organizer and lives in Cambridge, Massachusetts.

The Den, the Dining Room, and Saint Rose of Lima

Or, How My Confirmation Came to Pass

Elizabeth Duclos-Orsello

At fifteen I was confirmed wearing an appropriately modest pale pink dress. But the buttonholes along the bottom seam gave away its other side—it could be quickly buttoned up into one of those "bubble skirts" that rock stars and popular girls were wearing in the late 1980s. In its altered form the dress showed off my knees and my runner's legs. But this short version was not the version I showcased at confirmation. No, I stood before the bishop and spoke my confirmation name, Rose, in the longer dress, my knees well hidden. All the while I thought about whether I could live up to my chosen saint's standards and tried not to think about either how my dress looked or about what it meant that I was embracing a name tied to a life of self-sacrifice and celibacy.

I was proud and confused; I stood at the altar's edge as the daughter of a married priest and an activist mother. I believed saintliness was something to aspire to. And I believed that women were equal to men. I prayed to God the Father; yet I never doubted that there was a God the Mother somewhere. I believed I could outperform any male in the church—if only someone would give me a chance.

Why, as a budding feminist in 1989, did I so readily step up to the altar at St. John the Evangelist to be confirmed in the

Catholic Church? This question has plagued me for more than half my life, and none of the answers I've so readily meted out for years have ever struck at the heart of the matter. Certainly, I was raised Catholic and felt some degree of family and community obligation to be confirmed. Certainly, I was not well versed enough in Catholic theology and history in the tenth grade to understand all the implications of my decision. Certainly, I was swayed by the fact that my older sister had been confirmed the year before. But I did not grow up in a "traditional" Catholic household, I did not attend Catholic school, and on any given day I was hell-bent on proving myself to my male counterparts in the classroom, on the track, or in the church.

In 1989 I believed in equality of the sexes, I believed that women should be priests, and I believed that there was something wonderful about being Catholic. I was beginning to think of myself as a young feminist Catholic without knowing exactly what that identity meant—either to others or for my life.

"Catholic" and "feminism" were two words I heard often in my home—but never in sequence. On the hutch in our family's dining room sat a half row of books detailing the lives of saints, while on the bookshelves in the playroom and den at the other end of the house sat that anthem of Second Wave feminism, *Our Bodies, Ourselves.* These two rooms and these two sets of books were separated by the kitchen. Somewhere in this mélange of images and experiences of women, my feminist Catholicism was formed and my lifelong dis-ease about it first ignited. The physical distance that separated these two sets of books stood in many ways as the tangible manifestation of my bifurcated understanding of the role of women—especially strong-willed, intelligent, and ambitious women—in the Catholic Church.

The Catholic Church of my youth taught a sort of gender essentialism (the belief that there are "natural" differences between men and women that shape interests, aptitudes, and—ultimately—social roles) that was challenged but not overturned by 1980s-style feminism. Like the church's teaching, emerging feminist agendas also identified women as a unique group and encouraged each woman to know and celebrate her essential femaleness—but 1980s cultural feminists also tried to reappropriate essentialist arguments as a way to celebrate and validate traditionally diminished women's work and skill-sets. Yes, they agreed, women *were* essentially different from men (largely because of menstruation and childbirth), and yes, women had unique, innate knowledge and skills. But for these cultural feminists, these ways of knowing and these skills (many related to nurturing and caretaking) were powerful, important, and in some ways superior to men's.

In many ways, then, in 1989 it seemed entirely possible for me to reconcile a church that revered women as "different" and as a group "to be respected" with cultural feminists' calls for women to embrace their essential differences from men and come together to celebrate their unique skills, intuition, and collective wisdom. At the same time, the general feminist call for gender equality (at least of opportunity) could not be so easily reconciled with the limitations I saw each Sunday at St. John the Evangelist parish. Despite my observant and regular involvement in almost every ministry open to girls at the church—altar server, children's choir member, youth group leader, even pastoral council youth representative—I knew that *the* central spot on the altar could not be mine. Early on, I realized that without a phallus I would forever be barred from the priesthood.

How then could I have accepted and confirmed as my own a belief in the Catholic Church on that spring day in 1989? More important, as a friend of mine has recently suggested in her scholarship, *how* was I able to do this? *How* did I stay in the church?

Enter St. Rose of Lima.

I've begun to believe that taking the name of St. Rose at my confirmation made my Catholic identity possible. Rose was attractive to me because she allowed me to imagine a way of connecting the dots between the dining room and den, between the saints' lives books and *Our Bodies, Ourselves*. Rose allowed me to draw a line right through the kitchen, where the actual adult Catholic women in my life—my mother, grandmothers, aunts, great aunts, and family friends—spent a great deal of their time.

Over pots of pork and beans in this kitchen, I listened to and heard about my *ma tantes*, great-aunts whose convent years were full of prayer, service, and higher education. While rolling out crusts for *tourtière* I listened to my *Mémère* speak about living in physical poverty, never missing Sunday Mass, and never doubting that God and her own tenacity would provide. Her faith accompanied her as she, a working-class daughter of immigrants, raised three children and pursued a high school diploma in her sixties. With baby after baby—six in all—on hip, my mother chopped vegetables for soup and told me stories about her years with the Catholic Extension Society, serving and worshiping with Mexican migrant families in southwest Kansas in the late 1960s and her efforts to start a nonprofit in her twenties. While preparing for gatherings with family friends, I spent time with Sarah, our parish's faith-filled pastoral minister whose office in the church rectory held theology books and photos of her children. These were the Catholic women I knew. And these were Catholic women I admired.

These were the women I admired. Period. Catholic or not.

These women cultivated their own intellects, their passions, and their minds in ways that stuck in my head more than any discussion of the praying, sacrifice, or chastity that went along with their stories. But the Catholic Church was a key part of each story. In fact, this group of women—some of them the most adventurous and educated Catholic women I knew—found themselves and their voices *through* the church. Time spent in Catholic worship or ministry—time away or outside of the mainstream—provided possibilities and opportunities to grow and effect change. These women had either trained their bodies for celibacy or offered them up to the children they bore. They saw and felt suffering and believed in themselves enough to meet it head on. They took what life offered and made it into something better. I saw them as fully alive human beings, amazing models of secular feminism in action, and as engaged and inspiring Catholic women of faith. In them—in their bodies—I could see myself, my future, my power. The possibility of the church (broadly conceived) to stand as an alternative institution for strong women intrigued me, and I imagined a reconciliation between its patriarchy and its possibility.

I somehow saw all of this in St. Rose too. I did not pick Rose at random. I spent hours poring over those hutch-shelf books, reading and rereading the lives of every female saint I could find. Rose certainly wasn't quite as flamboyant in her saintliness as some saints (no dungeons like Perpetua or Felicity), nor as traditional as others (she wasn't a teacher like Scholastica). But she seemed to be just what I was looking for. In *my* reading of her biography, Rose, the patron saint of the Americas, was a teenager who had rebelled against the gender-based expectations her sixteenth-century, well-to-do parents had for her—marriage and childbearing—in favor of a life of her own choosing. So very strong was her yearning to love and follow God's calling that she dedicated herself at a young age to a life of physical mortification and sacrifice. Most compelling to me was the way she actively critiqued her culture's ideas about the social role of attractive women. When her beauty and her attendant marriageability were discussed, she cut her hair and marred her face with lye. She lived out her brief three decades of life the way she saw fit: living in a grotto, subsisting on little, serving the poor, and sacrificing her body for the glory of her God. The saints books celebrated her virginity, her work on behalf of others, and her willingness to eschew the temptations of living an easy life as a beautiful woman in Peru's elite class. I celebrated her dogged refusal to have others tell her how to live; she wanted to devote her life to the church and for that I admired her. Rose had understood the political power of her body and its beauty and instead of giving it to a man she did not love, gave her life and her body to God. She cut her hair, slept on glass, denied herself food. *This was a saint I could admire.* She had a body, she was smart, and she was faithful.

Like the women filling and filing through our kitchen, Rose offered me a limited and idealized view of Catholic women that supported women's difference from men and, as a result, celebrated the unique power and promise of women as women. Like the other Catholic women I admired, Rose's body (a female body) was the site of prayer, of service, of power, of life, and it was celebrated by the church.

On one hand Rose seemed to satisfy a Catholic view of women as profoundly and eternally different from men. But at the same time she seemed to me an embodiment of a late twentieth-century view of women as both *wonderfully* different from men and masters of their own lives, decisions, and futures. She fit into my definition of a feminist circa 1989: she refused to be married, argued with authority figures in order to live a life of her own design and on her own terms, took potshots at her contemporaries' ideas of acceptable behavior, and made a public name for herself in a nontraditional way. She controlled her own body and controlled her own destiny.

Rose was my fifteen-year-old way to reconcile the den and the dining room. And it worked—for a while. In fact, it still worked when I was twenty-five. That year, when I received my master's degree—based on a thesis about gender essentialism and feminism's Second Wave—I asked to have "Rose" included on my diploma. I wanted Rose in my life. I believed that she could help me make sense of the growing tension I felt as a twenty-something feminist who taught women's studies courses and also called myself Catholic.

But the tension grew. At twenty-nine, when I received my PhD, Rose was nowhere to be found. She never made it onto the diploma. I did not want her there. She lost her power of reconciliation.

As cultural feminism had passed out of favor in the waning years of the twentieth century, so too had both my intellectual fascination with theories of gender essentialism and my belief that women's separate but unequal position in the Catholic Church could be defended. And Rose was no help. Over time, I began to believe that she had been forced to give up too much to craft a life of her own making and she had been forced to endure too much physical denial in order to be venerated by the church. What would have happened, I began to wonder, if Rose had been able to put her intellect and body to work in the service of the priesthood? Might she have been celebrated as a public figure whose body and mind were nourished and taken care of instead of sacrificed? Would martyrdom have been her only path to celebrity?

As I thought more and more about Rose in light of my own exclusion from certain gendered positions within the Catholic Church, I began to realize that, although Rose had brought me to the altar on my confirmation day, she could not bring me to full inclusion in the church. As a woman, Rose's Catholic life was limited. As a woman, my Catholic life is limited. The altar is still male space. My body is still a mark of an unequal other. In the last few years, I have been looking for a new saint who can keep me in the church. While I still respect Rose, these days she is not enough.

And the kitchen that once bridged the den and the dining room is no longer a site of reconciliation between Catholicism and feminism for me. The kitchen in my childhood home is still the site of women's conversations, but these are not the same as they once were. The women themselves are different and their position in, and in relation to, the church is different. By the early days of the twenty-first century, my grandmother and great-aunts have died; one aunt has left the convent after more than thirty years; my mother is studying pastoral ministry and grappling with the limits of feminist theology; and Sarah, the woman who had served so many as pastoral minister in my parish, has been shut out of ministry in the diocese because she refuses to bow to a male view of God and the church. The kitchen no longer connects the dots for me. In that space, women's discussions have grown weary—and angry. As the church has become more and more entrenched in institutional tradition since 1989, I have become increasingly pessimistic about the possibility for a Catholic feminism that feels life-giving and is reflected in the structure of parish life and vocations. Real power and equality have not come to pass, and women's bodies remain the mark of exclusion. The essentialism that once linked the saints and *Our Bodies, Ourselves* in my mind is the very thing that I now see as conspiring to keep "Catholic" and "feminism" apart and that now leaves me increasingly skeptical of my own future with the church. I now believe that gender essentialism in any form can too easily be used to exclude women from full participation in the Catholic Church; its potential for empowering women is tainted by centuries of gender inequality both inside and outside the church. In my childhood home the saints' lives books still sit in the dining room while *Our Bodies, Ourselves* still holds its place in the den, and I am more aware than ever of the distance between the two.

Elizabeth Duclos-Orsello holds a PhD in American and New England studies from Boston University. She is currently an assistant professor of interdisciplinary studies and coordinator of American studies at Salem State College in Salem, Massachusetts, where she teaches many courses inspired by her time with the Jesuit Volunteer Corps in the 1990s.

Spaghetti, Steak, and Spirituality

M. Nelle Carty

A person is fully alive only when [she] experiences, at least to some extent, that [she] is really spontaneously dedicating [herself], in all truth, to the real purpose of [her] own personal existence. . . . A person finds [herself] and is happy, when [she] is able to . . . orientate her whole being toward the purpose which [she] craves. . . . The purpose is life in the fullest sense of the word . . . a life that transcends individual limitations and needs, and subsists outside the individual self in the Absolute—in Christ, in God.
– Thomas Merton, *The New Man*

Dinner at the Carty's

Whether my dad made spaghetti with sauce from a jar or my mom grilled steaks with her special mushroom sauce and made mashed potatoes, the Carty dining room table was where I first tasted what I consider to be "my purpose." Thomas Merton describes the movement of steering one's being in the direction of one's purpose "which [she] crave[s]." It is hard to describe what I consider my purpose in life without describing the formative years around the Carty family dining room table, where I learned to crave more nourishing meals.

Dinner was an everyday, compulsory part of being a Carty. Every family dinner started with a prayer, regardless of whether it was an informal meal at the breakfast table, whether there were guests who were not religious, or even whether we were at a restaurant and in public. Often, when my brother and I were embarrassed about having to say a prayer in public before meals, my dad would laughingly respond, "Well, you know how the saying goes, 'The family that prays together, stays together!'"

Nightly meals with my parents and my brother were not only nourishing because of what we ate; it was the haven where we shared our days' events, told jokes, acted silly, and let down our guards to be who we truly were. The dining room table also served as the negotiation headquarters for everything from driving and carpooling schedules to curfew agreements and college acceptance decisions. Our table hosted heated arguments, emotional breakdowns, encouraging pep talks, and family reconciliation services. As a teenager, I sometimes begrudged family dinners, wishing I could watch *Beverly Hills, 90210* or hang out with friends, rather than eat dinner with my family. In retrospect, I realize this daily Carty family ritual shaped who I am and how I live in the world.

Dinner at the Carty household occurred early some days and late others. My mom was a Catholic elementary school principal and often had school events during the week. My father was a marriage and family therapist in an ecumenical counseling center. He frequently worked in the evenings and ate dinner late after work. My younger brother and I were active in sports and extracurricular activities. So dinner was sometimes rushed, occasionally takeout, and often something that my mother cooked in advance and reheated in the microwave. On Sunday, however, everyone was home, the pace was more relaxed, and we even recited a special Sunday prayer, an e. e. cummings poem that my parents had said on their wedding day. Dinner during the school week was by no means identical every night, but it was always a ritual to eat at the table with the family, no matter how busy we were.

Since graduating from high school and moving away from home, I often crave Carty family dinners.

The Big News . . .

When I was in fourth grade, my mom, my dad, and I were sitting around the table in our usual places, my brother having already gone off to do whatever kindergarteners do. Having finished both dinner and dessert, the mood suddenly shifted. My parents looked at each other, and my mom said, "Nelle, there's an article coming out in the *Catholic Herald* next month that we need to discuss, in case any of your friends' parents read the article and mention it to you." My parents were always older than most of my friends' parents, and although I never really questioned it, I began to wonder at this moment if my parents had been married before they met.

Trying to anticipate what my mom was about to tell me, I blurted out, "What, were you married before or something?" My mom looked at my dad, and said, "Well, sort of." My mother calmly explained that she had been a nun. Then she waited for my reaction. My reaction was minimal. Then my father added that he had been a priest, and I recall feeling utterly confused. Imagining parents with previous lives can be difficult for anyone. Imagining *my* parents in religious orders before they started their married life seemed completely out of the ordinary for "normal" parents.

I grew up around a number of my parents' friends who were women religious and priests. Although I was comfortable around them and asked them many questions, I still had preconceptions about most priests and nuns and placed them in a separate category. *They* lived an alternative lifestyle that was countercultural to the norm of getting married and having a family. Who were my parents that had lived this religious, alternative lifestyle and then left to get married and have a family? From that moment on, I began to see my parents as people. I began asking my parents a variety of questions, actively trying to know who these *people* were.

My parents' story surprises many Catholics, particularly those who have seen any of the movies where the priest falls in love with a nun. My parents, however, were very open and quelled any imaginative stories I invented that could have been made into a primetime, made-for-TV movie. As I learned more about their story over the years, I realized the courage it took for my parents to leave their vowed lives and public roles as they sought to discover and follow their authentic vocations. I see my parents more clearly now as models of faith and pillars of support assisting me when I struggle with my own vocation and call to ministry.

I do not feel called to join a religious order for women, nor have my parents ever encouraged me to do this. Yet, there have been many Carty dinners where I have expressed my frustration at not having the option to discern my vocation to the ordained priesthood. The family dinner table is the place where my parents offered me a foundation for understanding myself, my spirituality, and the world; this foundation is undeniably rooted in the Roman Catholic tradition. Just as my parents both asked themselves whether they could remain in the Catholic Church after they left their vowed lives, I ask myself whether to remain in a tradition that does not allow women's ordination or married clergy. My parents have not and will not and cannot answer this question for me. My parents' continued devotion to discerning God's will for how best to live their lives gives me a model of how to approach the questions and struggles in my life. Although I cannot say what the future holds, at this time my call to be *in* the Catholic Church is greater than my call to the ordained priesthood.

The Advent Wreath

When I was growing up, my mom pulled out the Advent wreath every December. She pulled out the pink and purple candles and the little blue book with a picture of an Advent wreath and three children singing on the cover. For each day of Advent, there was a reading, a reflection and a song like "O Come, O Come, Emmanuel." Each evening before the meal, we would take turns reading from the book, which seemed more exciting and important than merely getting to say our everyday, "Bless Us, O Lord." There was an air of excitement that came with this change in our nightly dinner routine. Starting our meal with our little blue Advent book opened dinnertime discussions to questions about our faith.

I never heard my friends talk about lighting Advent wreaths at their homes, but this simple seasonal ritual is the perfect example of how my parents lived faith-filled lives offering an integration of everyday life and spirituality. I realize now that this simple, symbolic action of faith had a significant impact on my understanding of how to live out my faith and who I am.

In elementary and middle school, my friends and I played MASH, the silly game where you pretend to end up with a husband, a car, kids, and either a *M*ansion, *A*partment, *S*hack, or *H*ouse. We wrote down names of boys to be our "potential husbands" mostly because we thought these crushes were cute and funny. Sometime after college, I realized that I was developing a more intricate list for a future spouse that involved more than merely "cute" or "funny." My list expanded to include characteristics such as intelligent, good sense of humor, attractive, healthy lifestyle, ambitious, and avid traveler. I have met and dated some wonderful people, some of whom possess *all* of these qualities, but something never felt quite right.

One day, I was talking with one of my best friends in Chicago analyzing why none of the guys I met seemed to be Mr. Right. She immediately blurted out the one quality in a spouse that was glaringly absent from my list: "You need a guy who will light the Advent wreath!"

I never described Advent dinners at the Carty table to my friend, and I didn't even own an Advent wreath at that time. My friend's humorous attempt to pull me out of the single-girl blues made me aware of something that is fundamental to who I am: my faith. At that moment, I added it as the number-one attribute to my list of what I am looking for in a serious relationship.

Now, when I introduce someone new to my friends, within the first two minutes of the interrogation my best friends ask, "What about the Advent wreath?" They may be joking, but they know, as well as I do, that this is *the* crucial question. After all, the Advent wreath represents the importance of sitting around the table with family, having a meal, and sharing—which includes questioning—the faith.

Craving Theology

Not surprisingly, with my history of sharing and questioning my faith, I found myself interested in studying theology and involved in various ministries. I thought I could satiate my desire to understand my faith intellectually and to be involved in liturgical and social justice ministries during my four years at a Catholic college. I attempted to ignore, abandon, even fight my call to ecclesial ministry in order to undertake a more culturally mainstream life. Each time I veered toward a secular career, God managed to offer another entrance ramp onto a ministerial route.

Five years after graduating from college, I finally managed to find my path to ministry. I entered a two-year master's program at Weston Jesuit School of Theology (now Boston College School of Theology and Ministry), then transferred to the three-year, more pastorally focused degree program, the Master of Divinity. My brother joined me at Weston Jesuit during my second year of divinity school. I think he would admit that he too has a call to work in the church, most likely in education. One night during my brother's first year at Weston, we were having a typical graduate student dinner that involved tortillas, beans and rice, and maybe even some chicken. We were talking about future plans and career goals when the topic of vocation arose. My brother made the comment that it was "ironic" that *I* was the one who wished to discern the ordained priesthood. I smiled silently, mulling over, as I still do, this truth that seems like more than irony.

I still grapple with understanding my identity as a laywoman who aspires to work in and for the Catholic Church. My interest in being a lay ecclesial minister combines a call to serve, educate, and support others along their faith journeys. I have a deep admiration for the richness of the Catholic faith, but I also hope for change within the human institution. I call myself a "lay" ecclesial minister, but in truth I am not sure that is the most accurate description of my call. Am I a lay ecclesial minister only by default because my own ordination is not an option?

In the midst of my struggle to understand my role in the Catholic Church, I look to the Catholic mystic and theologian Thomas Merton. I view my calling to ministry in the Catholic Church as my way of "dedicating [myself], in all truth to the real purpose of [my] own personal existence." Living out our callings, or the purpose which we crave, allows us to become, as Merton describes it, "fully alive."

I feel most alive when I am ministering to others. I am continually amazed at God's presence in people I encounter and how God works through their lives. As a minister within the church, I am not arguing people into faith or convincing them of God's existence. Rather, I feel that I am helping them recognize, explore, and process experiences of the Transcendent that they have already encountered. This is the life of theology and ministry. This is what I crave.

Catholics believe that the Eucharist unites the members of the Body of Christ to one another and to the Divine. This sacramental worldview expresses and celebrates the mystery of the Christian faith. Just as the eucharistic meal is an interpersonal encounter that unites, transforms, and gives life, Carty family dinners bring my family together, allow me to enter into my faith and encourage me to live fully through my call to ministry.

When others discover that my brother and I are both studying theology, they jokingly inquire, "What did your parents feed you and your brother growing up?" My response, which is more honest than they can imagine, is, "Spaghetti, Steak, and Spirituality!"

M. Nelle Carty finished her Master of Divinity at the new Boston College School of Theology and Ministry (formerly Weston Jesuit School of Theology) in May of 2009. She is planning an extensive year of traveling coupled with ministry following her graduation.

No French Kisses

Sarah Keller

I had my first real date at the age of eleven and a half. I remember not being able to sleep the night before, a trouble normally reserved only for the night before school started again after a long and happy summer vacation. But the night before my first real date, I was more restless than ever, checking my book bag again and again, making sure that I had the five dollars that would buy me my slice of pizza, my slice of middle school heaven.

His name was John McGrath,* and my pack of girlfriends had cornered him on the playground during recess the week before and began the negotiations that would make him my official boyfriend. The terms of our agreement seemed clear enough. He accepted the proposal to date me because I was well versed in the Yankees' infield and because I showed exceptional skill at routine kickball games during gym class. I was not entirely bad looking, I was a tomboy, and I had not yet started to wear a bra (a fact that was readily observable, given the practical transparency of our thin, white uniform shirts)—these three things seemed to play to my favor. Not being particularly pretty, not being particularly endowed, and not being particularly a girl seemed to

---

* All names are pseudonyms.

make me agreeable to John McGrath. I must have seemed less scary than most of the other girls in our class, who were stuffing their bras and stealing makeup from their older sisters to share with each other in the bathroom at lunchtime.

The bargain John McGrath struck with my friends was straightforward—he would be my boyfriend as long as I didn't expect to hold hands with him on a regular basis. We would not talk on the phone. And we would never French kiss.

I was fine with his terms. Actually, I was elated. In my small-town Catholic school, there were only thirty kids in my class, the same thirty kids who had been there since the first day of kindergarten and the same thirty who would graduate eighth grade having gone through the best and worst parts of puberty together. There were only seven boys in our class of thirty. Seven. And by the fourth grade, girls had gotten pretty cutthroat to secure a boyfriend. Collecting and trading stickers was suddenly unpopular—collecting and trading boyfriends became the rage.

John McGrath was my boy of choice. Well, actually, he was always my *second* boy of choice. But everyone knew that Tim Johnson was off the market, maybe forever, since he had started dating Katie Lynn at the end of third grade and had seemingly never looked back. Since she was the most popular girl, and he was the most popular boy, we all assumed that nature would run its course, that they would get married and beget popular progeny. It was social suicide to even flirt with Tim Johnson. If you did, Katie Lynn would be sure to make the next two years of your life a living hell.

So John McGrath would do.

Our friends arranged for us to go on our first date the day school recessed for Easter break. On the days before Christmas and Easter breaks and on certain holy days of obligation, grades K–8 would pack into the church for an agonizing hour-long Mass before school let out at noon, the rare and wonderful half day. Since fifth grade, my parents had always let me walk to the pizza parlor down the street with my girlfriends for lunch on half days. They gave me five dollars and promised to punish me if I did not let the crossing guard help me across the small town's busiest intersection. We always had such adventures on those half days! We crossed the street several times over—first to the pizza parlor, then across to the ice cream shop, and then to the drug store for whatever candy we could afford with the change from our five-dollar outing. We marched happily from one side of Main Street to the other and back again, the sheer thrill of disregarding the crosswalk pulsating through our veins. We would sit on the benches outside the drug store, giggling with what felt like freedom, honest-to-God independence. We shook with laughter from the high of too much sugar and no one to scold us. We talked about boys, about Tim Johnson and John McGrath, about how we wanted to French kiss them (even though none of us had ever even been kissed on the cheek).

I was surprised that John McGrath agreed to come with us to the pizza parlor after Mass that day. Having already publicly stated that we were in a boyfriend/girlfriend relationship, our being in the same space, *outside* of school, made the trip an official date. Of course, he had agreed to come only if his two best friends could be there, a fact that delighted my girlfriends and kept them up at night from nervousness, imagining that they could date his friends and we could all get married together. We talked about how we wanted our wedding dresses to look and where we wanted to honeymoon. Nothing was happier to imagine.

When the big day finally arrived, I woke up extra early to get ready. I carefully put my hair up in my lucky yellow scrunchie. I wore my newest pair of uniform navy knee socks, the pair that looked the best. And I wore my favorite white uniform shirt, the one that was the softest, a hand-me-down from my sister that had seen at least six years of constant washes. I doused myself with the grass-scented perfume I bought at the Gap, and went to school knowing that it would be the single most important day of my life.

John McGrath did not look at me once during first period pre-algebra. He did not look at me during second period science, or third period history class. Only as we lined up at the front of the classroom to march into church did he smile at me, faintly. "I'm really looking forward to our date today!" I said too eagerly. He nodded once, and our teacher at the front of the line shot me a look that warned me not to talk again.

I sat impatiently in Mass for what felt like eternity, desperate throughout the homily for my world to officially start at noon. When we were finally set free, I waited on the playground for John to meet me so we could walk to the pizza parlor together. I wondered if he would offer to carry my books, like I'd seen in the old movies that my grandparents made me watch when I visited them. I rolled down my knee socks, exposing knees that were scabbed from soccer practice and a little fuzzy, having never been shaved. Rolling down my knee socks signified that I was done with school for the day, ready for adventure, ready for anything. My girlfriends were there with me, their socks clustered clumsily around their ankles as well. We were all wearing our lucky scrunchies. We were all wearing lip-gloss.

A few minutes went by before one of John's friends walked over to us with a message. "John can't walk with you to the pizza parlor. His mom is here picking up his older sister, and he can't risk being seen." John wasn't technically *allowed* to date until he was thirteen, at least that was the reason he used to explain to me that I was never allowed to call him on the phone and should never expect any phone calls from him, a blow that had initially devastated me, as routine phone calls were the hallmark of all the other couples in our class. But I had decided to take a positive spin on it all—he was dating me against the explicit wishes of his parents, breaking all the rules for our love affair. The whole thing seemed so romantic, so passionate and forbidden. "We'll walk there first. Give us a head start, and we'll see you over there."

We followed John and his friends to the pizza parlor, trailing them by twenty feet so that his mother would never find out about our date, about our undying love for each other. I tried to take in every detail of the walk, desperately wanting to preserve it forever in my mind and in my diary. I remember feeling a kind of happiness that I had never known before. I was closing in on the kingdom—popularity, boys, handholding; it was all within my reach. Nothing could break my high. But as we walked by the park where the public school kids had recess, I heard a shriek that brought me back down to reality: "Nerds! Ugly kids in your ugly uniforms!" The public school girls were taunting us as we walked by, still in school and angry at the freedom of our half day.

At the age of eleven and a half, I honestly believed that public school kids were a threat to society, fundamentally different than Catholic school kids. They hated us and we hated them. They would use our classrooms and desks during Sunday CCD, and I was always positive on Monday that they had broken the tips of my pencils on purpose, their initials carved into the top of my desk and fresh gum stuck to its underside. On the rare occasion that we saw each other and were unsupervised, it was all-out warfare. "Look at your stupid uniforms!" they laughed and pointed. "Look at your stupid socks!"

My friends were quick to yell back. "We can't even hear you! *We're* going to get a slice of pizza now. Because *we're* already done with school!" We stuck our tongues out at them, sliding them over our shiny, strawberry-flavored lips.

"Are you with those boys in the stupid uniforms that just walked by?" Now they were hitting close to home. "What? They won't even *walk* with you?" The girls howled and howled at us, as we stood there unsure of how to answer. It seemed silly to explain. Certainly, a rejoinder like, "He doesn't want his mother to see that he's madly in love with me, because love is more special when it is a secret," didn't seem like it would faze our antagonists. We opted for something more to the point.

"Sluts!" we screamed at them in a unison that must have seemed rehearsed.

"Prudes!" they screamed back, in the same uncanny harmony.

I couldn't shake the encounter off, even as I picked at my pepperoni pizza and John finished his Cherry Coke. I didn't really consider myself a prude. It seemed very clear to me that I was in a committed relationship with a boy I loved, a boy who was willing to risk being grounded to sit next to me at the pizza parlor. But still, I couldn't help but wonder why John had never tried to kiss me, and if he was ever going to. Our date was going smoothly enough. We spent the whole hour talking only to our own friends, and never to each other. Occasionally, I'd glance at him and he'd glance back. I felt positive that he was as in love with me as I was with him. We had a connection so powerful that we didn't even have to communicate it, or communicate with each other—at all. When the boys finished their pizza, we told them about our tradition of crossing the street and getting ice cream, an idea they seemed to like.

John told me that he had run out of money, that he had only brought three dollars for pizza, that he couldn't afford any ice cream. I remember that, that he used the word "afford," a word that sounded incredibly adult and important; I thought that it added to the legitimacy and maturity of our date. I told him that I would pay for his ice cream, since I still had two dollars to spare. He shrugged. "Are you sure that you don't want any ice cream?" It was clear that I would only be able to buy one.

"No, I'm totally full," I lied. I loved ice cream. But I loved John McGrath more.

"Okay then." He ordered a chocolate cone with sprinkles, and I handed the cashier my two dollars. As I watched John enjoy the chocolate licks, one by one, I felt like I was sacrificing for the one I loved, going without so he could be happy. It was an idea that was incredibly familiar to a kid in Catholic school—perfect love was always tied to perfect sacrifice. As he worked his way down the cone, I felt a strange sense of satisfaction. I was like Jesus Christ. I was like the Giving Tree.

The boys weren't done eating their ice cream when they decided it was time to leave. They were going to John's house to play basketball all afternoon. They simply could not stay a moment longer. John got up to go with them, but lingered a moment, chocolate stains from ice cream at the corners of his smile.

"I've got to go now," he told me.

"I know," I said. It seemed like the right thing to say.

"I'll see you at school," he told me.

"Okay," I said. "Have a good Easter."

He turned and took five steps away. And then he turned back to face me. Maybe it was because he felt obliged since I bought him ice cream, or maybe it was because his friends were egging him on, or maybe (as I thought then) it was because he really was in love with me with his whole heart—he walked up to me and kissed me quickly on the lips, no French kissing as per our agreement. He took off in a run, and his friends followed him.

My girlfriends crowded around me screaming and jumping up and down. "He kissed you! He kissed you!"

"I know! I know!"

"Well?" They waited for my response.

"He tasted like chocolate," I told them. And of course, he had tasted that way, needed to taste that way, to keep with the fantasy of it all, the innocent dreaminess of a first date and a first kiss, the strange perfection of crumpled navy knee socks and the high-pitched giggles of the girls who wore them.

I watched the boys run away, their light blue shirts untucked from their navy khakis, and faintly heard them tease John for the kiss he had just given me. "You're gonna *marry* him!" my girlfriends cooed and swooned. And I nodded in agreement with them, because (as I thought then) I certainly would.

Tonight, as I write this, I am twenty-three years old and engaged to a man who regularly holds my hand and French kisses me. As I tell him this story of John McGrath, of the unrequited devotion I managed to conjure up in my preadolescent self, he laughs and I laugh with him, at the unnecessary profundity I granted to forty-five minutes and a single slice of pizza. But even as we're laughing, I can sense that he is a little jealous, and maybe he should be. After all, you only get one first kiss in this lifetime. And mine will always be with John McGrath, in the parking lot of the town's only ice cream parlor. And though the entire scenario is funny now, I can't help but smile at the memory of the quick kiss, all of us in our plaid uniforms, taking ourselves so seriously, believing that a single kiss could and should change the entire world.

The thing about Catholic school, about growing up Catholic, is that it prioritizes the sacred, the ceremonious, the ability to create something holy out of otherwise profane time. What we are taught as easily as biology, as matter-of-factly as mathematics, is a sense of wonder, that there is a transcendent and overarching God at play, that love is what propels the universe. Every single memory I have of growing up in Catholic school is permeated with this strange and special love-wonder, a quality powerful enough to sanctify even the most unextraordinary first kisses, the most unenviable heartaches and hardships.

Sarah Keller contributed to Spirituality 101: The Indispensable Guide to Keeping—or Finding—Your Spiritual Life on Campus *(Skylight Paths, 2004) and graduated from Harvard Divinity School with her Master of Theological Studies in 2008. She graduated from the College of the Holy Cross in 2006, and is a writer/editor for SourceAid LLC.*

From Sacristies to Snow Angels
Finding God in All Things

Sr. Julie Vieira, IHM

When I was young, the inside of a church was as familiar to me as my own home. Because my dad was in the parish folk group—that curious ensemble of singers, guitars, flutes, drums, and tambourines—I had many opportunities to explore the nooks and crannies of the church while my dad practiced. As long as I didn't interrupt the musicians and singers or scandalize anyone, I had free rein of the church.

I took advantage of my freedom to roam. Sometimes I climbed up into the wooden pulpit that was only ever, in my experience, occupied by our priests or by the bishop. With reverence, I grasped either side of the pulpit just like the priest did. Standing on my tiptoes, I gazed out into the sea of empty pews. I sometimes pretended to read or preach aloud, oblivious of the guitars and bongos behind me. Other times I slipped into the sacristy, which was like the holy of holies to me. If I was lucky, I'd catch a glimpse of the chalices or other sacred vessels normally tucked away behind locked doors.

Wherever I went, the eyes of Jesus on the crucifix that hung over the altar followed me. Thinking this was nothing short of a miracle, I wandered from place to place in the church, checking to see if Jesus was still watching me. Even from the vestibule in the far back of the church, I could see Jesus making eye contact with me. It was unsettling and comforting at the same time. Was this what my teachers meant when they said that Jesus was always with me? Could Jesus see through the church walls into my everyday life too?

One day, while sitting in the front pew, I examined the intricate grill that separated the sanctuary from the choir area where my dad was practicing. My eyes settled on a large banner that hung behind the pulpit on the grill. The banner seemed to sparkle. It read,

> I asked Jesus how much he loved me.
> "This much," he said. And Jesus stretched out his arms . . .

Just as adults demonstrate to children how big something is by stretching out their arms ("The fish was *this big*"), I imagined Jesus smiling and doing the same. But there was a twist that I didn't expect:

> . . . and he died for me.

Time stood still as I realized that when Jesus stretched out his arms, it was so that he could be nailed to the cross. Jesus loved me so much that he was willing to die for me. I had heard this said at Mass but the weight of it sunk into me like a stone dropping into a well.

As I sat stunned in the pew, I felt like the church building had just yielded its greatest secret. That simple, worn banner had become a vehicle of Jesus' presence and love for me. If Jesus could reach out to me through burlap and felt, could he be discovered through the other "stuff" of Catholic life?

Everything about the church—every statue and cross-engraved pew—reminded me that I was part of something bigger than myself, something I didn't quite understand but that was a part of me. My whole life was marked by these things—holy water at my baptism, kneeling in the confessional, holding the chalice for the first time at Holy Communion. Being in church reminded me of these important moments of my life and was also a tangible connection to my family, friends, neighbors, and schoolmates who were part of the parish community and who had modeled the reverence I felt within me.

By exploring and literally feeling my way around the church building and its mysterious contents, I immersed myself in the deeply sacramental nature of the Catholic Church. Of course I didn't know that at the time; I was just a kid waiting for her dad to finish up so we could go home. My regular explorations into the inner world of the church environs combined with the weekly rhythm of the celebration of the Eucharist and the sacraments. These etched themselves into my memory and my imagination and my whole way of thinking about myself and the world.

I began to recognize this sense of mystery and awe and beauty not only in church but in other places in my life, especially the outdoors. One of my favorite things to do as a child was to lie nestled in a huge drift of snow and stare at the noontime sky. I was overwhelmed with the vastness of the sky, amazed that the sun could reach out and touch my face from millions of miles away. The snow insulated me, warming me and creating a space of silence. It was as if I was in my own world yet intimately connected with everything around me.

Over time, I realized that my experiences—the awe I felt exploring the church and celebrating the sacraments and the stillness I felt nestled in snow—were connected to one another. Each was part of an ongoing relationship with God. Each was an opportunity to get to know God deeper and deeper—and to fall in love with the One who loved me more than anything I could imagine.

Now, I can't help but see God's hand in all of my life and the world around me. Even in the darkest moments when it feels like God is not there, I remember that sliver of light burning next to the tabernacle—the ever-lit lamp that reminds us of and honors God's presence with us and all of creation.

The tabernacle lamp is just one of many sacred signs, or sacramentals, that light my imagination and remind me of God. I love the palms used at the start of Holy Week on Palm Sunday, the incense burned on high holy days, and the images of Jesus and the saints adorning our places of worship. All of these things are tangible reminders of who we are and *whose* we are. Such sacramentals can help us grow in a life of prayer and recognize the presence, love, and activity of God in our lives—within the church and beyond. Seemingly ordinary moments—sharing a meal with a loved one, dipping one's toes in the refreshingly cold lake water, feeling the rough bark of an old tree beneath one's fingers—become sacred vehicles or reminders of God. Even the physical motions of our sacramental lives—kneeling, shaking hands, bowing—can also be sacred vehicles in our everyday lives, such as when we kneel to speak eye to eye with a child or are brought to our knees by a personal tragedy.

Those many hours of waiting for my dad were some of the most formative of my young life. Being free to roam the church was like being schooled in the sacramentality of all of life. By my own lights, I would not have come to this conclusion or to the depth of its meaning. I had the feeling that Jesus the Christ was not only following me but guiding me and drawing me in.

Every moment of every day holds this kind of depth to it— the opportunity to meet God personally and to respond to the call to be transformed. Maybe it happens while praying from a worn kneeler in church or while waiting in the rain for the bus to come. No matter, it is God who is reaching out to us with love beyond what we can imagine.

Being Catholic has formed how I perceive the world and my place within it. It has given me multiple languages with which to articulate my experience including the language of words, gestures, and images. It has opened my life to recognizing God in all things—that there is nothing so ordinary or "secular" that it cannot be a vehicle of God's presence, love, and activity in our lives.

Sister Julie Vieira, IHM, is a member of the Sisters, Servants of the Immaculate Heart of Mary of Monroe, Michigan. She is author of the popular blog www.ANunsLife.org and also ministers at Loyola Press, a Jesuit publishing company in Chicago.

Faith in Action

Bless us, O Lord, and these thy gifts,
which we are about to receive from thy bounty,
through Christ our Lord.
Amen.

When I (Kate) was a kid, my mom insisted our family always say grace before meals, even at restaurants. Embarrassed by this public display of religiosity, my sisters and I quickly and quietly mumbled the prayer, "Bless Us, O Lord," at our laps, ramming the words together, willing our friends not to walk by.

Catholicism is a religion of public displays. Two summers ago, I participated in an outdoor Mass and procession through downtown Juneau to celebrate 125 years of Catholic Mass in Alaska. The annual Maryknoll-led School of the Americas protest draws thousands to what sounds, looks, and feels a lot like a Catholic funeral Mass at the gates of Fort Benning. A vocal commitment to serving the poor is another example of Catholicism's public force. Catholic social teaching articulates this commitment and makes me proud to have said grace into countless restaurant tablecloths.

Catholic social teaching also taught Kate Lucas that doing justice is an intimate part of being Catholic. As Kate Lucas found new ways to be Catholic in the ideals of Daniel Berrigan and

45

Dorothy Day's social action, Kate Barch Heaton was also soaking up the story of Day and the Catholic Worker movement. This kind of public display of being Catholic—this willingness to, as Barch Heaton and her growing family do, invite a homeless man to share a meal and sleep on the couch inspires their religious identities. This outward display of her Catholicism helped Lucas appreciate the value of the tradition's contemplative practices. And it helps keep Barch Heaton eager to challenge the status quo.

Like hundreds of other young Catholics who volunteer after college, Johanna Hatch joined the St. Joseph Workers—a one-year volunteer program run by the Sisters of St. Joseph of Carondelet. She joined to serve the women at a women's shelter. But it turned into so much more—she learned "there is a little bit of God in washing the windows and making the beds. Maybe, even, there's a little bit in me, too."

When I (Jen) arrived that Saturday morning, the air was thick with dirt and dust. It was the beginning of my senior year of college, and I joined other students on a weekend service trip to an unincorporated community near Tijuana, Mexico. After crossing the border, we joined members of that community in laying the foundation for what would become a schoolhouse. While some of our group protected their eyes with t-shirts and bandanas, others of us were ushered into a playroom with the children. Although, admittedly, I was somewhat relieved not to be working outside, the idea of spending the day in that room with so many small children was a daunting one. Settling into a chair that brought my knees too close to my chin for comfort, I shared crayons and paper with one of the little girls. "Mariposa," she explained, pointing to her first piece of artwork. Above her butterfly, I colored a bright sun. "Sol," we agreed.

As the morning went on, we tired of this game, and I tried to think of activities I enjoyed at her age. Recalling the countless recesses my friends and I had spent playing pat-a-cake and singing the silly songs that went along with it, I turned to my new friend and instructor. We arranged our awkward chairs to face one another, and I clapped my hands together once. She responded in the same way, and eventually we clapped slowly and at the same time. "Uno," I said and clapped her right hand against my own. "Y. . .," I said, clapping close to my chest, ". . . dos," clapping our left hands against one another. Soon we found our rhythm, singing, "Uno y dos, uno y dos, uno y dos, unidos, unidos, unidos." One and two, one and two, one and two. Together, together, together.

Participating in public displays of faith-filled Catholicism translates into meeting the needs of marginalized women and playing pat-a-cake with children in under-resourced areas, but it also means using our voices to advocate for our own needs in the institutional church. Tefi Ma'ake writes of her culturally diverse experiences in the church—from Tongan Masses at home to *Posada* processions with her students, from multicultural Masses in Santa Monica to the warmth of African-American Gospel Masses in Oakland. These challenge her and the church to consistently extend that welcome.

For Nancy Olivas, the church has often been a place of welcome—but eventually the patriarchy and machismo in the church overwhelmed her into action, urging the institution to extend a more open welcome to women on the altar. Emily Jendzejec was looking for a welcome too when she wrote countless letters to her diocese, requesting information about her own ordination. Frustrated and disappointed by the injustice of her exclusion from the discernment process, she had to look inside the quiet of herself to remember how Catholicism helps her connect to God. And this journey continues to draw her in to a faith that constantly challenges her to grow in ways unanticipated.

With the women in this section, we offer a communal, "Bless us, O Lord, and these thy gifts"—the gifts of seeing God in daily rhythms, in prayer, and in voices that ring out in public proclamation of both faith and action.

Sacraments at Sarah's

Johanna Hatch

Baptism

As I park my car in front of Sarah's . . . an Oasis for Women on my first official day as a full-time volunteer with the St. Joseph Workers, I stop to take in the beauty of the place. It's an old convent of the Sisters of St. Joseph of Carondelet on a quiet residential street, surrounded by flowers, fruit trees, and peace prayer flags. No one would guess from the exterior that it is home to an ever-changing group of women, including survivors of torture and abuse, most of whom are immigrants and refugees from around the world. These are the women I have committed to serve. I feel like I'm walking into uncharted territory. I come only with my feminist conviction, a passion for service, and the hope that I might stumble upon my faith again.

As I enter the house and walk through the halls, I read off the names of the women who live here—Selamawit, Samrawit, Raessa. The names sound new and awkward in my mouth. It's so important to me that I pronounce them correctly, and I repeat them over and over in my head.

My first days are full of meeting new people, meeting the women who live at Sarah's and trying to learn all the agencies the women use and how to get to them. And then it begins. "Johanna, will you help me?" Some things are easy for me. I type resumes, I show women how to use the internet, and I check English papers for grammar and spelling. Some things are more difficult. I have never used the city bus line before, and someone needs to know how to get to ESL classes. I don't know the difference between an asylee and a refugee, and people are asking me about immigration forms. Suddenly, my privilege is my ignorance. However, these women choose to trust me anyway. The questions keep coming, some gentle, some forceful and demanding. So I must keep figuring things out and finding the answers they need. One woman says to Sister Maggie, our director, "Johanna knows everything." What a huge responsibility!

Reconciliation

The Minnesota legislature had a late start, so the state is trying to get the business done in two months that it usually does in four to six months. Throughout March and April, I am at the state capitol at least once a week. The scope of issues that affect the lives of the women who live at Sarah's leads me everywhere from crowded committee meetings on "sanctuary laws" that help cities serve their immigrant citizens to a sparsely attended rally for more funds for AIDS prevention.

Reconciliation is the process of healing our relationships, and I see my legislative advocacy as part of healing society's relationship with the marginalized among us. The lives and well-being of the women I work with are not on the top of any legislator's agenda. My citizenship and my ability to speak English gain me surprisingly easy access to the halls of government. As I sit with our state senators and legislators, I begin my introductions with, "Let me tell you about the women I know at Sarah's in Highland Park." I tell them stories about their immigrant neighbors, the dreams and hopes these women have for their lives.

The charism of the Sisters of St. Joseph of Carondelet is, "Love of God and neighbor without distinction." By advocating for just laws and allocation of resources, I attempt to reconcile my neighbors and community with God by working to change the structural injustice the women at Sarah's encounter.

My legislative work is not limited to visiting the state capitol. After committee meetings, I come back to Sarah's and write up letters that Sister Maggie, the staff, and the board will send to their state legislators. I monitor national legislation and write letters to our representative and senators. The most moving occasion of our legislative advocacy comes when Sister Maggie asks me to make postcards asking President Bush to take decisive action to help end the genocide in Sudan for the women to sign. I type up a simple message, print it on postcards, and place them on a table in the dining room. One by one, the women sign their names to the postcards—some with elegant script, some with unsure penmanship, just having learned to write English letters. Women from across Africa, many with terrifying stories of their own, take a stand for women suffering the same fate.

Communion

Sophie's curly hair bounces around her face as her strong arms roll out the dough for the meat pies. The kitchen is filled with the smells of meat simmering and rice with vegetables bubbling in pots. Wednesday dinners are always a special time in our house, especially when the women cook. We share meals from Cameroon and Thailand, but some of the most unexpected delights come from immigrant interpretations of American favorites. I ask a woman to make a vegetable salad to go with dinner. When I take it out of the refrigerator, there is no lettuce, but boiled eggs and potatoes, sliced tomatoes, green pepper flowers, and lemon and oil dressing. Two young women tell me they will make spaghetti sauce. In it, they substitute traditional Italian spices with the East African favorite, *berebere*. It was delicious, but best eaten with lots of bread and cheese!

No matter what is served for dinner, our rituals and traditions stay the same. Sister Susan sets the tables and lights a candle on each one. Sister Maggie comes in the kitchen and inspects all the covered pots, "What's that delicious smell? What's in here?" One of the women takes the bell and walks through the house, knocking on doors, making sure everyone knows dinner is ready. As the women slowly trickle in, we gather around the center table filled with food. We join hands and Sister Maggie leads us in prayer, "God of all people, we give thanks for our lives today." We give thanks for our food, our safety, and our homes. We pray for the women around the world who live without all that we have. Every prayer closes with, "May peacemaking prevail on Earth today." We share in a tradition as old as the Christian tradition—we break bread, share our food and our stories, and there is always enough to feed us all.

We celebrate our community with food, and also with prayer. Sarah's is a multifaith home, with women from Islamic, Roman Catholic, Orthodox Christian, and Protestant traditions. To celebrate the International Day of Peace, we gather around the peace pole planted in the garden by the front door. I ask for volunteers to read peace prayers from different religious traditions. After passing out the slips of paper, I ask each woman to read her prayer. A Muslim woman reads a Jewish prayer, a Christian woman reads an Islamic prayer, and the birds sing in the trees above us. Across our religious traditions and the borders of our home countries, we pray that peacemaking will prevail.

Confirmation

"Johanna, my daughter, how are you today?" Cecile asks as I walk into the kitchen.

"I'm doing well, Cecile," I say with a smile. "How are you today?"

"Wonderful. It is a beautiful day." Good things have been happening for her. Her son's immigration case has been moving forward, and she is preparing to move into a new apartment with a bedroom for them. The teamwork Cecile and I put in together—making copies and writing letters for her immigration case, finding apartments and filling out applications—has paid off. I'm lucky, I get to see the work I do making a difference in someone's life. More important, though, I get to see Cecile making a difference in her own life. I get to be of assistance and empower her to succeed, providing a bridge with internet searches and access to a copying machine along the way.

However, the term of affection she chose took me aback. She fled her home country, having to leave her children behind. To call me her daughter must take great faith, bravery, and love—crossing lines of race and nationality. It also imparts great responsibility to me: to honor my new mother, to continue to advocate on her behalf, to continue to honor her stories and struggles and accompany her on this part of her journey.

One weekend a month, I spend the night at Sarah's. One evening, I set up a pizza party in the dining room, complete with art projects and music. As I turn up the stereo and take the pizzas from the oven, the young women begin to arrive one by one. Yassah picks up a piece of pizza, and so does Marjani. We begin drawing; we are making quilt squares for an exhibit at a local college. I encourage them to draw something about their experiences as women and as immigrants. Yassah draws a woman sitting on a step with her eyes cast down. "This is what it is like to be an immigrant," she says. "Sometimes you feel so alone." She thinks for a moment, draws a flower blooming in the woman's line of vision, and adds, "But it's not always this way."

Fatima walks in quietly and inspects the pizza before sitting down with us. Marjani begins drawing an elaborate cross and writes in Amharic, "The cross is power." The strength these women draw from their faith often sustains them and, in turn, sustains me. When faced with the choice to give up or struggle through, even in the most overwhelming circumstances, these women choose to keep going, knowing their God will see them through. With the comparative life of privilege I have lived, who am I to give up in the face of that?

Fatima picks up the markers and draws a rose blooming with the words, "I love Sarah's." As she looks up and smiles, the veil covering her hair slides off, and she doesn't move to adjust it. For some Muslim women, the presence of the veil can be a division between public and private, removed only at home, with other women. Without saying a word, she welcomed me into that home.

As the night goes on, Ethiopian CDs come out from bedrooms and dancing begins. At first, it is just Yassah and Marjani, then they pull Fatima in. Laughing, dancing, chatting in Amharic, they suddenly turn to me. "Johanna! Come dance with us!" I'm shy and self-conscious, but they don't let me off the hook. With the beats thumping from the stereo, they show me how to move my shoulders and shake my hips. I'm sure I look ridiculous, when Yassah says, "You're doing it!" I laugh—I really am doing it!

Vows

We have all, staff and residents alike, come to view Sarah's as our mother's home, a place we can always return to for love, praise, community, and a good meal. Sarah's is, of course, named for the biblical Sarah, wife of Abraham who welcomed strangers with good food and laughed at the impossible. My experience at Sarah's was a bit of a family reunion—all of us, daughters of Abraham, reaching out to each other, seeking to heal the wounds of division among us.

When I first began my service at Sarah's, I was seeking a deeper understanding of God. As I struggled with the ugly reality of rape and torture, domestic abuse, a cruel immigration system, and racism around every corner, I was afraid that I would find myself angry and would blame God. Instead, I found God hiding everywhere at Sarah's. God in laughter, God in music, and God in women's joy as they found jobs or graduated from college. I found God in the healing that women found and in the celebration of our community. Sarah's is soaked in the Divine.

My year of service at Sarah's came to an end, but my devotion has not. In my life as an activist in college, I was never forced to reckon so deeply with so many of the harsh realities women in our communities are living with, especially immigrant women. As a teenager and young adult, I railed against God for not seeming to notice the abuse, torture, and humiliation so many of my sisters face. Through my time at Sarah's, I have learned that there are no easy answers, no quick fixes, and no use in blaming God. Instead, there is community, there is a safe place to ask for help, and, in time, there is healing. My faith is no longer one based on demands and immediate results. It is messier now. The charism of the Sisters of St. Joseph is to love God and neighbor without distinction; we believe this because we often find God hidden in the dear neighbor.

For me, God is no longer a cloud-bound old man, separated from our daily lives. God, perhaps, is a woman taking the bus to English class or a Ugandan auntie taking a big pan of rice out of the oven. There is a little bit of God washing the windows and making the beds. Maybe, even, there's a little bit in me, too. As I bid farewell to a place I love so much, I promised to return. I promised to continue to work for justice and safety of the women who have blessed the place with their presence. No matter where I go, I carry their holy names with me, blessed to have found my faith in the hands of my sisters.

Johanna Hatch is a writer, feminist activist, and St. Joseph Worker alumna currently residing in Verona, Wisconsin, with her beloved, Evan Creed. In her free time, she knits and crochets gifts for the people she loves and is working toward becoming a certified doula. She believes another world is possible.

My Narrow Escape

Kate Barch Heaton

I was fully immersed in a mundane household project, my head and torso lunging into the depths of our dark and congested closet, when a familiar sort of spiritual wrestling pinned me to my knees. It was a Saturday morning in February, and the month's characteristic bleakness had taken leave of Boston for a short time; sun revisited our windowsills and left us with a generous patch of warm floorboards. My husband took his full coffee mug and loitered near the drafty windows, his chest bathed in light and his back turned, not coincidentally, to me and my futile endeavor.

The excavation had begun near dawn when, sleepless and achy, I decided to turn our single closet upside down in search of baggy sweatshirts and other remnants of my early nineties apparel—anything that might fit over my swollen belly. The sixth month of pregnancy did not veer from the books' descriptions; I was charmed by the movements within me, though vexed by the hasty expansion of my skin and by thoughts of how our lives would be stretched in unsettling ways. On this particular morning, I took to the obscurity of the wardrobe, trying to make sense of our material world, one I thought I could simplify and subdue. But as I unearthed the contents of each tattered box and overstuffed bin, I was overcome; now on all fours, spelunking beneath hanging pant legs and occasion dresses, I muttered my disgust with our cluttered lives. When did I start to spend my weekends taming and pruning the contents of our small apartment? Was I allowing my life to become this narrow—this insular?

Kneeling on a pile of down vests and ski parkas, I nervously collected my unruly hair into a neat ponytail and wiped a few tears of frustration from my cheeks. *The coat that hangs in your closet belongs to the poor.* It was not uncommon for me to entertain thoughts of my favorite gutsy Catholic. Just hours before, her face had appeared to me from beneath a collection of literary magazines. This was no apparition, just the fortuitous uncovering of a five-by-eight-inch icon depicting the earnest face and steely locks of Dorothy Day. I positioned her in the sunny dining room atop a roughly hewn sweater chest; here, I thought, her face might remind us that this good life could be shared, in some small way, with others.

Sunday's hearty stew, whose simmering steamed these broad windows and flushed our faces—this was a thing to be shared. The fine blouses and brand new mittens and scarves we hoarded in the deep recesses of our home—all things to be shared with a broader community. I felt enlivened just realizing that I still had these magnanimous desires, but had I already become too practical to live as my heroine had lived? *Damn it*, my husband heard me growl from my position in the darkness. And perhaps he thought I had stubbed my toe or bruised my unwieldy belly in an act of clumsiness. But this was frustration of another kind. Was it too late for me to become Dorothy Day?

Like other Catholic women I know, I became enchanted with Dorothy's story the first time I heard it. She bore all of the attributes of Josephine March, Anne of Green Gables, and other sweet but feisty childhood heroines. Dorothy sounded bold, determined, and unconventionally loving, but unlike Jo and Anne, she was real! It was 2002, and I was staying at St. Francis Farm, a Catholic Worker project in upstate New York, when I first heard of Day's uncommon life. I am sure that I romanticized the tale, imagining that Dorothy gave assiduous attention to each of the poor people she met and fed, then retreated to a quiet study where she would smile to herself and write neat columns about her noble day's work before nestling into a cozy gingham bed for the night. Biographies like Dorothy Day's are easy to manipulate, especially with a fertile imagination. But it did not take me long to realize that my heroine's raw love for the poor and marginalized must have ushered her into a rather raw life. A woman who offers hospitality to the homeless cannot hide from foul odors, heart-wrenching decisions, or sleepless nights. And a woman who tends, not her own household, but the household of God's poor cannot become as complacent as a woman like me.

The morning had passed me by, and it was nearing one o'clock. I reassembled our closet, made a grocery list on the back of our church bulletin and grimaced as I thought of the itinerary of errands awaiting me. There were wedding registries to visit, bills to mail, and baby shower gifts to return. I had intended to visit my elderly friend, Raphaela; she passed her quiet days in a spartan apartment down the street. Raphaela loved to have me in for tea, at which time she would pull a not-so-dainty bottle of sherry from beneath her kitchen sink and offer me a shot to go with my scone. I had owed her a visit for weeks, but perhaps I would spend another weekend doing meaningless things instead.

I once poked fun at our neighbors, Richard and Saria, a gentle Syrian couple who used to invite all of us to long, lazy barbeques until they became like so many other Americans, spending their Saturdays at Wal-Mart and their Sundays at Home Depot or IKEA. Heading back from my run in the local arboretum, I would catch a glimpse of Saria hoisting voluminous plastic bags from the trunk of her Camry and dragging them into their tiny, lime-green house. I would wave and wonder, where does it all go? Rashad would busy himself with the upkeep of their quarter acre, raking and re-raking his turf or blowing pesky leaves and refuse out of their little Eden and onto our dead-end street. Within a year of their arrival in the United States, they had acclimated; they no longer engaged our socially inept neighbors in conversation or extended courageous invitations to the reticent condo-dwellers. They were Americans now, so they tended to their home and lavished gifts upon their two-year-old. It occurred to me now that I was becoming just like them.

Was my world narrowing before me? If so, I knew that living more radically for a community would broaden my family and me. How sorely we needed such a challenge. And I was not without a model, for I had lived in a Catholic community just three years before. Just beyond the chaotic borders of Port-au-Prince, there lies an oasis for Haitian children. It was my privilege to live and volunteer there during one academic year. From the moment that my flip-flop clad feet hit the tarmac in Haiti, I was asked to give myself over to the needs, whims, or fancies of others. What a different lifetime that was!

Sitting cross-legged in the parched central courtyard of our school, *l'Ecole Louverture Cleary*, it was easy to feel purposeful, for I was never without a throng of attention-seeking students. Though the school, which offers the slums' children a rigorous, free, Catholic education, is sequestered in an unremarkable *quartier* called Croix-des-Bouquets, I can remember feeling as though I were at the center of some very important place. As the news about Haiti's woes emanated, like a dirge, from *Radio Internationale*, our children went about the business of learning three languages and singing proud anthems of their beleaguered nation.

Life was very demanding for all of the Haitians and Americans who contributed to the life of the school, but we learned to live, almost instinctually, for the other. By five each morning, the students were bathing loudly in the shower stalls below our residence's windows and I was roused from a fitful night's sleep. By seven, I was ushering twenty-seven boisterous middle schoolers into our open-air classroom for French lessons, and by noon, I was hauling buckets of cistern water up the stairs to wash dishes or flush our temperamental toilet. And when I thought I had it bad, I looked at my colleague, Joanne, a young Haitian woman who had unwittingly become the housekeeper to all.

Pretty and slight, dressed in delicate hand-me-down sundresses, Joanne did not at first appear the shrewd and sharp-tongued taskmaster we later found her to be. She quickly befriended each comfortable, corn-fed American who joined the faculty, then stripped us of our luxuries and put them to work for Cité Soleil's children, our desperately poor student body. She suggested that we scrub the tile floors more frequently, keep tighter control over our pupils, and abandon some of our gluttonous ways. I will never forget the day that Joanne lectured three Midwesterners on their frivolous use of toilet paper. This commodity, in her estimation, was to be the financial ruin of the school.

Every few weeks, on going-to-market day, Joanne would enlist my help. Perhaps she saw me as an ally, despite my wanton use of bathroom tissue and cleaning products. Before we left the walls of the school, Joanne would have me translate the wilted grocery lists into French or broken Creole. No menial task made me more nervous; I was the first to tell Joanne if some New Yorker had requested poultry or breakfast cereal or if the Midwesterners were sorely in need of potatoes. When this unpleasant exchange had passed, she and I would escape, happily, into the wilds of the marketplace. As we waded through the puddles and pitted roadways of Croix-des-Bouquets, Joanne greeted the children who joined us in our stroll. She knew their names and their families, and she didn't seem the slightest bit troubled to see that some of the five-year-olds were playing with machetes or that none of the girls were in school. Until she fell into her arduous position at *l'Ecole Louverture Cleary*, this was Joanne's world, and she altered her stern demeanor, greeting the needy neighbors with joy.

Amidst the bustle of the marketplace, we haggled for mangoes, plantains, and pounds of rice. We scoured the sun-baked tables and stalls just to find the smallest potatoes that an American has ever seen. Each truck that rumbled past us tossed blinding clouds of dust into the air, and a school bus, being washed in the river next to some bathers, honked abrasively. Nothing distracted my companion from her procurements. With the vendors, who sat on their haunches and squinted at us, Joanne was tough, but fair. She bristled at inflated prices and spoke of the importance of securing enough *blé* (a wheat-based starch) and oatmeal for our three hundred students. Joanne was the first to tell me that school meals were important for the dozens of pupils who were not able to eat on the weekends when they went home. These were *her* children, it was clear.

Joanne taught me that there is nobility in our most tedious tasks, so long as they are done for rich and poor alike. Looking back, I know that Joanne was our steward and our nurturer; she was our Dorothy Day.

◆

It is an unfortunate trend that a life lived "in community" is something we must contrive. Must we go to great lengths to manufacture such an experience if we want to live in relationship with all manner of God's people? My life tends toward insular habits unless I pay close attention to how I spend my time, efforts, and resources. And I should not have to fly to Hispaniola in order to live for others. As I have spoken with other people of faith, I have realized that I am not alone in this grappling.

Not long ago, my husband and I decided that we should imitate, if ever so humbly, the example of my heroines. We had come to know and love a member of Boston's homeless community, a tender and thoughtful man named Robert, and we had built a trusting rapport with him. Knowing that it would be good for all of us, Robert kindly accepted our invitation; he came for dinner and spent the night on our couch. As I lit candles in the dining room, sliced a loaf of crusty bread and wrapped our sofa in flannel sheets, I came to know a new type of hospitality. The evening that followed was memorable, and there has been another like it. Even though our commitment to Robert's basic needs was intermittent, I know that the relationship was heartening to all involved.

As our family grows and I become tethered to many daily responsibilities, can I sustain a connection to those who live lonesome or agonizing lives? It will be difficult, I think. Most of the young families I know are so mired in the maintenance of their own schedules and upkeep of their own homes. They are unavailable to those less privileged. When my time is dedicated to a family and a career, will I still think of those who have neither? Will my children ever see me lend hospitality to the poor or comfort to the forlorn? It is anyone's guess. But I have hope, born of inspiring role models, that even my cluttered life can make room for forgotten ones. The knowledge that I *can* live courageously for God, sharing my home and comforts with friends rich and poor—this knowledge sustains me as I cross into a new phase of life.

Kate Barch Heaton lives in Boston, Massachusetts, where she coordinates community service projects for high school students. She is studying theology and pastoral ministry at Boston College.

Between the Lines and in the Margins

Kate Lucas

What you need is absolute, unmixed attention. This is prayer.
—Simone Weil, philosopher and Christian mystic

I think art has something to do with the arrest of attention in the midst of distraction.
—Saul Bellow, writer

religion

dust motes glow
above workbooks
while pale Mary stands
at attention
scent of brownies
and tater tots drift
amidst the tinny cadence
of children
we are many parts
and all one body,
the gifts we have
were given to share,
the river of love
makes a swan indeed,
now A to Z line up
for lunch

I grew up on a Catholicism that centered around my cheery little grade school and the big brick church next door. For the most part I thrived there, traveling up the ranks each year with the same small cohort of students. My teachers were mainly young and kind and motherly. I relished the good food cooked by mothers of my peers in the sunny basement kitchen, with its linoleum floors and spearmint green walls and dusty pipes crisscrossing the ceiling. I devoured the shelves upon shelves of books in our little school library that kept my imaginative mind engaged. I fell into the rhythm of weekly Mass and especially loved being appointed a lector, when I could stand on the footstool at the pulpit and speak slowly and clearly into the microphone so my voice rang out into the sanctuary.

Yet from an early age, there were things about school and church that rankled me, made me feel out of place. I loved most of my classes, I loved learning, but religion was by far the least interesting class. On my First Communion I tried to feel inspired but felt mostly awkward in my white dress and veil. Each Christmas I watched with a mixture of admiration and envy as some serene girl was picked to play Mary and hold the little baby, the newest addition to the parish. Deep down I knew I would never be picked. I wasn't the peaceful, agreeable type they were looking for. Even at that young age I knew I didn't fit into a neat mold of pious religiosity. The model presented to me at this point was serenity—quiet, peaceful goodness, which felt too much like a bland and boring kind of surrender. I had too many opinions, too many questions. And the cartoonish drawings in our religion book carved out a very simplistic and two-dimensional understanding of religion. These classes seemed to be mostly stories to memorize, behaviors to imitate. We did not talk in a language that helped me to name awe or wonder around me. We did not explore in a way that engaged my mind and heart.

In high school this two-dimensional picture lost any prominence as I moved beyond the comfortable confines of my little school. With no parochial high school in town, I attended the public school and religious education on Wednesday nights.

Seemingly numb and indifferent parents led us through workbooks and dull videos in a windowless basement room; no service projects, no engaged conversations, just painfully awkward,
boring dullness. The tired exercises and anecdotes, void of context, put into question any import or relevance of a Catholic
spirituality; there didn't seem to be anything of meaning, nothing
to engage the mind or spirit in this wasteland.

liberation

tofu simmers
with kale and potatoes,
a photo of Dorothy
hangs at attention
over talk of
Emerson, Jonah House,
consumption
and swords pummeled into
ploughshares,
since many stones
can form an arch
though singly none,
singly none,
and we won't study
war no more
just botany
for the test
day after tomorrow

   When graduation came, I went on to a Catholic college mostly
by accident, where suddenly, surprisingly, my mind was engaged
by spiritual and theological explorations. Finally I discovered the
lively, cantankerous, radical, challenging experience that Catholicism can be. Asking big questions, arguing about them. Having
my very fundamental life choices challenged by Catholic social
teaching. Working alongside the poor in a Catholic Worker house.
Reading about Dorothy Day and Daniel Berrigan. Protesting the

School of the Americas, standing for peace and nonviolence. Distinguishing vertical theology (seeking heaven in the hereafter) from horizontal theology (working for heaven here on earth). During college I finally started to see a glimmer of what I had found so lacking in religion in my younger years—wholehearted engagement. I discovered myriad ways to engage my mind and spirit with spiritual and theological questions. But nearing the end of school, I became weary of so much talk. It became clear that I needed action; I needed to live out the bookish and abstract ideals I had uncovered in college. I wanted to volunteer, live in community, experience living simply.

So I did. I moved to Denver and joined a volunteer community. During the day my housemates and I worked with the poor at different agencies around the city. At night we ate dinner together and reflected on our days. Once a week we celebrated Mass with guests in a small upper room, then shared a simple dinner in the big dining room below. There was something very basic and solid about our weekly rhythm that my gut agreed with. I was engaging my whole body, my whole life, in convictions that I believed in. Perhaps more than any other time in my life, during this volunteer year I felt certain I was exactly where I should be.

Still, this remained a primarily intellectual endeavor. I often reasoned that it wasn't for wholly religious principles that I was doing what I was doing. I sometimes pontificated in my journal and in conversations with more liberal-minded community members that I could use logic to explain the need to care for the poor; I didn't need religious texts. But interestingly, as the year wore on, I theorized and pontificated less. I became increasingly drawn to poetry as a form of discovery and expression. It came to feel like the only way to adequately and humbly capture the bigness and intensity and reality of the things I was observing and experiencing—the pain and need, the bravery and grace, of the people we worked with each day. The short form, it seemed, was the only one with enough space and expansiveness to reflect these moments and people.

And then my attention opened up in an entirely new direction. We went on retreat at Snowmass, a Cistercian monastery in the mountains outside of Denver. I had read about meditation in an Eastern philosophy context, intrigued by its simplicity and depth, and now here were these Catholic monks living out the contemplative experience. Suddenly I was experiencing a tradition first-hand that I learned was decidedly rooted in the Catholic tradition. I ate it up. It was nothing I had ever seen within the Catholic tradition. We learned about the monastic life of silence, stillness, and routine. We met Thomas Keating, one of the most notable contemporary voices of contemplative prayer within the Catholic tradition, who said that since God is everywhere, you can listen to God anywhere. He talked about prayer as "listening with rapt attention." Brother Micah told us, "You can't say what God is, only what God isn't. God is more than all-powerful, all-loving. So what do you do? Fall silent." And Theophane, wiry and frail with piercing gray eyes, challenged us to name an undefining definition of God; he said that language limits, and we try to use it too much. Besides these conversations, we spent most of our time in silence, following the rhythm of the monks, waking before dawn for morning prayers, walking down the gravel road to the chapel to sit amidst the measured cadence of their singing. Surrounded by those big skies and hills, I soaked in the experience of that place, and it was profound.

One early morning as we walked toward chapel under the white circle of moon, the smell of damp earth a richness all around, the only sound the puff of breath and crunch of gravel underfoot, I turned to my friend to whisper something—about the smell, or the view, or the crisp fresh air—but I stopped myself before speaking. There were no words to describe the beauty of that moment. We walked on in silence. I wrote later in my journal that my only hope was to summon a piece of it, between the words on the page, and behind them. The joy of the poet, I wrote, is not to lament the extreme paleness of words, but to have the ability to create the space where one can look beyond them. In this process, there is a great amount of reverence. Snowmass connected many things for me, but I don't think I realized the irony for quite some time: during a year where I intended to get my hands dirty engaging in what I believed was a pretty radical horizontal theology, I was touched perhaps most profoundly in solitude and silence, way up on a hill outside the city.

solitude

sunday, december
a chill in the room,
my feet soak up cold
from the floorboards
a car passes by
then nothing
no sound
while under the circle
of light at my desk
since we are the voice
of the living
god and my pen keeps moving,
my head remains bowed
since once it was dark
but now i'm in light
and i journey,
onwards and up

But of course I came down the mountain soon enough. Our year of volunteering ended and we all scattered to the four winds. Now several years after volunteering I have entered a somewhat dull isolationism of a different kind than I experienced in high school—that of the single quarter-lifer. And so going to Mass on Sundays is a very disengaged experience again. I know no one, I am very conscious of coming and leaving alone. I listen to the readings and the homily, but I am not brought into the fold of a community or spurred to an engaged spirituality. But. Something about the incense, the candles, the songs that I know and have sung for years, these things tug at my heart. And so I

continue trying. The imprint of those reverent and cheery moments in grade school, the passion and conviction discovered
in college, the groundedness of volunteering, these memories
call me back.

The experience of Snowmass continues to resurface too, most
recently in the words of Krista Tippett in her book *Speaking of
Faith*, when she talks about rethinking religious truth. I came
across Tippet's work when I started listening to the Sunday
morning broadcast of her public radio show of the same name.
I joked with friends that the show was my way of honoring the
Sabbath during that time, an avenue to create space in my busy
week to sit and grapple with religious and spiritual ideas with all
manner of theologians and spiritualists and academics brought
onto the show. I found Tippet's spiritual conversations to be a
wonderfully nuanced engagement of the mind and heart, the
academic and the spiritual. So I picked up her book recently, and
discovered one especially illuminating passage. Tippet describes
how we can discover truth in the "insides and edges of [religious]
words and ideas" that are humanity's humble attempt to articulate an understanding of God on earth. She says that there are
lots of ways in which religion and art come from a similar place.
We speak from our heart in poetry, and so too are religious ideas
written in metaphor and parable and verse. Then she takes it
one more step: she says that we understand the mystery and
truth of it all as much in the words as we do "beyond them," that
silence is "a reality that does not negate reason and argument
but puts them in their place" (48–52).

And it all comes together for me in these ideas. While the
wealth of theology was invigorating and enlivening in college,
and I needed that, after a while I became caught up in my head,
awash in argument and theory. For a while I believed everything could be interpreted and experienced at this heady, academic level. But while volunteering, I began to discover this
wasn't sustainable—or that in daily lived experience, God could
be present in much more subtle and mystical and intangible
ways, and that perhaps I was missing it. Writing poetry—and

entertaining silence—helps me to stay attuned to this, and to try to point a finger toward it.

So I have come to visit the ritual of writing with some regularity. There is form and intellect to poetry, but there's also a very mystical, ethereal, "between the lines" quality. Right brain and left brain have to work together—quite literally. I recently learned the biology behind this oft-repeated axiom, and it seems a telling metaphor. With language centers in the left hemisphere and creative centers in the right, hither and fro the synapses must travel across the messy connectors of the corpus callosum. Perhaps more than any other creative endeavor, writing requires the messy unity of these two poles.

Growing up Catholic gave me a container for spiritual expression, and that container, the rituals of Catholicism, grabbed me to a degree. And yet, I was conscious from a very young age of the potential for it to be stifling, or the feeling of being only partially embraced in its context. So perhaps all along I have been seeking a way to merge the ritual and the creative—a way to engage to a certain degree in the structure but also to open it up, find it illuminating and changeable and alive.

My friend Christine reminds me that a healthy spiritual life is one where we live on the edges. Those who don't are mostly just putting in time, not really engaging. Living on the margins, she says, is all about the tension between the institutional and the spiritual, and it's a part of the maturing spiritual process. In grade school and junior high I yearned for this engagement, but I didn't know quite how to make it happen. In poetry I have found a practice that allows me to do this—to recognize ambiguity, struggle, paradox—and find the beauty and the bigness in it. And in this, I have found a holy kind of reverence.

remembering forward

here still is that girl
in her communion dress
stiff and anxious,
trying so hard to listen

with rapture
i say she can tie a red sash
round her waist,
and kick off her shoes in the corner
dash out to pick wildflowers
for the carnation bouquet,
stomp round the indifferent among her,
sit still with the woman
who claims the same pew each week,
squeeze her hand when they
mention the loved ones
then slip out the side door
to lay in the field
where all the ends
have seen the glory
and wonder at the
blue dome above her

Kate Lucas served in the Colorado Vincentian Volunteers after graduating from the College of Saint Benedict. She now lives in Minneapolis, Minnesota, where she writes grants and other communications for Common Hope, an international NGO that supports impoverished communities in Guatemala. She scratches out poetry and tutors young writers in her free time.

Welcomed Home
*The Multicultural Embrace of
the Catholic Church in the United States*

Tefi Ma'ake

I slid into an empty seat amid the lively congregation gathered for the young adult Mass at St. Monica's parish in Santa Monica, California. As a first-timer, I wasn't quite sure what to expect, but the energy radiating from the sea of smiling faces that filled the church excited me. I flipped through the worship aid, something I have done before Mass for as long as I can remember, hoping to find an old, familiar favorite. Surprise struck as I read the Tongan words of Jesse Manibusan's *Misa del Mundo*, *'Oku, 'Oku Ma'oni'oni.* Excitement overflowed within me as the assembly later sang these words, *Holy, Holy God*, and welcomed my Tongan heritage. With just a few words, the faith that I had come to love embraced the culture that was so much a part of me.

My childhood experience of the Catholic faith and tradition was so intertwined with my Tongan heritage that I never questioned where one ended and the next began. No separation existed for me; my Catholic faith was part of my Tongan culture. These few words at Mass happily reminded me of my childhood, and in an instant I was swimming in a memory of the Tongan Masses I grew up with.

As a young girl I never found it strange that my family room was often transformed into worship space. I remember the smell of the woven mats laid out on the floor, the busy-ness of cooking all day, and the warmth of so many people gathered in one place. I remember the tower of shoes piled high outside the door, sitting barefoot on the family room floor, and children fidgeting in their parents' laps as they waited for Mass to begin. I remember the harmony that rang out between the men's and women's voices as they passionately sang hymns etched on their hearts and memories since they were children. And while I couldn't understand the Tongan words they sang, I needed no translation to understand the emotion behind them. I felt genuinely connected to the beauty of the ritual unfolding in my family room, to the beauty in the voices that glorified God without worship aids or accompaniment, to the beauty in this community grasping onto their traditional worship, despite the miles that separated them from the islands of their homeland. This beauty was faith, in such a profound and yet simple way. This was my faith, my culture—my experience growing up Tongan American and Catholic—and in my family room-turned-church, I was home.

"Hi, Ms. Ma'ake," Karina whispered as I crept out the back door of my classroom and joined the procession that had already begun. As president of campus ministry, Karina was one of the students who had organized this Friday afternoon *Posada*. About sixty Bishop Conaty-Our Lady of Loretto High School students, faculty, and staff had stayed after school on this sunny California December afternoon to remember Mary and Joseph's journey into Bethlehem. We sang and sought shelter, moving from classroom to classroom. Turned away from door after door, we continued our pilgrimage.

I smiled at Karina and the other students who had taken the initiative to hold this event. Their passion and desire to share this celebration with the school had amazed me when the idea came up at our weekly campus ministry meeting. They planned all of the details of *La Posada*, received permission from the administration, gained support from faculty members, and rounded up a remarkable number of students to participate on a Friday afternoon.

We neared the gym door, our final destination, singing. *En nombre de cielo, les pido posada. Pues no puedo andar, ya mi esposa amada.* We sang, seeking shelter, a place of rest, a home. *In the name of heaven, I ask you for shelter. My wife is tired. She can go no further.* With this, the students threw open the gym doors, exclaiming in song. *Entren, santos peregrinos, peregrinos a este humilde rincon. No de mi pobre morada, morada sino de mi corazón.* Mary and Joseph, and all of us gathered were welcomed inside. *Come in pilgrims, holy pilgrims, holy pilgrims, in this nook take your part not alone of my poor dwelling, my poor dwelling, but take also of my heart.* "But take also of my heart"— the same gift my students had offered me.

Karina ran up to me with a hug. "It was great!" I exclaimed. And it was.

Throughout the four years I spent as campus minister at Bishop Conaty-Our Lady of Loretto High School, a predominantly Latina school in inner-city Los Angeles, "my girls," as I affectionately named them, shared their culture and opened their faith to me. They reaffirmed the profound simplicity of faith enlivened by culture and culture enriched by faith. Their faith, their culture, became a part of me. As the celebration that followed the ritual began in the school gym, I realized that, as in my family room-turned-church, I was home.

I settled into the pew, surrounded by bright colorful dresses and big matching hats. A buzz of happy chatter swirled around me as I explored St. Patrick's, an African-American parish in Oakland, California. Mass began as the gospel choir, adorned in white and green robes, danced up the aisle, leading the procession of lay ministers and Father Greg. Everyone was on their feet, hands clapping in unison, bodies moving, voices lifting in song. Since moving to Berkeley several weeks before, I had been searching for a church to call home, and suddenly I knew—St. Patrick's was the parish for me.

My heart pounded and tears fell from my eyes, when a young girl no older than seventeen led the congregation in the Memorial Acclamation. *"Jesus died upon the cross, Christ arose from the dead. And just as sure as the sun will rise, Jesus Christ my Lord, my Savior, will come again!"*[1] I looked around, and a palpable grace danced throughout the room. It seemed as if the whole congregation was holding our collective breath. "Amen!" "Alleluia!" community members shouted, moved by the truth of that moment and the reality of the words we had just sung.

A few moments later, everyone moved out of the pews for the sign of peace. Eighty-year-old women—pillars of the St. Patrick's community—and their five-year-old great-grandchildren alike doled out hugs and kisses, handshakes and smiles for a good ten minutes. "Welcome, sister!" the handsome man seated behind me beamed. "Beautiful necklace. . . . Welcome to St. Pat's," said the choir-robed woman with magnificent dreadlocks. I smiled to myself, loving that it took Father Greg another five minutes to get everyone back in their seats. This energy was a lived and active faith clothed in the rich fabric of African-American culture.

Mass came to an end, and Mary Washington made her weekly announcements. There was a crab feed reminder—tickets were still available. Male volunteers were needed to mentor the youth basketball league. The choir sang "Happy Birthday" to everyone celebrating during the upcoming week. And finally she exclaimed, "Last but certainly not least, we would like to acknowledge our visitors. Please stand if this is your first time at St. Patrick's." A few of us stood, and the congregation erupted in applause. I sat back down. "Thank you for being with us today. If you are searching for a parish, please consider St. Patrick's your church

---

[1] "Jesus Died upon the Cross." © 1980, Grayson Warren Brown. Published by OCP Publications, 5536 NE Hassalo, Portland, OR 97213. All rights reserved. Used with permission.

home!" I exhaled, resting in the peace I had just encountered, ending my search. Again I was welcomed, embraced by a culture that was beautifully new and a faith that was comfortingly familiar. I felt it. I knew it. I was home!

Growing up with Tongan Masses in my family room, celebrating *La Posada* with my students, and being welcomed into the arms of the St. Patrick's family have given me only a few glimpses of how the beauty of different cultures enrich the Catholic tradition. I have been blessed not only with the opportunity to work with many diverse students, but also to make friends who have contributed to my appreciation of a culturally enriched faith, whether their background be Vietnamese, Mexican, Filipino, or Nigerian. The diverse and multicultural membership of the Catholic Church today has been, and continues to be, both gift and treasure to me. I love that regardless of where we all come from, we sit down at the same eucharistic table and share in a faith that truly is universal in all of its diversity. Our Catholic Church has the awesome duty and responsibility of fully embracing and becoming the multicultural reality of its members, one that works toward an ideal community not bound by language, skin color, or ethnic background. Our church is called to be a place of welcome that calls each of us to share our differences and embrace the beauty of so many parts becoming one body.

I am grateful for the blessings of welcome I have received from these many faces of the church I call home, and I can't help but question what this welcome then requires of me as a Catholic. What does it mean to truly welcome another? To open up home and church and heart to someone new? As I try to answer these questions, my thoughts turn to the immigration histories of so many of my students, friends, and, most important, my own family. Traveling in search of new opportunities, new freedoms, and new lives, many immigrants bring with them cultural identities rich with tradition and value systems based on faith. Whether coming to America to pursue better economic opportunities, to fulfill educational dreams, or to escape political turmoil and warfare, the importance of the homegrown faith and the welcome of the church in the United States is a common thread in so many of the migration stories I have heard. As in my Tongan living room Masses, the practice of faith is a link to the homeland left behind and a means to uphold culture and tradition. The unique matrix of culture and tradition carried here and welcomed by the church enrich and reshape the face of American Catholicism.

Since its beginning, the Catholic Church in the United States has played host to people from countries throughout the world, helping to establish parishes and schools to support immigrant groups. Such history holds important implications for each of us as members of the Catholic Church in the United States today, where immigration concerns dominate the evening newscasts, lunchroom chatter, and political ballots. What role does the church need to play in supporting the multitude of Catholic migrants entering the United States from Latin America, the Caribbean, Africa, the Middle East, and the Pacific Islands? What voice must the church be for voiceless immigrant communities, facing a variety of obstacles once in the United States, and the countless others still seeking refuge outside its doors?

In their pastoral statement *Welcoming the Stranger Among Us: Unity in Diversity,* issued in 2000, the United States Conference of Catholic Bishops calls for a renewed welcome—a new embrace of cultural diversity. The church and each of us as its members must more consciously and actively invite all, especially the immigrant, into our living rooms, our school gymnasiums, our church pews, and our eucharistic table. This renewed welcome is an opportunity for mutual enrichment, stemming from the gifts all have to offer, as we reshape our church into a place for all to call home.

As I contemplate the renewed welcome required of each of us, I am reminded of the wisdom of ancient Tongan voyagers that was passed down to me through story. While navigating new and challenging waters, Tongan voyagers were often forced to seek safety on unfamiliar shores. Upon this new and seemingly uninhabited ground, they not only found safety and rest, but also the necessary resources to continue on their journeys. Planted food crops, fresh water, and dry firewood had been left by travelers who had previously walked on the same sands. Gratefully and wholeheartedly, the voyagers received the gifts of those who had come before them and made sure to leave new gifts in place for all those who were still to come. They experienced true hospitality and welcome—community from strangers—and they returned it in faith, hope, and love to strangers yet to come. The members of the Catholic Church are called to be voyagers—both welcomed home and welcoming home.

Tongan mats on a family room floor, *champurrado* in the school gym, the warm embrace of a gospel song. Home! Welcome! This church I call home.

Tefi Ma'ake is the oldest child of a Tongan father and a Swedish American mother. She was born in Hawaii, grew up in San Diego, and currently resides in Los Angeles where she works as campus minister and theology teacher at Notre Dame Academy. She holds a Bachelor of Arts in sociology and theology and a Master of Arts in secondary education from Loyola Marymount University in Los Angeles, and a Master of Theological Studies with a specialization in multicultural theology and religious education from the Franciscan School of Theology in Berkeley. In her spare time, Tefi loves to read, experiment in the kitchen, and spoil her nieces.

Mi Condición Femenina, y Mi Fe

Nancy K. Olivas

I am a Mexican-American Catholic from Los Angeles—quite a cliché. In this diverse city, we are the dominant ethnicity and religion. That's a fact I am quite proud of. It feels secure to be part of the masses. But unlike most Mexican Americans in this city, I am an eighth-generation Angeleno, while most others are first- or second-generation.

My family has been here since before the movie stars.

There is a machismo, a sexism infused with patriarchy, in my culture that is nearly unrivaled by any other community. Only in the Catholic Church do I encounter a similar machismo. My life as a Mexican-American woman parallels my experience as a Catholic woman—in both, discrimination is shamelessly present, and there is a constant reminder that women are second-class citizens because of our gender. This ordering is dictated from the pulpit with the expectation that it be lived out from the pews, as if this is the way the world was meant to be.

But my recognition of this machismo came later. Growing up, the church was a safe haven for me in so many ways. I loved Catholic school, confirmation class, and camaraderie with the other Mass-goers. My home life was unhappy, so this warm, communal atmosphere soothed my inner wounds. My Catholic community cared for me. One afternoon my high school counselor at Bishop Montgomery High School pulled me out of class to talk with me about my relationship with my father, which she knew was strained. She just wanted to let me know that she was on my side and would always be there for me. The church was a gift to me—a place of solace and comfort.

As I grew older and immersed myself in further education, I began to question the discrimination of women within the church. It felt personal. How could this place that brought me so much comfort shut the door on other women and me, just because of our gender? Even though I've never felt called to priesthood, why should I follow such a blatantly discriminatory teaching?

I have been to confession twice in my life. The intimacy of this sacrament, of telling my sins to another human, makes me hesitate. I can only confess to someone whom I can relate to. How can I relate to a priest? His life experience is vastly different from mine. Once, I confessed to women who worked in the church. This was a defining moment in my life—the realization that I could open up about my darkest places to a woman confessor who simply *got* me, but was held back by these rules of the church. What a weight off my shoulders, sitting and talking with these women who offered motherly guidance. So I fulfilled the sacrament of penance, but on my own terms.

So there are these things.

I cannot let go of my religion. It is just in my blood.

In my early twenties, I was in an abusive relationship for three and a half years. That infamous machismo reared its ugly head. He was bigger, stronger, and believed my existence was solely to serve him. When I finally ended this relationship, I ran back to my safe haven—the church. But I ran right into it. That machismo. I sat and knelt and stood in Mass at a man's request, a man whose right to have that power rested in his maleness.

One Ash Wednesday morning, I received a call from my ex-partner. He reminded me why I left him by blatantly stating that he would travel several miles to patronize a community because they subjugated women.

Ash Wednesday has always been a meaningful Mass to me because it symbolizes change—the beginning of a new season. As I sat in Mass that evening, I realized that the way the church was treating me—excluding me from the altar—was an extension of my abusive relationship. I decided to leave the church.

But three years later, I wanted my community back. I missed my congregation, the energy I feel among a large worshiping group of people. I missed the Eucharist, the union with Jesus Christ on a regular basis. And I missed the social justice teachings of the church. I have never experienced the generous nature of the Catholic Church anywhere else. I was ready to return.

On one condition. I promised to do my part to change the church's machismo. I could not play the role of passive resister. I rejoined my parish and joined the Women's Ordination Conference, and have remained active in both for the past four years. This gives me the benefit of practicing my beloved religion with the hope that one day things will change.

Nancy K. Olivas is an active member of the Women's Ordination Conference and a team leader for the Young Feminist Network. She lives and works in Los Angeles, California, and enjoys the beach, travel, and wine.

Challenging the Church, Finding My Faith

Emily Jendzejec

The door opened and Natalie came out with her head hung low, looking sheepish. She flashed me a grin as she made her way to the altar to do her penance. It was my turn now. A nervous and awkward preteen, I shuffled into the sacristy for my first confession.

The priest was waiting and he motioned to the empty chair in front of him. His gray hair shimmered from the candles behind him, creating the illusion of a holy glow that did not help my nervousness.

"Bless me, Father, for I have sinned." My voice was shaky as I crossed my hands and looked down at the floor.

"Good God, child! Your mother lets you out of the house with nails like that? Girls these days!" I froze in shock as the priest shrieked in disgust. I looked down at my nails. They were a rainbow of colors that I had just carefully painted before I had come to the church. I quickly hid them in my sweatshirt pocket, embarrassed but defensive.

"I am sorry if I offended you, sir!" I retorted and stood up to leave. With tears streaming down my face, I ran past the other children straight to the bathroom, with Natalie in close pursuit to comfort me. No man who judged my nails was going to judge my sins.

◆

Four years later, I was prepared. Next in line for confession, I had no sins to share, just one simple question to ask. Natalie opened the door and, with her head hung low, made her way to the altar to do her penance, flashing that same annoyed grin only a best friend can understand. I walked into the room where the priest sat yawning in sync with the creak of the door as I shut it behind me. A shy preteen no longer, my confident high school attitude empowered me to stare that same priest who had berated my choice in fingernail polish in the eyes.

I leaned forward in a challenging manner. He shifted uncomfortably in his chair, knowing he was in for something. I pulled out my Bible with passages hinting toward the subjugation of women bookmarked.

"In God's eyes, are men truly meant to have power over women?" I inquired.

"That is what the Bible says and we must believe it to be so."

I waited for him to say more; but as silence lingered, my heart sank and I got up to leave. My religion let me down once again. I wanted so badly to love this God, to embrace this faith, but this second incident again stood in my way. I shrugged and stood up. I managed to murmur, "Thank you, Father," as I left the room, closed the door and with it, decided to try to shut the church out of my life.

As I sat in a pew, swearing off the church, memories of the Catholicism I cherished swirled in my head. I was fascinated with the rituals at Mass, adored the stories in the New Testament, and was in awe of the pope in Rome. Natalie came up and sat next to me, putting a comforting hand on my shoulder. We had been best friends since we were five. We could giggle for hours and share long conversations of our struggles and joys with the church. Even as I fumed over the priest's response, the two of us whispered about the pilgrimage to Rome we were about to make together, laughed as we recalled the numerous youth retreats we had attended, and remembered being introduced to "faith through deeds" through Habitat for Humanity trips in impoverished areas of Appalachia. Natalie's help recalling these positive experiences throughout the years was a reminder of why I loved her and why I decided to not shut the church out of my life.

I started my freshman year of college a self-proclaimed "spiritual, but definitely not religious" person, since I still struggled with the hierarchical, institutional face of the church. Natalie and I chose different colleges, and Catholicism wasn't in fashion with the feminist circles I was now trying to join. Without my family and without Natalie by my side, embarrassment of my faith forced me to lie about it; I swept my true feelings under the rug. I sipped cappuccinos at the local java spot, nodding my head in agreement while my hip new friends denounced organized religion and jeered at the students making their way into the church across the street for Bible study.

But I was a closet Catholic. I attended Mass, sometimes twice a week, and just stared in awe at the paintings of the Blessed Virgin Mary, truly yearning for more. Church had always been my place for meditation, and a time to find solace and peace within myself, no matter how stressed or upset the world made me. The beautiful traditions of the Eucharist and the radical messages of the readings nourished my so-called nonreligious self.

I allowed myself to fall secretly in love with the saints, with Catholic social teaching, liberation theology, and especially Jesus. Here was this man—pacifist, feminist, and activist—who embodied the greatest type of love, unconditional love, for every person he met. I sat in theology class reading Gustavo Gutiérrez's *A Theology of Liberation*, soaking in every word. We discussed the Works of Mercy and peace: feeding the hungry, clothing the poor. Through justice comes peace. Jesus had it right, I thought, but the world still isn't listening.

Although I didn't have Natalie by my side anymore, I began to meet new friends who sat scattered in the pews and desks around me. Fruitful discussions brought a new flame to my spiritual life. I was thirsty for more; no longer ashamed of my faith, but still critical of the institution.

◆

Kneeling at Christmas Mass, home on my Christmas break, my hands began to sweat as I clenched them tighter and tighter together, not in deep prayer but in deep frustration. On the altar stood that same old priest from my first confession, praying for an increase in priestly vocations. "Hey, right here!" my inner dialogue shouted back. But then I remembered I couldn't, I didn't have that one essential organ. Natalie knelt a few rows back with her family, and I turned around to give her a discreet eye roll in response to the priest's message.

It's kind of funny, don't you think, God? But not even She was listening.

I shrugged and stood up for a closing rendition of "O Holy Night" as members of the church filed out to get back to the turkey in the oven or, in my family's case, the traditional Polish Christmas *perogis*.

Back at school after break, I was still upset over the prayer at Christmas Mass. I decided I couldn't stay silent any longer. I had to take a stand and not leave the church. Quite the opposite—I had to be a voice of change within the church. I became what I like to call "a thorn in the church's side." I started applying to the priesthood. I mailed dozens of letters that read:

To Whom It May Concern:

Although I know that at this present time the Catholic Church forbids the entry of women into the priesthood, I feel that I am qualified and able to serve God in this way, as are many lay women leaders in the church. It only seems right to allow a devoted servant of Jesus to serve the church and her people, regardless of the gender of the person. While I understand that the sisterhood is a respectable option, it prohibits women

*from truly taking her place in all celebrations of the church,
especially the Eucharist.*

My fire burned more brightly as rejection letters came back to
me. *I appreciate your desire to become a priest, but the Catholic
Church bars the way for you, as you recognize it forbids the entry
of women into the priesthood. . . . Sorry I cannot be of help,
maybe you should look into becoming a nun. . . . In his Apostolic Letter* Ordinatio Sacerdotalis, *Pope John Paul II stated that
the Catholic Church does not have the authority to confer priestly
ordination on women.*
This one really got to me. If the church does not have authority, who does? Guess we have to wait for Jesus to come back.

I continued these escapades throughout college with only a
few scattered replies. Most lacked empathy and none contained
the answers I wanted to hear. I continued to go to Mass, but still
I felt thwarted. Frustrated with my beloved church, I questioned
whether it was worth being part of an institution that preached
justice and equality but did not practice it within its own walls. I
prayed for answers and listened in vain to the silence, in search
of a reply.

Truly listening to the silence eventually did yield an answer. A
few days before I started a three-day silent retreat, my spiritual
director, Tammy, encouraged me to pray for guidance. Tammy
was a beautifully spiritual woman who had stuck it out in the
church and lived her faith with grace and conviction. I admired
her ability to question the authority of the church while humbly
working for justice through both prayer and action.
Tammy gave me Dorothy Day's *The Long Loneliness* to read.
Dorothy's words and Tammy's encouragement affirmed a feeling that I had held so dear all my life—that working for justice
and peace is what Catholicism is truly all about.

I kept Tammy, Dorothy, and Natalie in my prayers as I entered the silence. I lay on the rocks on a deserted beach during the weekend retreat. Without voices covering the sounds of nature, I could truly listen, absorb, be at peace. I closed my eyes and felt the rays of sunshine warm my cheeks, eyelids, lips. The cool winter breeze rushed over my body as crisp ocean mist sprayed my face. My body shivered as I began to focus my thoughts on opening my heart to the light.

Despite my lifelong struggles with the church, I always have carried a deep sense of faith. So I opened my mind and let myself pray. I sat for an hour, just breathing and communicating with God. It was such a peaceful and comforting hour that I wanted to stay in it forever. I realized that this feeling of acceptance did not have to go away. As much as the institutional church frustrates me, many friends and role models truly make up this church. And I love and belong to this church. I smiled and let out a joyful sigh of relief. I walked back toward my cabin with my head up high and my footsteps a bit lighter.

◆

A few years later, I am sitting among fifteen hundred other "progressive Catholics" at a Call to Action Conference in a crowded convention hall in Sacramento, California. We spent the weekend discussing the actions we need to take to cultivate a church of love and acceptance without losing the sacred traditions that draw many of us to Catholicism. I turn my attention to the priest near the altar as he begins the prayers of the faithful. He prays for an increase in priestly vocations. I cringe a bit, but he continues his prayer, "and for equality and the end of oppression both outside the church and within." My response is a resounding "Lord, hear our prayer!" To my joy, those around me sing out just as loud.

Mass ends, and I go straight to call my old friend Natalie. I tell her of the conference and the amazing conversations and debates it sprouted. I explain that I think I can safely say I am a

Catholic now. It is not a perfect religion by any means, yet it is the one I feel most drawn to. I can't abandon it.

"I guess we are both in it for the long haul!" she chatters back, bursting of news of the Jesus fish tattoo that now decorates her ankle. She giggles, using her knack for making light of the situation. I smile and realize we are not going anywhere. We were born into Catholicism. And are choosing to stay.

After graduating from Boston College in 2006, Emily Jendzejec spent a year with the Jesuit Volunteer Corps in Sacramento, California. She currently lives in Portland, Oregon. She is passionate about working for systemic change within the church and society, riding her bicycle, and dancing wherever, whenever possible.

Being a Catholic Woman

Our Father, who art in heaven,
hallowed be thy name.
Thy kingdom come, thy will be done,
on earth as it is in heaven.
Give us this day our daily bread
and forgive us our trespasses as we forgive those who trespass
against us.
Lead us not into temptation, but deliver us from evil.
Amen.

To be a young Catholic woman, as Margaret Scanlon describes it, is to live "with the ambiguity and messiness of it all, stuck between what the church is, and what the church could be." We grow up being told we can be anything we want to be—and then realize the church does not agree. Meagan Yogi's parents always encouraged their three daughters to do whatever made them happy and fulfilled. And Meagan believed it was possible, until her parish priest told her First Communion class that women can't be priests.

Being a Catholic woman often has the same startling incongruity that comes from hearing a group of women pray the Our

Father. Jessica Coblentz became aware of this paradox when she realized that the institutional church isn't always as loving and embracing as the Jesus she experienced during her struggle with anorexia. How could a church founded on the Jesus who showed her how to love exclude her from the pulpit?

I (Kate) used to braggingly complain about how much more housework I did than my younger sisters. My mom often chided, "Ah, don't be such a martyr, honey." And I never quite understood—the martyrs I knew of were usually saints, glorified in stained glass and in saints-of-the-day calendars. Martyrs sacrificed themselves for God and for others. They forgave trespasses and their model was supposed to help lead us away from temptation. We prayed for their guidance in glorifying God, Our Father, at every Mass. Wasn't sacrifice a good thing?

During my sophomore year of college, I discovered why some feminist theologians refuse to spend much time thinking about the whole "Christ died and rose" part of the Christian story. The glorification of sacrifice, as read by too many women for too long as instructions for being a good person has left too few women able to stop abuse of various forms. As a sign of solidarity, my twenty-year-old self decided to be silent during the eucharistic prayer, resisting the glorification of sacrifice.

This resisting sacrifice, it's a slippery slope. It so easily becomes ideological. All of a sudden, I didn't know if I was living up to my protest if I sacrificed time alone for time with a friend in need. It has taken me a while to understand what feminist theologians and my mom must already know: there is good sacrifice and bad sacrifice, good suffering and bad suffering, and the lines are blurry—the challenge is to lean toward the good kinds.

For years, Deborah Heimel worried about how the Boston LGBTQ community would receive her deep appreciation for all things Catholic. She hid her Mass-goings and her desire to participate in Good Friday processions, sacrificing her Catholic identity for her lesbian one. And it was the bad kind of sacrifice, the kind that suffocated her, the way sacrifice has a tendency to do to women. She eventually came out as Catholic because she could no longer ignore that being Catholic is as much a part of her as being a lesbian—both, she realized, are her daily bread.

Halfway across the country, Kerry Egan sat in a rocking chair, breastfeeding her newborn, basking in the 4:00 a.m. stillness of a Midwestern winter. She fed her baby, urging him, "Take this and eat it; this is my body," and she suddenly understood eucharistic sacrifice. And it was the good kind, the kind that nourished her and her son.

Figuring out how to hold the tension between the institution's gender norms and our twenty-first-century expectations of being a woman in the tradition is a lifelong experiment for young Catholic women. And figuring out how to be a healthy Catholic, faithfully reciting prayers to Our Father requires the practice, patience, and persistence of strong young Catholic women.

Why I Stay

Margaret Scanlon

Not too long ago, I met my friend Jake for our monthly Friday lunch date. We placed our order while updating each other on the hurried details of our lives, but as the waiter walked away, my companion suspended our game of catch-up. "What's with the clam chowder? I thought you said you were hungry." I quickly reassured him that, no, I wasn't on a diet; I was "on" Lent. It was Friday, so I was having a light lunch without meat—question answered, or so I thought. I tried to move our conversation back to where it had been (in the middle of a particularly juicy story involving his roommate), but instead, Jake, who is usually one of the most open-minded men I know, asked, *"You're* Catholic? *Why?"* My face flushed and my ears rang. Why, indeed.

I would have loved, at that moment, to have a snappy retort. One akin to the responses all liberated women are taught to use for similarly awkward social situations. You know the ones. When asked why you're not married yet, the recommended acidic response is, "Because I just love hearing that question," or, "Just lucky, I guess!" And if nosy folks want to know why you haven't popped out any kids, just reply, "And have sex? Yuck!" Issue deftly skirted.

Did I say I would have loved a *snappy* retort? I mean to say, at that particular moment, I would have settled for *any* retort. As I stammered like a moron, Jake followed up his awkward *"Why?"*

with a backhanded compliment. "But you're so smart," he said, with an incredulous tone. Oh, the irony! Jake was complimenting my intelligence while I could barely string a sentence together.

But the thing is, he was right. I *am* smart. I'm not brilliant, but I don't often doubt my intelligence or play dumb, either. I've loved learning as long as I've been a student—both in and out of school. And when I am lucky enough to find myself in an academic setting, the process thrills me. I love it all: the frustration of wrestling with new terminology, the late-night study sessions, the sleep deprivation I self-inflict to meet a deadline. I thrive on the new questions that arise from a good class discussion; I skim the new arrivals shelf at the library; I underline and mark obscure footnotes. In short, I am a nerd. And a Catholic one.

So do I agree that intelligence and Catholicism are mutually exclusive? Of course not. Implying that a woman's intelligence should keep her from being Catholic is a bit like implying that a woman's attractiveness should keep her from being single— a blatant mistake. Persuasive argument, right? Eloquent case, obvious line of reasoning? Perhaps. Irrelevant, however, if all this good sense occurs *only in my head.*

Sitting across from Jake, nothing resembling coherence came out of my mouth. Instead, I hemmed and hawed while I stared at my friend, obviously struggling to answer his question. Typically, Jake and I both agree that I am funny, articulate, engaging. Just not at that point. Not handling this question. Which is why it is unfortunate that we Catholic women don't have zingers readily available to fire back at our inquisitors. When fielding questions like, "Why are you Catholic?" the phrases, "Because I like patriarchy!" or, "Who doesn't like celibate men dictating the rules about sex?" just don't seem to have the right amount of chutzpah.

And maybe there's a reason for the lack of witty repartee.

You see, half the time, I'm not really sure why I'm Catholic either.

Let me be clear. There are moments, Masses, months, when I am overcome with the beauty I find in my faith, in the "smells and bells" of it all. On occasion, nothing strikes at my core more than the smell of incense, or singing *Pange Lingua Gloriosi* on Holy Thursday. Liturgy and sacrament are part of the magnificence—I routinely cry at baptisms and weddings, I love the self-reflection that miraculously emerges during Lent, and I am filled with hope in the resurrection at Easter Vigil. Each time I receive Eucharist I am enveloped with a peace I haven't yet encountered elsewhere. These flashes of grace are so nourishing, and bring such a feeling of being enfolded in God's very self, that the thought of leaving becomes incomprehensible.

Then there are the moments when I am infuriated. When I reflect on the sexual abuse scandal so fresh in the memory of the American church. When I read and reread, easily picking apart the arguments opposing women's ordination. When I am told the contradictory message that I am made in the image and likeness of God, but that the way I am made in God's image directly hampers my ability to stand *in persona Christi*. When the institutional church cannot keep its mouth shut about sexual practices between any and all human beings, but does not speak loudly (if at all) to rail against rape. When our "culture of life" condemns the evil of abortion, often without addressing any impetus behind such a painful decision—to say nothing of our too often quiet acquiescence to the death penalty. When as a female Catholic, I am routinely told to model Mary—woman par excellence—instead of her Son, the Christ in whom I profess my faith.

And occasionally, there are moments when I am more than infuriated. I am insulted, despondent, and heartbroken. Jake asks, "Why are you Catholic?" and to be honest, when I think of all the church's failings, his inquiry becomes something of a mantra inside my head. In the end, the feeble response I gave Jake during our lunch wasn't much of an answer, and I would change that if I could. Today, instead of tripping all over myself, I would tell him very simply, "I am Catholic because I *am*." I wish I could be more lucid, but there it is. I'm a cradle Catholic; for better or worse, my religion so deeply permeates who I am that I can never entirely be free of it. That includes living with the ambiguity and messiness of it all, stuck somewhere between what the church is, and what the church could be. I wrestle with it, I question it, I rail against it—but only because I am entirely devoted to it. Staying isn't easy, but it *is* the choice that I make, over and over again.

I would tell Jake that I simultaneously love and loathe my church. Is it perfect? Far from it. Then what makes me stay? It's the knowledge that my church—for all its imperfections, sins, and failings—is part of my genetic code. My insides. Not only because it is both my biological and spiritual family, but also because it is where, to my chagrin, I feel God speaking to me and molding my life. What's more genetic than that?

Something from within, something hereditary, tells me that any church staking a claim on the Gospel of Jesus Christ is meant to be more than what ours currently is. I would tell Jake about the people I celebrate Mass with, the faith I am so honored they share with me, and the hope for the future that they instill within me. I would tell him that, for better or for worse, my church is, at its root, a community of people just like me. We attempt to respond to God's love for the world, as best we know how, in our everyday lives. *That* is Good News. And so, Jake—yes, I am Catholic. I stay.

Margaret Scanlon recently earned her Master of Theological Studies from Weston Jesuit School of Theology. She currently lives in Cambridge, Massachusetts, and is completing her second year of teaching theology at Boston College High School.

Nursing, Eucharist, Psychosis, Metaphor

Kerry Egan

Because there was no shade on the window, winter moonlight poured onto the rocking chair and onto the baby and me. It was below zero, as it often is at four o'clock in the morning in December in Iowa, and cold seeped through the glass. The baby didn't seem to mind. In the blue light his mouth looked like a tiny morning glory flower planted on my nipple, and his hands held and stroked my breast, as six-month-olds do when they nurse. Every now and then he stopped and opened his eyes. When he saw me he would smile for just a second and resume suckling at twice his former speed.

In a few minutes he fell asleep again. As his mouth went slack and his face fell away from me, a trickle of milk flowed from his mouth down his cheek.

Even after he was done nursing, I stayed in the chair, my feet up on an ottoman and a blanket thrown over both of us. Not quite awake but certainly not asleep. For months, this hour that was not quite morning but no longer really night was the only peaceful time of the day. It was the only time my brain would slow down, the only time that memories of my son's birth did not dominate my thoughts, crashing through and leaving me shaking, crying, in a state of confusion, unable to function, terrified and terrorized.

On this night a thought seeped through. By the time I noticed it, I had been repeating a phrase over and over again: "Take this and eat it. This is my body."

I looked down at Jimmy as he clung to me. "Oh," I nearly shouted. He stirred, lifted his half-closed eyes to me, and then rooted around until he found the nipple again and settled back into my armpit.

"So that's what that means," I said out loud.

After thirty-one years as a cradle Catholic, the Eucharist finally made sense.

When Jimmy was born by emergency C-section, the anesthesia failed mid-surgery. When my legs began thrashing on the operating table, the anesthesiologist gave me two hundred milligrams of ketamine, a powerful hallucinogenic drug that knocked me into a psychotic break so severe that it functioned as a sort of dissociative anesthesia. Basically, I no longer felt any pain because my mind had been chemically severed from my body.

On ketamine, I had no body but was immersed in a small pink tunnel that swirled around me. The tunnel was some sort of an entity, also bodiless but somehow all encompassing and alive. I was suspended in this being and I was asking this thing questions. Very patiently, and with a bit of sadness, the entity answered me.

"This can't be all there is," I said, over and over again.

"Yes, this is it. This is the only thing that's real."

"But what about the world?"

"No, that's not real."

"But it is real. I've been there. It was real."

"No, that all comes from your imagination. This is what's real. The rest is just what you want to be real. You made all that up."

"And so there's no meaning to it at all? It all means nothing?"

"That's right. There is no meaning. None of it's real. All the things in the world—you people just made that up to make yourselves feel better."

"This just can't be. This can't be all that is real."

"No, this is it."

And so on, over and over for what I thought was eternity. The entity, either unable or unwilling to comfort me, just kept repeating that it was the only thing that was real.

Nothing mattered; nothing was real. All of existence was a misperception. If nothing else was real, if nothing else mattered, then what was the point of my life? What was the point of life at all?

I had built my adult life around questions of meaning. I was a hospital chaplain. Day in and day out I sat with people as they struggled with questions of suffering and purpose—of their lives, of their illnesses, of their deaths—and it was my job to help them construct meaning out of painful realities. Just a few days before the birth, I had sent in to the publisher the final revisions of a book I had written about grief and prayer. This was the work I had wanted to devote my life to: to give meaning to loss and suffering. My faith had meant everything to me, and now I was terrified that what this entity said was true. I was terrified of God. I was terrified of life. I lived in a perpetual state of fear and confusion, unable to trust even my own experiences. I didn't know what was real anymore. My waking life felt like sleep, and the desolation of the tunnel was reality.

"Psychosis" literally means soul sickness, and the infection that caused the disease was this: the idea that all of life meant nothing, that reality was just a dream, and that God did not care one bit what suffering this might cause. The infection seeped into every thought, every feeling, every moment I was awake.

The half-life of ketamine is about twelve hours, but for months after it was physically out of my system, its effects remained. Drug-induced psychosis turned into untreated postpartum psychosis. For most of the day, I was disconnected from my body and seemed to be floating around it. I was often unable to understand what other people said to me. I could read individual words but couldn't comprehend sentences. Sometimes I couldn't muster the energy or desire to move. Images of the pink tunnel burst into consciousness a dozen times an hour. I could drive these images away by shaking my head violently back and forth, but whenever my mind wandered toward prayer or even thoughts of God, my heart would pound and every cell of my body burned with terror and I would have to run away from the thought, either out the front door and into the street, or into the bathroom where I could cover my head with a towel.

But nursing Jimmy in the darkness, half-asleep in the glider, I was in my body and terror never intruded. Sometimes I even felt something akin to happiness.

I remember as a child and even into my teenage years craning my neck during Mass at the time of the transubstantiation, waiting to see or feel something when the little bells rang. "Take this and eat it. This is my body, given up for you." As far as I could see, nothing happened. Certainly no alchemical change from bread to body. In theology classes at my Catholic high school, the more the teachers insisted that the bread and wine literally turned into flesh and blood, the less meaningful the whole ritual became for me. Any person could see that it was a piece of wafer and bad wine.

In college religion and theology classes, the Protestant ideas that God is with and around the bread and wine, or that it was a ritual of remembrance, seemed to make much more sense. And the criticism that the Eucharist was cannibalistic seemed uncomfortably accurate. I became embarrassed of the Catholic insistence on transubstantiation.

As I grew older I did find some meaning in symbolic understandings of what communion meant. But the literalism at the heart of the Roman Catholic assertion that bread and wine become the substance of God, and that substance is flesh—is the body of Jesus—was not just creepy but unfathomable.

When a woman holds her breast to a baby's mouth and patiently strokes the nipple across a newborn's lips, she is telling the baby to take this and eat it. That it is her body and she wants her baby to have it. There is joy and solace and peace in offering your child your body for her sustenance, for her comfort, for her strength.

I nursed Jimmy for the first time in the neonatal intensive care unit, where he was taken at birth because of meconium aspiration syndrome and two collapsed lungs. He was four days old and I was topless. One nurse held Jimmy, wrangled the various tubes and wires connected to him, checked to make sure his oxygen saturation didn't dip too low. Another nurse adjusted pillows and me, showing me how to position the baby so that no monitors were set off. A lactation specialist dripped sugar water on my breast and tried to coax Jimmy's mouth open with her other hand. Suddenly, and almost roughly, she shoved the baby onto my breast and he clamped down. He sucked for perhaps a minute and then fell asleep. It didn't seem as though anything had happened, and yet when the nurse took him from me, there was the thin, white liquid drooling from his mouth and drops on my skin.

As strange as it was to think that my body had created this new person, it was even stranger to have milk dripping from me. It seemed miraculous and magical and even a little bit frightening that my body—any mother's body—could be food for someone else. But by the time a mother and baby hit the two-month mark, nursing is pedestrian and routine, even as it remains intimate and cozy. There is nothing creepy or cannibalistic about it at all. It is both mundane and sacred.

It was the literal understanding of the Eucharist that was salvific for me in the months of untreated psychosis. The Roman Catholic insistence that this is not symbolic, this is not just an idea, this is not a metaphor for the love of God—that this is literally the substance of God you ingest that becomes a part of your flesh—was something that made sense in my body when my mind was broken.

As I sensed it that night, if Christ wants to nurture me with his body, and I want to nurture my baby with my body, then God must feel for me something like I feel for my child. In those hours God was no longer terrifying, no longer cold and uncaring. If I felt this way about nursing my baby, how must God feel about me?

At a time when I was struggling with delusions, many of them religious in nature, and at a time when I dealt with depersonalization, derealization, and dissociation, a corporeal understanding of God was something I clung to for months and years as I clawed my way out of postpartum psychosis. I was nursed that night by God just as surely as I nursed my child.

Cloistered monks and nuns pray throughout the day and night. They rise every three hours, believing that their prayers are transforming the world they cannot see. Mothers of newborns are also up every three hours, day and night. I've come to think of those four-in-the-morning nursings as prayer at a time when I could not pray as I once did.

Jesus said that we must be like little children to enter the kingdom of God. Perhaps like suckling infants.

This idea was new to me, but it wasn't a new idea. The importance of nursing as a metaphor for the love of God is found throughout the history of Christianity, in medieval and Renaissance painting, in the poems and theological reflections of mystics, in the Bible.

References to nursing are sprinkled throughout the Hebrew Bible. Some scholars have suggested that *El Shaddai*, a name of God translated as "God Almighty," is derived from the Hebrew word for breast, *shad*, and should be poetically understood as referring to a God who nurses and nurtures his (her?) people. Though there is disagreement about whether this etymology is correct, there are even more explicit Biblical references to breastfeeding.

The psalmist tells us, "But I have calmed and quieted my soul, like a weaned child with its mother; my soul is like the weaned child that is with me" (Ps 131:2). And the prophet Isaiah, speaking of Zion: "Rejoice with her Jerusalem, and be glad for her, all you who love her; rejoice with her in joy, all you who mourn over her—that you may be satisfied from her consoling breast; that you may drink deeply with delight from her glorious bosom" (Isa 66:10-11).

In Catholic theology, the church has long been described as a mother nursing her children, the faithful. Nursing has also been an important trope in the cult of the Virgin Mary. The classic Renaissance image of the Madonna and Child shows Mary bare-breasted, encouraging her baby to nurse. A fat naked baby boy stands or sits in his mother's lap, one exposed breast, round and pale, at the center of the image. The image of Mary nursing Jesus was present, though rarely used, in Christian art since the second century. In the early fourteenth century, however, a veritable deluge of paintings of the *Madonna lactans* burst into Tuscany. The pictures were something of a visual revolution in theology at the time. Previously, Mary was usually depicted as the Queen of Heaven, with crown, splendid robes, and a retinue of angels. When she was depicted with her baby, both were usually formally posed, staring stiffly at the viewer. The Christ Child usually looked more like a miniature king with regal bearing, standing tall on his mother's lap, than a hungry baby.

At this time wealthy Italian women did not nurse their own babies. If the family could afford it, a wet nurse moved into the parents' house to breastfeed the child for up to four years. In most cases, the infant was sent to the home of a nurse and her family out in the countryside. The image of Mary nursing her child told the viewer that she was a common woman who could not afford a nurse. The image of Christ as a baby hungrily nursing told the viewer that Jesus was a vulnerable infant like any other human. The popularity and importance of these images of *Madonna lactans* is hard to overstate.

During the Council of Trent, part of what is known as the Catholic Reformation or Counter-Reformation, a decree that restricted nudity was issued about the portrayal of sacred figures in art. And so the *Madonna lactans* faded in iconographic importance in the Catholic imagination. The mother and child were increasingly painted all covered up. Recently, a friend who is a parish priest in Houston, Texas, commissioned a statue for a new chapel to Mary in his church. All three models proposed by artists, of Mary nursing Jesus, were rejected by his congregation that stridently protested the idea of a bare breast in the church.

Medieval mystics embraced the breastfeeding metaphor. Catherine of Siena and Teresa of Avila wrote about God's nourishing breasts. It was Julian of Norwich, a fourteenth-century English anchoress, however, who wrote of a maternal God more than any other person. An important part of her theology was Jesus as nursing mother. In her thought, Jesus nurses us not with milk but with the blood of his wounds: "The mother may lay her child tenderly to her breast, but our tender mother Jesus, he may only lead us into his blessed breast by his sweet open side."

Girls and young women entering the convent were sometimes given toy cradles and dolls of the infant Jesus that they could take care of, pretending to nurse and swaddle and rock the baby as a spiritual devotion. A crib and doll given to a German nun named Margaretha Ebner in 1344 led to a series of mystical dreams in which she was awakened by the Christ Child in his crib and breastfed him back to sleep.

But there is, sometimes, something not quite right in these images and ideas of breastfeeding. They are beautiful, surely, but they can be sentimental, idealized, romanticized into a picture of nursing that many women might not recognize as anything resembling their experiences trying to breastfeed their children. We never see Mary's cracked nipples, the psalmist never complains about plugged ducts or mastitis, and Julian never addresses the issue of what it would mean if the milk never came in, or supply was too low and the baby began losing weight.

When my daughter was born a little more than two years after Jimmy, I looked forward to nursing. I stood in the shower one day at the end of the pregnancy, rubbing my nipples to try to bring on labor, and had a sudden physical memory of nursing and a rush of joy and anticipation. But it was different with Mary Frances. Almost from the beginning, we had trouble.

On November afternoons, when it was dark by four, we sat on the couch in our low-ceilinged living room, trying to nurse. A stream of *Sesame Street*, *Blue's Clues*, and *Boohbah* blared from the television every day.

"Me play Mommy," Jimmy said, at first plaintively and then angrily. "No nurse baby," he yelled as he pulled on my shirt and pants. "Please Mommy Mommy Mommy."

"Okay Jimmy, just watch TV, sweetheart, please," I begged as Jimmy cried and Mary screamed and twisted and arched her back till she almost fell out of my arms. Nursing was not warm and cozy for either of us. Mary would nurse for a few minutes, and then pull away to scream and arch, then come back to the nipple to nurse for a little while longer, crying while she drank, tears smearing across my breasts. She clawed my skin, drawing blood, and mashed my nipples between her gums. She often spit up while trying to suckle, and choked herself on her own vomit. We have very few pictures of her first months of life, and in those that we do, her eyes are always swollen half shut, her face is a mottled red, and she is grimacing. She sometimes stopped in a moment of calm and looked at me. I thought I saw reproach and devastation in her bloodshot eyes.

The three of us drove around in the car when we couldn't take being trapped in the house anymore. Mary screamed. Jimmy threw crackers at her, tried to pull her car seat over, and shouted, "Stop it baby!" I turned up the stereo as loud as it would go and clutched the steering wheel with arms straight out in front of me and elbows locked, pressing my body hard into the seat. I curled my fingers around the wheel till the nails left deep purple crescents in my palms. I learned that Pearl Jam is by far the best music to drown out a colicky baby. My pediatrician suggested getting a coffee for me and munchkins for Jimmy at the Dunkin' Donuts drive-through, and then parking the car and standing outside of it for fifteen minutes. This way I could still see the baby but her screams would be muffled. Anything to not shake the baby.

"I'll stop nursing, if that would be better. I'll do anything."

"Don't stop nursing. If you think it's bad now, it'll be far worse on formula. Just keep trying," the doctor said when I brought the baby in every week, convinced she was dying.

I stopped eating onions, I stopped drinking milk, I stopped drinking caffeine. I nursed her on only one side at a time, I pumped for five minutes before nursing her, I spooned watery oatmeal down her gullet. I propped her up into a sitting position to nurse, I wore her hanging upright on my chest until I could no longer raise my arms from the pain in my back and shoulders. Nothing changed. We tried Zantac, then more Zantac, then Pepcid, then Prevacid, and then more Pepcid.

On the high dose of Pepcid, after months of screaming in pain, things finally started to change. Mary still vomited at least half of what she drank, sometimes spraying it out five feet across the floor and couch and dogs, and she still sometimes cried inconsolably, but only for twenty minutes at a time, instead of hours. At four months, she began to smile.

But the damage seemed to be done. She hated to nurse. She began losing weight, ushering in blood tests and weekly weigh-ins. I started supplementing with a bottle, popping it into her mouth every chance I had, when she was distracted by toys or Jimmy and wouldn't notice that it was a bottle and not a pacifier in her mouth, just to get a few more milliliters into her.

She nursed less and less, and I produced less and less milk. She turned her face away from me and would not latch on, much preferring her bottle filled with a thick, nasty-smelling cereal-soy formula combo. Finally, there was no milk left. I didn't cry like I did the first time I weaned a child. I was relieved, and I imagine maybe she was too.

I felt like the life had been sucked out of me when Mary finally stopped screaming at eight months. I felt like I had failed her. And I am ashamed to admit it, but I resented the nursing battle, and sometimes I even resented my baby. I resented how needy she was, how she fought me with all her might when I was trying to help her, how she alternately demanded and rejected me.

The eighteenth-century English novelist William Makepeace Thackeray wrote, "Mother is the name for God in the lips and hearts of little children." That's a heavy burden to any mother, especially the mother who cannot comfort her child, who comes to resent needing to comfort her child.

Does God ever feel this way about me? I wondered. I hoped not. The question that was comforting the first time I breastfed a baby was now dispiriting. The more I thought about this nursing and Eucharist analogy—the more I tried to make it fit into a logical framework—the less sense it made. And so my metaphor falls apart at some point, as all talk about God eventually does.

Metaphor is a product of the mind that can extract a concrete image from an ineffable experience, the mind that can extrapolate from symbol to symbolized, and discern idea from reality, hope or fear from delusion. Metaphor inhabits the realm of reason—the place that becomes sick with psychosis. Flashes of grace—a wash of peace or forgiveness or even clarity that comes from outside, that descends upon you at times unsuspecting, that jolts like a shock of static electricity—these flashes of grace bypass that place. They can speak to a part of the soul and brain that does not depend on healthy, abstract, or rational thought— the part that can be comforted in mental illness.

The metaphor falls apart, but the experience—the clarity, the comfort— remains crystallized in my mind.

I cannot offer any systematic, theological explanation of what the Eucharist means. I cannot even explain what it means in my own spiritual life, three years after psychosis. I'm no closer to being able to explain what I learned that winter night in Iowa when I was so sick than I was the day after it happened. I have no clarity to offer on the mysteries of the Transcendent or the mind. I spend my days in an endless cycle of cooking, feeding, playing, cleaning, and washing. I watch my children grow up. How they can change so much every morning from the night before is enough mystery to fill my head.

The other day, Mary sat in her high chair in the kitchen in our house in Massachusetts eating lunch. She picked up her last glob of smushed lasagna, reached out, and offered it to George the dog. George, of course, gobbled it right out of her hand. When she realized that she had no more food on her tray and that George was not going to give the lasagna back, she began to cry. Jimmy approached her and patted her hand, murmuring, "It's okay. It's all okay." It's what I used to sing-song over and over, as much to myself as to Mary when she sobbed while nursing. I didn't know Jimmy had been listening to me all those months until I heard my son mimic me in comforting his sister. It reminded me of Julian's most famous words, growing out of her maternal God imagery: "All shall be well, and all shall be well, and all manner of thing shall be well."

The promise of the Eucharist—the words a woman unthinkingly murmurs to soothe her child, a morsel of hope in the pain and terror of psychosis—that it will all be okay.

Kerry Egan graduated from Harvard Divinity School with her Master of Divinity several years ago. Her senior thesis became Fumbling: A Pilgrimage Tale of Love, Grief, and Spiritual Renewal on the Camino de Santiago *(Doubleday, 2004), and she is now a senior editor with Iowa Wordwrights.*

Coming Out Catholic

Deborah Heimel

May today there be peace within.

Several times a year, different family members or friends forward me these words over email. They are the first lines of a prayer attributed to St. Therese of Lisieux, a Carmelite nun who lived in the late 1800s. She is known as the "little flower" because she said she could best give glory to God simply by being her little self, even among all the other flowers. She accepted herself for who she was and knew she was beautiful.

I first read St. Therese's autobiography in college, during a semester abroad in Berlin, Germany. It was one of a handful of books I took with me on the trip. I don't recall how I initially acquired it, but I remember thinking the semester would be challenging and I should take something that would give me strength and reassurance. A book about a saint seemed like a good idea. As I read the autobiography, I judged her a little wacky. Her prayerful words made me uncomfortable. But I did like her sense of self and was amazed by how aware she was of her thoughts and feelings, even acknowledging ones I am often too afraid to admit. Somewhere in the middle of the book, she won me over. I finished it, impressed by her attitude and trust in God.

May you trust God that you are exactly where you are meant to be.

My post-college adventure into the real world began with the Jesuit Volunteer Corps (JVC). I received a long list of placement options from JVC and indicated an interest in almost every job related to housing and homelessness. Many of the other placements were in service areas I was unfamiliar with—working with children, doing community organizing, and assisting with legal or immigration issues. While I had no experience in housing either, I thought the learning curve might be smaller. I simplified it by thinking, "I could talk to women living in a shelter or I could be responsible for keeping people from being deported." Talking won, hands down.

I waited eagerly to see what job I would receive. I chose to stay on the East Coast to be near family and friends, but in JVC terms that meant anywhere from Maine to North Carolina. Maybe a shelter for women in DC? Or a transitional program in Philly? And then I got the call. They wanted me to work at a shelter for men in Hartford, Connecticut. This was one of the few housing jobs I had *not* checked because the learning curve for this particular job seemed pretty steep. They said it was intense and one of their best placements on the entire East Coast. I sensed they used the word "best" in a different way than I did. Best like fun, easy, happy? Or best like you'll be pushed so far out of your comfort zone you may never find your way back?

Four months later I attended JVC's orientation retreat. I had a hard time concentrating on the events of the first few days. Not only did the thought of the job make my stomach lurch, I had to tell my new housemates I was gay. I had only been out to myself for less than a year, and out to friends for a few months. I didn't have a lot of practice at coming out, especially not to people with whom I would pool money, as is JVC policy. I feared they would show their discomfort with my sexual orientation in subtle ways, like ignoring my additions to the grocery list. Staying in the closet didn't seem so bad if the alternative was to go without Coca-Cola.

One by one my roommates arrived and I listened attentively to their every word. JVC is filled with socially conscious people, but it is also based on the theology and teachings of the Catholic Church. Did an interest in serving others necessarily mean an acceptance of different sexual orientations? Or did an interest in a religious organization mean they were homophobic? Although *I* knew that being gay and Catholic could go together, I was aware it wasn't a commonly held belief.

May you not forget the infinite possibilities that are born of faith.

One recent Good Friday, I was at a dinner party with a gathering of lesbians and allies. One woman mentioned that on her way to the dinner, she passed a group of people carrying a huge cross up a hill. As she described the scene with derision, I felt a longing to be on that hill. But, as my dinner companions rolled their eyes, I kept the thought to myself.

Good Friday is one of my favorite days of the year. The solemnity takes my breath away, and I cry every year from pure gratitude. This is confusing to some, especially to those who know that I look forward to Good Friday processions as much as I look forward to annual gay pride parades.

When I first meet people, I find ways to talk about my partner or my work for the Boston Alliance of Gay, Lesbian, Bisexual, and Transgender Youth—as a way to casually out myself. Outing myself as a Catholic is harder. Phrases like, "I attended church on Sunday" or "I believe in Jesus" don't flow in most of my conversations quite as well, nor do they do justice to everything I feel. I don't talk about being Catholic because I don't know what to say, where to begin.

When I do tell someone I am Catholic, I often sense they assume I mean this in a purely cultural way, that I couldn't possibly mean it in a spiritual way. In their heads, they see it as a simple logic problem. I know you're gay, and I know that you can't be gay and Catholic, so therefore you can't be Catholic. At least not *really* Catholic.

But I am. I am culturally *and* religiously Catholic. I love the Stations of the Cross. I love the smell of incense and the quiet of Midnight Mass on Christmas Eve. I love the rituals and traditions and feel of a Catholic church. It feels familiar and good. I have tried other churches, worshiped in a variety of places and styles.

None of these feel like a religious home for me. The Catholic Church is my fallible, often frustrating vehicle to God.

May you use those gifts that you have received, and pass on the love that has been given to you.

The Catholic Church hasn't always felt like a home for me. Growing up, I arbitrarily identified as a Catholic because my parents took me to Mass on Sundays. Every Sunday we went, despite snow, errands, or vacations at the beach. The ritual was there. But the personal meaning for me was not. Then I went to college.

My first year, I joined InterVarsity Christian Fellowship (IVCF). I was curious about other types of Christianity, and I also wanted to be with people who were *excited* to be praying and singing about God. I often wished for a little more interest from the people in the pews at Mass and figured it was easier to go where the enthusiasm already existed than to try to create it. I got a little more than I bargained for with IVCF and I frequently felt overwhelmed and uncomfortable there—people openly talked about God and being saved, they prayed and sang with hands held high, and quoted biblical passages. I felt awkward in their company, but I kept going back anyway. It felt peaceful, loving, and spiritually fulfilling.

After my freshman year, I had the opportunity to go to Paris for World Youth Day, a gathering of Catholic youth from all over the world. My sister and I traveled with a group of nuns, students at Cabrini College, and members of the Cabrini Mission Corps from all across the world, including Israel, the Philippines, and Nicaragua. Everyone had their own story and I slept very little that week, trying to learn as many as I could. We talked about religious orders and discernment. We talked about how Masses differ by countries' customs. We talked about abortion and birth control. The conversations were fascinating and I loved every minute of them. What I loved the most was realizing how different we could all be, yet still be united in the Catholic Church.

IVCF was so different from my religious experiences in the Catholic Church. This conservative nondenominational Christian community filled a hole I didn't know I had. I didn't know if Catholicism could fill me in the same way. But World Youth Day answered that. I realized that some Catholics do sing with their hands in the air. They read the Bible. They *are* excited to go to Mass.

During this time, I realized I loved going to Mass. I loved it so much I often went *twice* on Sundays. I would go in the morning to the local Catholic church and then, at night, to the Mass on campus. I went twice because I loved the community that I experienced at Mass. I loved being a part of the Catholic community on campus and sharing time together in such an intimate setting. I also loved the community at the local town church. I didn't feel as much a part of it, but I loved to watch it—the ushers who knew everyone, the families who came and always sat in the same pew, the conversations about school or Girl Scouts between mothers on their way back to the parking lot.

Maybe I could be spiritually fulfilled as a Catholic. But did I want to? I began to address my complacent Catholicism. One friend really pushed me to think critically about my religion. He constantly challenged my understanding of the church and my faith: Why does the Catholic Church give out ashes on Ash Wednesday? Why is there a pope? Why do you confess to a priest? I was at a loss to answer most of his questions, to his satisfaction and my own. I wanted to answer the questions and I wanted to know if I agreed. So I started to research and read.

I took a course in American Catholicism. I read books and articles from different perspectives. I read about Vatican II, celibacy, and Pope John Paul II's papacy from conservative and liberal viewpoints. I read the *National Catholic Reporter* and the *National Catholic Register*. I read biographies of Dorothy Day, Oscar Romero, and Joseph Ratzinger (as he was known at the time). And I read about St. Therese of Lisieux.

May you be content knowing you are a child of God.

I don't remember spending a lot of time obsessing about or denying my sexual orientation, in part because I didn't understand that my feelings were different from anyone else's. I used to think all women shared my attraction to other women. I loved that women could compliment each other on their looks, try on clothes in the same dressing room, or snuggle while watching a movie. It's part of the female culture. But near the end of my college years I began to realize that maybe everyone didn't have *quite* the same feelings that I did.

Aside from my naïveté, it was also easier for me to accept my sexuality because I had already wrestled with the theology of it before I knew I was gay. As part of my research into Catholicism, I read several books by Henri Nouwen and Joan Chittister. As members of Catholic religious communities, they showed me a Catholicism where people could be committed to the Catholic Church and have a strong personal relationship with God yet be liberal in their theology.

At the end of my junior year, I went on a retreat. One day, everyone gathered to listen to a retreat leader speak. She spoke about a serious and meaningful romantic relationship she had with another woman when she was in her twenties. She left the relationship because she thought it was against God's will. I listened to her speak with an open mind, but I was not convinced that she had to leave the relationship to live a Christian life. As she talked, I felt a deep sadness for her.

The feelings from that speech reinforced what I was already thinking—being gay is not a sin. Months later I realized I was attracted to a woman. I was worried about the reaction of my friends and family, but this realization was made easier because I didn't have the internal religious conflict to worry about at the same time.

Let this presence settle into your bones, and allow your soul the freedom to sing, dance, praise, and love. It is there for each and every one of us.

I love the variety of people recognized as saints by the Catholic Church. It speaks to the multitude of ways we can live our lives as Catholics and shows the importance of valuing our individuality. My identity as both a Catholic and a lesbian is confusing to people who have certain ideas of Catholicism or certain ideas of gay and lesbian people. I might not fit the mold or follow the expectations that people have for these two groups, but I am following the path that is right for me.

May today there be peace within.

Deborah Heimel graduated from Drew University in 2000 and went on to serve as a Jesuit Volunteer in Hartford, Connecticut, in 2000–2001. She is now the director of operations at REACH Beyond Domestic Violence in Waltham, Massachusetts.

To Share a Meal with Jesus

Jessica Coblentz

When I close my eyes, I can still see myself standing there, fourteen years old, looking down at the glowing red numbers.

It is the fifth time I stand on the beeping black scale today. I cannot help it. *112.5*. I sigh, stepping off the box into my loose denim jeans. I always remove them to weigh myself. Turning, I toss my hair in the bathroom mirror, smile, and open the hallway door. I am starving.

The house sits atop a hill in a bustling Seattle suburb full of charming parks and walking trails, friendly neighbors and golden retrievers. Thanks to my parents' unceasing support throughout childhood, at age fourteen I am an outgoing leader and a passionate student with an amiable personality. I have played competitive soccer and taken on leading roles in local musical theater productions. On one hand, it has been a wonderfully pleasant upbringing.

On the other hand, the blind suburban bliss of youth has finally caught up to me. In junior high school I find myself amid a daunting depression. Injuries have pulled me from club soccer and school volleyball, and a new academic track has left me isolated from the comfort of scholastic ease and my long-standing clique. Without the busy-ness of the everyday and a collection of medals dangling around my neck, life seems immensely unfulfilling.

Attempting to ward off my depression, I do what many young American teen girls do: I don name brands and too much makeup, and embark on a more active quest for popularity. Absorbed in new ventures, I distract everyone—including myself—from the eating disorder I am secretly fostering. I like the affirmation I feel as I drop pounds and denim sizes. It is enough to sustain me throughout each day, even as my stomach churns. Between reps at the gym, I tell myself I need *this*. I do not need food, I need to be happy; I need to be so beautiful I am happy.

But the emptiness inside me is unrelenting. Despite thinner thighs, I still cry myself to sleep, quietly hoping that there is something more—that self-worth is not meant to be this hard.

One day I read the caption below a smiling, pale-skinned complexion in *People* magazine. It reads, "This is so-and-so at 103 lbs. At this point, she consumed 400 calories a day." That was more than I had eaten the day before. And she recently died. In spite of my obsession with mirrors, I truly see myself for the first time in a long time. *I have tried dangerously hard to fix things*, I think to myself, *and I am still so unhappy.*

Frightened and ashamed, I decide to battle my destructive habits. I am still depressed, though, and even more discouraged than before. I lose motivation for the activities, abilities, and social life that I once turned to for affirmation—all of that proved fleeting.

During lunchtime I find refuge on a smooth bench near the school parking lot. It is far from the noisy screams, fights, and giggles of the cafeteria—a room that only reminds me of how out of place I feel. For some reason I feel safer outside, alone. It becomes a routine. Day after day over good books, I wrestle with peanut butter sandwiches, and slowly, I begin to pray.

It was not really the first time I had *prayed*—my mother, a cradle Catholic, and my father, a convert, raised me in the large wooden parish church just a few minutes from our home. Years of Mass and religious education taught me my Hail Marys and

Our Fathers, but I had never prayed like I prayed during those lonely lunch hours. Against the drone of passing cars and the scent of impending rain, I experienced the most natural, stirring prayer of my life. I simply realized God was there, all of a sudden, like a pleasant stranger who politely invited herself to sit beside me one day, and just never left. Maybe because I was unfettered from my previous, consuming devotions—from the secret rituals of disordered eating and the sacred traditions of the all-too-comfortable church—I was able to hear God—a gentle, compassionate God who loves me. *Me.*

The *me* who had withered at the hands of my depression and disordered eating found new life in this divine companionship. During the months and years following my schoolyard prayers, generous ministers, our local youth group, Scripture, and continual prayer nurtured in me a deeply devoted Catholic faith. I found a mysterious, sustaining coherence in this conversion—a narrative that made sense for my life, my hopes, and the foundational truths I held about humanity. The more I encountered the gospel message of unconditional love, inclusivity, and compassion, the more I felt freed to love myself without the contingency of achievement or status. *If the God of All is mysteriously and joyfully a part of my existence, of what have I to be so ashamed? What part of my life is useless, or without hope?*

Sophomore year world history class interrupted my faith. The Crusades. The Inquisition. Excommunication. Indulgences. I had heard of these things, but they had never affected me like this. The church had never before been *my* church, so its active role in these events had never been so personal. *No,* I found myself thinking, screaming on the inside. *No! No, something is not right with all of this.* I had become deeply devoted to a *liberator* Jesus. The freedom granted by his message was intrinsic to my sense of salvation—my belonging in the church, and in this world! But here, in my history book, I found an alternative tale of Catholicism. God's church was the oppressor—the voice saying, "not like us," and, "not good enough"—words that had haunted me for years. *I thought Christianity calls us, the church, to be above this sort of hatred, this contingent self-worth!* Isn't that what Christ did for me?

My stomach hurt. The grace-filled Catholicism that saved me on that bench appeared further and further from the institutional church I found in textbooks. This disjunction compelled me to reexamine my faith more critically. My parish was notably affluent, and I did not see sufficient attention to aiding the impoverished and abused. Catholicism claimed to be universal and inclusive, yet my faithful Protestant friends could not receive the Eucharist with me at Mass. I thought the Bread of Christ was for everyone.

Over the next six months I continued to panic as I tumbled, uncontrollably, down the growing chasm between my experience of the Gospel and my view of the church. One hot June day, my parish youth minister, Laura, found me sobbing on the concrete steps in front of her office. She hugged me, and I confessed, "I'm sorry, Laura. I can't be confirmed next year. I'm so sorry. I don't know if I can be Catholic anymore." The church that saved me from physical starvation now seemed the cause for a different sort of deprivation—a spiritual starvation. Catholicism lacked the love that had once revived my waning spirit. I felt like I had to choose: it was either the Catholic Church, or my fundamental belief in Christ's inclusive and liberating message for *all* people—for *me*.

Later that week, I told my parents I was leaving our parish.

Two years later, in 2004, I arrived at Santa Clara University bursting with both enthusiasm and acute hesitation. It was my ideal university—ethnically diverse, politically and socially engaged, academically rigorous with intimate classes.

Except it was *Catholic*.

I spent the last two years of high school growing in my Christian faith, finding a spiritual home at a progressive Protestant church. This young congregation met in the gymnasium of my junior high school, the location where I had once met God so powerfully. It was directly across the street from my family's parish, but that felt worlds away to me. Meanwhile, I continued to navigate questions regarding my Catholicism: "So . . . *are* you Catholic?" friends inquired. "Were you? What *are* you? *Why?*" I did not know what I was. I remained uncomfortable with Catholicism, yet I recognized its role in my faith formation, a faith on which my life depended.

Despite Santa Clara's appeal, I feared spending the next four years at a Catholic university trying to explain this to a group of reactionary skeptics. It never occurred to me that much of what drew me to SCU might actually be its Catholic affiliation. Things like "social justice" and "unconditional love" were no longer a part of my concept of Catholicism.

This Catholic university quickly surprised me, though. The young Jesuit priest who taught my first theology class was inquisitive, caring, and compassionate, shattering the vision of Catholic clergy and religious I had long fostered from a distance. He was not patronizing or detached from the difficulties of life and faith. And Santa Clara's ethnic diversity exposed me to thriving Catholic cultural traditions like *La Posada* and devotion to the Virgin. I made friends who were strict, conservative Catholics; others were progressive high school converts. There were even some, like me, who had spent time in Protestant traditions. At the student Mass on Sunday evenings, I prayed with my eyes open, watching the sway of the diverse communion lines. Amid this array of Catholics, I saw a church that challenged the desecrated image I brought with me to college. *There are so many different settings at this Holy Table*, I thought, *maybe even one for me.*

Still, disparities between the church and my Christian experience remained. Catholicism's treatment of women became a central disappointment. At times in the Protestant community, I had dreamed of becoming a pastor. It seemed natural—I had always been a leader among peers; I loved to study and teach Scripture and theology. I was good at it. Why would Catholicism prevent me, or any of the exceptional women preachers and pastors I had encountered, from employing these gifts?

My angst culminated one March afternoon. "Female leadership is the biggest problem in the American church," proclaimed one male friend. "That's why the church is not growing. Too many women in leadership roles."

After this conversation, I could no longer contain my frustration and despair. How could Catholicism deprive people of genuine spiritual gifts and vocations? The conversation brought me to tears and eventually to one of my favorite professors in the religious studies department, Dr. Catherine Murphy. I was enrolled in her course on gender in early Christianity, where we studied controversial topics like feminism and sexuality in the early church. I also knew she was a practicing Catholic.

I distinctly remember the sincerity and candidness with which she spoke to me about my concerns. We dissected the biblical verses my friend had cited to support his views on women and talked about the various possibilities for interpreting those lines. Our conversation culminated with the same underlying question that had plagued me since high school: "But how can you be Catholic, Professor Murphy, when the Catholic Church's patriarchy, moral teachings, and history so often contradict the inclusiveness we recognize at the heart of Christianity?" She told me the story of her Catholic faith, one that celebrated the divinely ordained gifts of all people.

Through the friendship of numerous gay and lesbian Catholics at SCU, I realized that women were not the only group that struggled to reconcile their identities with the church's imperatives. "What keeps you Catholic, Greg?" I asked my openly-gay spiritual director, a long-time university campus minister. I shed tears of solidarity with him as we mourned the treatment of marginalized Catholics. He too had a perception of Catholicism that included all of God's blessed children.

I was surprised by Catholics like Dr. Murphy and Greg, who felt a sincere connection between their Catholic faith and issues of justice and inclusivity. When we told our stories or prayed together, I did not experience the restless hunger, the *lacking* that had defined my previous Catholic experiences. The church's positions remained the same, but these relationships dramatically changed my understanding of Catholicism. There was something mysteriously satisfying for me here—*because* of these Catholics, not in spite of them.

A few weeks ago at the Easter Vigil, the most liturgically extravagant and engaging Mass of the year at Santa Clara, I stood in the front row of the congregation and watched my friend, Brandon, receive full initiation into the Catholic Church. It had been a long time since I saw a confirmation—a few years at least—and the last one I witnessed was from a pew somewhere in the back of the large Spanish Mission where our campus worships each week.

Knowing how much this ritual meant to my friend, a fellow Catholic with a strange faith journey like mine, I eagerly anticipated the neat, glistening cross the priest would paint on Brandon's forehead. It would be the cross I would receive on my own forehead in only four weeks at another confirmation ceremony. The presider lifted his hand, fingertips covered in sweet-smelling olive oil.

What I saw was not neat. The priest pushed the oil into my friend's hairline, across his brow line, from temple to temple, into his long, straight locks. I shook as I stood watching; it was so different from what I had imagined it would be. I wondered: If I had known confirmation to be so *messy*, would I have postponed it for so long?

In reflections on faith throughout my life, from the junior high park bench to these years of collegiate theological studies, I have been baffled by my own, messy faith story. How could my faith, full of questions, doubts, and objections, fit into Catholicism—a tradition of supposedly unchanging, orderly absolutes? Am I Catholic? What am I? Why?

In witnessing this single, sacred moment of confirmation, I was reminded of what my years in and out of Catholicism have led me to believe today: my messy faith is, really, not unlike the Catholicism that I see at Mass every Sunday, that I read about in the history books, and that I see in my Catholic friends every day. The church has always been complicated; it has just taken me a long time to see it for what it is. Only after encountering courageous, nontraditional Catholic seekers—feminists, queers, and other pro-change believers—did I recognize a place for everyone at the Table. I needed only to claim it for myself. *I am Catholic too. We are Catholic.* Their perseverance, faith, and joy overwhelm the "not like us" and "not good enough" that still lingers in our communion.

Each week, now, I join the messy feast to share a meal with Jesus, the God who first dined with me as a hungry teenager. This loving God and I watch the colorful crowd gathered around the Table in love. We smile, and I am not starving anymore.

Jessica Coblentz graduated from Santa Clara University in 2008 with a double major in religious studies and women's and gender studies. Since then, she has interned with the Archdiocese of Los Angeles in Young Adult Ministry while preparing for graduate studies in theology and continuing writing projects for young-adult Catholics.

Encountering a Priesthood of All

Meagan Yogi

On a winter night seventeen years ago, I sat next to my mother in the back room of our local parish. Around us, other children and parents sat at various tables. Many of my friends from school were there, and getting to see friends on a school night was rare.

We were taking First Communion preparation classes. Excitement was in the air. Finally! Finally I would be allowed to proudly march up the aisle with the rest of my family and receive the Eucharist. I would wear a beautiful puffy white dress and a veil, I would now get a snack during church, and what I was doing seemed to please my mother. We had shiny, gold, hardcover workbooks filled with pictures and prayers—a definite upgrade from the silver paperback ones we had for First Reconciliation.

I liked this room—it permanently smelled like the doughnuts and coffee that were served after Mass every Sunday. In middle school, I would dance with a boy for the first time in this room. In high school, I would prepare to confirm my commitment to the Catholic Church in this room. This room was familiar. I usually felt at home and happy there.

But in just a matter of minutes during that First Communion preparation meeting, I went from enthusiastic and encouraged to confused and uneasy. This room no longer felt like home to me; I became just a visitor there. One brave mother asked our priest to share his thoughts on women's ordination. He paused, thinking about what he was going to say. Perhaps he noticed that nearly all of the parents in the room were mothers; only a few fathers attended. He explained that he *personally* did not feel comfortable with the idea of women as priests. Then he added, "But I'm old and set in my ways."

As an adult looking back, I can appreciate this second part of what he said. He was acknowledging his own humanity and his biases. But in that moment, my second-grade self was perplexed. Women cannot be priests? Perhaps I had never heard it stated so bluntly before. I have two confident older sisters; we were raised to believe that we could become whatever we were called to do, whatever would bring us joy and fulfillment. My parents graciously affirmed our every goal or dream, no matter how outlandish. But here, my priest, a man whom I was taught to respect and admire, was putting a limit on my future. I felt confused and sad. Had I done something wrong? Had we girls done something wrong?

Over a decade later, I sat in quite a different room, though the topic of conversation was the same. Working on my bachelor's degree in theology, the course was Catholic Feminist Theology, and though men were welcome, none had registered. Most of the women in the class were Catholic, and many had the same concerns as I had begun to have about our church in second grade. Many of us had had life-changing experiences doing service with our church, we had been inspired by the writing of Dorothy Day, we had been moved by Pope John Paul II's efforts to improve relations with other faiths and speak out for the poor. But we were frustrated too. We were frustrated that women seemed to do nearly all of the service in the name of the Catholic Church, but rarely received credit. We were frustrated that our church could not understand how banning contraception decided our futures for us. We were frustrated with the inconsistencies and hypocrisies of an institution that is supposed to follow the teachings of Jesus. And, sitting in that class ten years after I received my First Communion, I remembered my priest's attitude on the ordination of women and how it had planted a seed of doubt in my nine-year-old sense of self-worth.

But I did feel a renewed sense of faith to be surrounded by other young women who understood my joys and frustrations with Catholicism. We could empathize with one another's experiences, both positive and negative. Our professor, a committed woman religious, was able to wisely lead us in discussion, validating our criticisms of the church while maintaining her devotion to it. She gave us space to wrestle with our relationships to the church.

We studied the church's teachings on women's ordination. Our assigned reading included *Inter Insigniores* (Declaration on the Admission of Women to the Ministerial Priesthood, October 15, 1976). One day, the following passage became the focus of our class discussion:

> The same natural resemblance is required for persons as for things: when Christ's role in the Eucharist is to be expressed sacramentally, there would not be this "natural resemblance" which must exist between Christ and his minister if the role of Christ were not taken by a man: in such a case it would be difficult to see in the minister the image of Christ. For Christ himself was and remains a man. (5)

Many of my classmates were angry; I suppose I was too. But my overwhelming emotion was hurt. It was like I was the little girl all over again, feeling rejected and not understanding why.

"It's stuff like this that makes me want to leave the church," said one young woman.

"I just wonder what I'm supposed to tell my daughters," said another.

One young woman who always made us laugh said, "So I guess Freud was right; it really does just come down to the penis."

We all laughed, but I could not stop thinking about this passage. My *gender* hinders my ability to represent Christ? But I thought that, as a Christian, as a person baptized and confirmed in my commitment to the church, I was called to represent and follow Christ's example. Why does my church, my church that has been a gift in my life, urge me to embody Christ's Spirit and yet undermine my ability to do so?

Later that year, I uncovered some clarity. I was in a room where I could not have felt less comfortable, less at home. It did not smell like doughnuts and coffee—no, it smelled like illness and poverty. I was in Haiti, working in Mother Teresa's Home for the Dying in Port-au-Prince, the poorest city in the Western Hemisphere. This room was filled with cots that were filled with people, sometimes two people to a cot. Though the sisters here could not offer much medical care, they could offer the poorest of Haiti a dignified death, an escape from literally dying on the street. In this room, where I couldn't understand the language and could hardly stand the suffering, I saw the embodiment of Christ more clearly than ever before. I saw the face of Christ in the faces of these sisters as they cared for the sick. I saw the face of Christ in the suffering of the patients. I saw the face of Christ in the priest as he gave patients the anointing of the sick and tenderly prayed over them. I felt the Spirit of Christ within myself, pushing me to let go of my fears and let the compassion and love inside me pour out.

I approached one woman sitting on a cot. Her face was beautiful; she looked about seventy but was probably younger. She said something to me in French Creole, I responded in French, but it became clear that we would not be able to communicate verbally. I knelt down in front of her rusty cot and she looked at me with pain and fatigue in her eyes. She lifted up her ragged hospital gown to reveal to me that her body was literally rotting away. I was completely shocked. "I'm sorry, I'm so sorry." I remembered she couldn't understand me and I fumbled to grab her hand. I wanted to run, but something held me there. She held my hand tight as a few tears fell from both of our eyes. In that moment I let my walls down, and I was able to simply be with this woman. Not just sit with her, but really be present to her, soul to soul.

This humbling moment, sitting fully present with the woman in Haiti, is perhaps the most sacred in my life. It was the gentle whisperings of what I now see as a call to a vocation. This moment connected me to the Divine in a way that I had never felt before. It connected me to my own pain, my own power, and my own worth. This moment connected me to what I see as the true spirit of the Catholic Church and the personal transformation that is possible within it. This moment helped heal the nine-year-old inside me who knew, instinctually, that we can all be priests. Christ is embodied in each and every person in this world if we just open our hearts to see it.

Meagan Yogi is currently a chaplain resident at a community hospital near her hometown of Seattle, Washington. She is happy to be back in the Northwest after graduating from Harvard Divinity School with a Master of Theological Studies in June of 2007.

Vocation

Hail Mary, full of grace, the Lord is with you.
Blessed are you among women,
and blessed is the fruit of your womb, Jesus.
Holy Mary, Mother of God, pray for us sinners,
now and at the hour of our death. Amen.

In parishes across the country, Catholics pray for an increase in vocations—forty-six dioceses in the United States have written their own prayers. These prayers often ask the Virgin Mother to guide her sons to priesthood, praying, "Holy Mother of the Good Shepherd, turn your motherly care to this nation. Intercede for us to the Lord of the harvest to send more laborers to the harvest in this land dedicated to your honor," and imploring, "O Virgin Mary, Mother of the church, teach to all those the Master calls to say a joyful 'yes' as you did at the Annunciation."

As young women faithfully add their voices to this intention, the irony of being barred from the priesthood requires Kate Henley Averett to use "every ounce of energy not to cry, scream, or laugh." When Kate Henley Averett and Pearl Maria Barros were little, they both presided over unofficial Masses in their homes—Pearl transubstantiated banana slices and Welch's grape juice for her grandma and Kate secretly fed Cape Cod potato chips-turned-holy to her family members. And today, both struggle to channel that might-have-been priest energy into their daily lives.

Vocation, of course, is not only about priesthood or ordained ministry. At my (Kate's) Catholic college, campus ministers encouraged young women to listen to our inner selves to discern our vocations. The Benedictines worked hard to make sure we understood that vocation is a journey of exploring how we are called to serve God and the world. We meditated in quiet rooms, listening. In that quiet, some women heard a call to academia, to art, to service work. And some women heard a call to priesthood, an ordination that can only be, as a friend of mine once described it, "an unofficial ordination."

I (Jen) found vocation on my last trip to Georgia, the year it rained. It was November of 1999, and four of my classmates and I had traveled to Fort Benning to honor the Jesuits, their coworker Elba Ramos, and her daughter Celina, who had been murdered in El Salvador ten years before by graduates of Fort Benning's School of the Americas. We gathered with almost 3,000 others. In that place so marked by death and destruction, we held a vigil and protest, a witness to life and creation. The culmination of the weekend vigil at the gates of Fort Benning is the Sunday morning procession, when resisters commit civil disobedience. Crossing the white line that separates the military base from the rest of the community, many are dressed in black, carrying white crosses bearing the names of those who have been killed at the hands of the graduates of the newly named Western Hemisphere Institute for Security Cooperation. I remember the chanting of the names of those killed and our simple response. Celina Ramos, 16 years old. Presente. *As we sang and as the resisters marched, a light rain began to fall, and remnants of my third-grade imagination pushed themselves to the fore.* Elba Ramos, 42 years old. Presente. *I wasn't unique in my childhood conviction that God lives among the clouds.* Amando López, 53 years old. Presente. *When it rained, I thought God was crying.* Ignacio Ellacuría, 59 years old. Presente. *In that moment, surrounded by so many people who were there to be sure we never forget the atrocities that had been perpetrated in our names, I felt the innocence of that childlike sensibility return, telling me that God was weeping, indeed.* Juan Ramón Moreno, 56 years old. Presente. *God felt the pain of their loss and mourned with those who lived.* Joaquin López y López, 71 years old. Presente. *God raged against a political, military, and economic system that perpetuates this violence around the world.* Ignacio Martín-Baró, 47 years old. Presente. *God experienced the simple joys of working for justice.* Segundo Montes, 56 years old. Presente.

Looking back on experiences like this one, I hear God calling me to be the kind of theologian who engages with the realities of kyriarchy, or intersecting oppressions—of sexism, racism, militarism, classism, homophobia—and grapples with the implications of being a bicultural woman living in the United States.

Our vocations often come to us in fleetingly powerful moments. Claire Bischoff tells the story of realizing her call to become a theology professor during an 8:00 a.m. Old Testament lecture—years of pre-med preparation washed away in an instant. At a Benedictine monastery's retreat house outside Chicago, Felicia Schneiderhan realized writing is more than her profession; it is her vocation, the way she connects to God. Rebecca Curtin spent years trying to distance herself from thinking about being Catholic. Yet, as she looks forward, she cannot imagine her life without studying and teaching Catholicism. And Sarah Gottfried stumbled into a job as a caregiver for people living with HIV/AIDS. In striving to love and care for them as Jesus would have, she is learning, "This work is my calling. I get to honor my true self while vowing to constantly seek God, pay attention to and honor God through all people and all things. I wash feet; I care for the sick and learn from all of those who have known isolation and marginalization from their families and communities." These are stories of vocation.

In the biblical roots of the Hail Mary, Elizabeth rejoices in Mary's pregnancy—"Blessed are you among women" (Luke

1:42). It is a sweet song of thanksgiving and hope, a prayer young Catholic women know well. We have said it hundreds of times as we listen to our callings with open hearts—standing at the gates of Fort Benning, sitting in a lecture hall. With an open heart, Mary responded to the angel affirmatively with faith in things not seen, ready to move into a space despised by the society of her time.

Mary went to Elizabeth's house to offer companionship and care for her pregnant cousin. And there, unexpectedly, her cousin deepened her understanding of her call to be Jesus' mom— "Blessed is the fruit of thy womb!" Kate Henley Averett and Pearl went to Mass and then to graduate school. Claire went to her Old Testament class. Rebecca went to New Orleans, and Jen went to Georgia. Sarah applied for a job she didn't expect to love. Kate Dugan went to quiet rooms, and Felicia went to the monastery. We are examples of women whose openness to the Holy Spirit brings us to our vocations, pushing the boundaries of what the culture and the church are ready to accept.

Of Memory and Vision

My Grandmother's Legacy

Pearl Maria Barros

My love of theology began in my grandmother's living room, where I, an obstinate seven-year-old girl in pigtails and a purple jogging suit, argued with a tired but patient eighty-year-old woman about whether God would send anyone to hell. It was a simple room with many plants and a hodgepodge collection of furniture. The walls were decorated with family photos and various religious paintings. I like to think that those walls were the first to teach me about sacramentality—there was a painting of Mary pointing to her Immaculate Heart with my parents' wedding photo on her right and a photo of my cousin holding a doll on her left; the sacred and "secular" surrounding each other. Thus surrounded by a cloud of witnesses, we debated issues in theology ranging from heaven, hell, and purgatory to whether eating meat on Friday was truly a sin. Ironically, while my grandmother's pre–Vatican II worldview maintained a narrow image of God, her living room walls spoke to me of a God beyond all limitations. They spoke of a God who could not be entirely known through the black-and-white answers of the *Baltimore Catechism*, but who lived at the heart of all questions and was waiting for those who had the courage to raise them.

I remember raising a plate of sliced banana pieces above my grandmother's kitchen table, my hands reverently holding this paten made of simple white porcelain with pink roses along its border. "This is my body," I would solemnly say. Then, taking a small glass filled with Welch's grape juice, I would raise it just as reverently, saying, "This is the cup of my blood, the blood of the new and everlasting covenant. It will be shed for you and for all so that sins may be forgiven. Do this in memory of me." Although I was only seven, I had memorized the entire eucharistic prayer and delighted in saying Mass. The only problem was that I really didn't like bananas. So after I finished praying, I would approach my grandmother whose experience of growing up in a small Azorean village had taught her never to waste anything, especially food. Raising a banana slice in front of her face, I would say, "The Body of Christ," and despite her questioning look, she always said, "Amen."

Until one day when she didn't say anything. Staring at me in silence for what seemed like an eternity, she finally asked me, "Do you want to be a priest?" Interestingly, the thought had never before entered my mind. True, I enjoyed saying Mass, but somehow I always thought that anyone who wanted to say it could do so. After a moment of hesitation, I answered, "Yes, why not?"

"Because you're a girl. That's why," my grandmother said.

"What do you mean?" I asked.

"Girls, women, cannot be priests. Only men can be priests," she stated.

"Who made that rule?" I asked sharply, ready to begin one of our usual debates.

"The church and the pope," she said.

"Oh," I said, somewhat defeated.

I did not know how to fight her on this issue since it really wasn't her rule. No running in the house, no talking to strangers, no loud noise—those were her rules. But no women being priests, well, that was a church rule, that was different. All I could do was walk back into the kitchen to clean up my mess.

Looking down at the paten and chalice in the sink, I saw them for what they were: a plate and a cup. Dirty dishes needing to be cleaned like the dinner dishes that the men in my family ate on and the women washed. Hands that once consecrated bananas and grape juice were now submerged in soapy water, trying to wash away any remnants of this childhood ritual, any possibility of women being priests. I dried the dishes and put them away in the cupboard; everything was back in its place. Walking out of the kitchen that day, I realized that I would never play Mass again. What I did not realize was that the messy struggle for women's leadership within the Catholic Church remained in me. And no amount of soap and water could possibly wash it away.

Rejecting the domesticity of soapy dishwater, I turned my attention to the waters of baptism in my teenage years by discerning a call to religious life. At the time, I believed in a dichotomous worldview and the false piety that it often engenders. I believed that religious life was *the* path to holiness. I now know soapy kitchen water to be just as holy as the water in any baptismal font; I now know that religious life is not the only way of living one's baptismal calling. But coming to such an insight involved a long, and sometimes painful, journey. And so I walked into religious life at the age of eighteen, ready to begin my first year of college and to embrace this life that would supposedly lead me to immediate holiness.

I entered a small Franciscan community because I appreciated its charism rooted in simplicity and humility. Simplicity and humility were virtues that I desperately sought. All my life I had been told that I was not humble enough for a woman—I thought too much, I asked too many questions. In retrospect, I see that I ran to the convent because it seemed like a fresh alternative to the patriarchal church; it provided a space where women decided matters for themselves, free from the control of men. Or so I thought.

It took only about two weeks of living with the sisters to realize that matriarchy is not necessarily preferable to patriarchy. While no men lived in our midst, the hierarchical model I associated with "them" was completely evident. I was shocked. In my naïveté, I had presumed that women would never imitate the very structures that oppressed us, that somehow by our nature we would create a space of equality. Instead, I found myself asking the local superior for permission to use the internet, praying for "us men," and, to my great dismay, doing far more dishes than I ever anticipated.

When not doing dishes, I was reading for my classes. Reading was a welcome escape from the anti-intellectualism that surrounded me. In my time with this Franciscan congregation, I realized that they did not value education as a means of liberation, but as a means of securing a profession that would provide steady income for the community. When I tried to share the theological questions that were arising in me with my sisters, they perceived it as pride, or doubt, or fear. They seldom perceived questions as grace. And that's why I had to leave. I could not pretend that I wanted to spend my life believing everything that Father said, or excluding "laypeople" from our table in order to preserve the "sacredness" of cloister. I left the Franciscans so that I could become the person that I felt God calling me to be.

While my time with the Franciscans taught me that religious life was not the only path toward holiness, I still felt the desire to be a vowed religious. So, after leaving the Franciscans, I discerned membership with another religious congregation, one far more avant-garde and committed to education. During my time with the Sisters, Servants of the Immaculate Heart of Mary (IHM) of Monroe, Michigan, I witnessed a religious life that was dynamic and exciting. I lived with women religious who dared to ask questions and who never dissuaded me from my own. I saw in these women the desire to be completely open to God, even if such openness meant having to let go of beloved traditions. I watched them renovate their motherhouse so that it would be entirely ecologically sustainable. I observed eighty- and ninety-something-year-old sisters reading the latest theological works in order to update their own educations. I heard their dreams for the future of religious life. And as much as I longed to participate in their life, I realized that I could never be a vowed religious.

Like the calling that initially led me to discern religious life, this realization came to me slowly. It came to me in moments of silent prayer when I felt myself seriously questioning whether I wanted to give up the prospect of marriage and family. It came to me during community meetings when I heard myself talking about religious life on an intellectual level without feeling it in my heart. And that's what scared me the most: not feeling it in my heart. I had met too many women religious who went through the motions of religious life. They are the cold, prude-like nuns depicted by popular culture. I had no desire to be a stereotype. I wanted to be alive like the IHMs, whose passion for religious life was so palpable that I could not help but feel warm in their presence. I recognized that passion because it was the same passion I felt for theology, for writing, but not for religious life. And that was the unexpected fruit of my discernment: the realization that my vocation was to be a theologian and a writer. My time discerning religious life with the IHMs enabled me to glimpse the church for which I desperately hoped. It enabled me to begin developing a feminist consciousness, a consciousness that would be nourished and challenged during my undergraduate career.

Convinced that the church was capable of conversion, I eagerly pursued the study of feminist theology as an undergraduate. Within this academic context, I expected that my questioning of the Christian tradition and attempt to reappropriate it for women would be welcomed and nurtured. And it was, in many ways. But it was also challenged in ways that I had not anticipated. Whether it was a male professor commenting to me about the clothing of one of my female colleagues, "She really doesn't have the body to be wearing those kinds of clothes," or the rude and frightening comment of another such professor, "I can close my office door with you—you won't cry rape," I realized that the patriarchy I was fighting against within my theological studies also shaped the very environment in which I studied it. Alas, the academy could be just as confining as the convent.

Despite the restricting aspects of the academy, I have decided to continue pursuing theological studies at the graduate level with a concentration in feminist theology. My reasons are not entirely masochistic, but rather, rooted in those early childhood memories of debating with my grandmother. I think it rather providential that my love of theology began in a common place, a living room, and that it took place in conversations between two women struggling to articulate their religious beliefs. True, my grandmother did not question church authority, she did not encourage me to become a priest; in fact, she was probably glad that I stopped wasting so many bananas, and that I finally learned to do the dishes. To most people my grandmother was a conventional Portuguese woman whose strong Marian devotion, rigid morality, and loyalty to church teachings would make her anything but feminist.

Still, if I have learned anything from my studies in feminist theory and theology, it is that there is often an untold story, a pause in the sentence, a look, a sigh that signals the unconventionality of so-called conventional women. In my grandmother's case, her willingness to engage with me in dialogue and her constant encouragement of my formal education testified to the fact that this woman wanted a different future for her granddaughter. She may not have explicitly dreamed a future in feminist theology for me, but she did dream a future for me free of the struggles she endured: a lost dream of becoming a teacher, a difficult marriage, and a forced abandonment of her homeland. She dreamed that the sexist tendencies of religion and society would not harm me as they had hurt her. And that was the unconventional legacy she left to me: memories of struggle and strength, and visions of a different future.

Although far from my grandmother's living room, I carry her legacy of memory and vision with me at all times. This legacy strengthens me in the midst of the constant backlash against feminism. This legacy enables me to do theology—I do theology in memory of her so that we women can reenvision ourselves.

Pearl Maria Barros earned her BA in English and religious studies from Santa Clara University and her Master of Theological Studies from Harvard Divinity School, where she continues her theological studies at the doctoral level. When not reading, writing, and researching, she enjoys traveling, spending time with family and friends, and relaxing at her favorite coffee shop.

Mass in the Dining Room

Kate Henley Averett

When I was about eight, my dad went away on a business trip. This wasn't an especially rare occurrence, but I was worried. He would be away over a weekend on this trip, which meant that my dad would miss Mass. A rather serious eight-year-old, I worried over the state of my dad's soul. So I decided that when he returned from his trip mid-week, I would say Mass for him in our dining room. The plan seemed flawless. To be prepared for the Liturgy of the Word, I would swipe a missalette from the pew after Mass that Sunday and return it before Mass the following Sunday. Nobody would ever have to know it was gone. And as for the eucharistic rite, well, that part was simple—didn't all Catholic kids have the priest's part memorized by age eight?

I relayed my plan to my mother, knowing that I would need her help to pull it off—after all, I couldn't very well be the lector, the server, *and* the priest all at once. It was then that my mom delivered a shattering blow: only ordained priests, she explained, could say Mass. The news made my little world feel like it was spinning out of control, but that wasn't enough for my mom. She then delivered an even harder blow: only men could become ordained priests. It was a tough one-two punch to take. Not only could I not say Mass in the dining room for my dad that week, but I would never be able to say it. That whole "girls can do anything boys can do" thing they had been feeding me was complete bullshit.

◆

I'm pretty convinced that, had I been a boy, I would have been fast-tracked to the priesthood. I showed all the signs of a child with a vocation. In the weeks before my First Communion, I clandestinely practiced distributing and receiving the Eucharist with Cape Cod potato chips. I could recite all the words to the Mass along with the priest from an early age. I had secret fantasies in which the priest would collapse during Mass and, as he was unable to go on, I would run up to the altar and finish the service for him. I yearned to become an altar server in the days when girls were still not allowed to do so in our diocese.

By the time girls were allowed to serve in my parish, I was well past the age of normal altar server recruitment, so I only ever experienced the thrill of being at the altar once. When I was ten, my cousin in New Jersey got married and asked my eleven-year-old brother, the only other male cousin on that side of the family, if he would serve. My brother, however, didn't want to do the job. When the priest still couldn't convince him to do it only a few minutes before the Mass, he looked over at me and uttered the magical words I thought I would never hear: "Would you like to serve?" I must have immediately looked excited because I remember my mother interjecting with a comment about how girls couldn't serve in the Boston Archdiocese, and were they allowed to here? The priest responded, "No, not yet," and with a warm and almost impish smile, ushered me to the sacristy to prepare me for the Mass. I felt triumphant and subversive to be breaking the rules. I've never lost sight of the fact that my first feminist-activist act took place during a Catholic Mass, with a priest as my accomplice.

Had I been a boy, these early expressions of interest in the Mass would have been a cause for celebration, special attention, and encouragement to discern a call to priesthood. But because I was a girl, my desires felt somehow wrong and unnatural; their expression seemed dangerously subversive. And they often made me feel invisible to those around me, who were busy looking elsewhere for boys who showed the promising early signs of vocation.

This isn't to say that my desire to serve the church went entirely unnoticed, but the attention I received took a different form than the prodding toward priesthood that boys received. Many people encouraged me toward ministry, constantly reminding me—with mixed parts cheerfulness and resignation—that though priesthood was not an option, "You could always be a pastoral associate!" A campus minister in college urged me to consider youth ministry or campus ministry. But when I was nineteen and my childhood pastor, with a twinkle in his eye, finally asked the heretofore unspoken question of whether I had a calling to the priesthood, I didn't know how to answer him. I think I just laughed in discomfort, knowing that my answer was entirely irrelevant.

I finally began to wonder if I *might* have a vocation to the priesthood during one of my college summers, which I spent in South Bend, Indiana, taking part in a philosophy and theology intensive at Notre Dame. Of the twenty of us in the program, ten were Catholic and of those, seven were male. I'm pretty sure that all the Catholic men in the group either had spent or were spending serious time discerning whether they had a call to priesthood. We seemed to speak incessantly about vocation that summer. It appeared to be something of a rite of passage in the life of young Catholic men to discern priesthood, and I was jealous that I hadn't been invited to partake in this ritual.

My roommate had recently done her fair share of discernment about religious life and marriage, and I peppered her with questions about vocation. Her advice to me was simple and followed a clear logic: God would not give you a vocation that you could not possibly fulfill, and since women cannot be priests, women cannot be called to priesthood. Therefore, I didn't have a call to priesthood. Case closed.

Still, I could not help but wonder if my roommate was wrong; not wrong that God would not give you a vocation you could not fulfill, but wrong about women not being able to be priests. What if God gives women vocations to priesthood to make the point that women *should* be ordained? Didn't the fact that I couldn't stop thinking about it mean anything? Why was I feeling such a pull if such a vocation couldn't exist?

That summer, and throughout the following year, I finally began taking seriously that I might have a vocation to the priesthood. And then I started to resent the institution. Posters encouraging young men to consider priesthood enraged me to the point that I could not even bring myself to do what my feminist-activist consciousness urged me to do: tear off one of the reply cards and send it to the vocations office. Maybe I'd be a source of annoyance or humor to those who received it, but the larger statement I was trying to make would fall on deaf ears. It took every ounce of energy not to cry, scream, or laugh every time we prayed for vocations to the priesthood from our parish during the prayers of the faithful. It wasn't so much that I felt sure I had a calling to priesthood; all I really wanted was for my potential vocation to be taken seriously and my time of discernment to be acknowledged, honored, and supported.

I have sometimes been able to harness my sadness, frustration, rage, and resentment at the exclusion of women from ordination in productive ways, allowing them to fuel a larger critique, in both academic and activist circles, of the gendered injustices built into the structures of the church. Ironically, I am almost grateful to the church for inadvertently shaping me into such a strong-willed feminist. By simultaneously encouraging me to use all of my gifts and then barring me, and many other women, from doing so, the church provides exactly the right blend of factors to motivate me to action.

My anger and hurt, however, have been further exacerbated by my experience of being gay in a church that seems to work hard to offend and alienate its gay members at every chance it gets. At times, I've been so angry I've wanted to leave the church altogether, and sometimes I even have. But I can never stay away for long—I always feel pulled back to the church that helped raise and form me, the way we feel drawn back to our families, even after a bitter fight. Though I go to Mass with trepidation and often leave feeling upset or disappointed, there are always moments, especially during the eucharistic rite, in which the rhythm of the Mass just seems to breathe *home*.

That's the frustration of feeling called to the very thing I critique and at times even despise. My passionate ambivalence about the Catholic priesthood is enough to drive me crazy: I find it maddening that we Catholics are so overly reliant on this group of men called priests and I yearn to break free from their grasp. And then I realize I'm also angry that, because I'm gay, I won't have the option of having a Catholic priest officiate at my wedding. Sometimes it's enough to make me think that the best form of spiritual practice I can hope for is to learn to appreciate the great irony of resenting exclusion from the very church that I often wish I had never been a part of.

I carry this tension with me, my anger and hurt both motivating me to seek justice and reform within the church and distancing me from the very ritual that pulled me into this state to begin with. Or maybe the tension will motivate me to harness both the call to say Mass that I felt as a child and the subversive impetus I felt at my cousin's wedding sixteen years ago. Maybe I will finally swipe that missalette from the pew and say Mass in my dining room.

Kate Henley Averett earned her BA in Religion from Mount Holyoke College in 2004 and her Master of Divinity in 2008 from Harvard Divinity School, where she studied Catholicism, queer theology and experience, and the performing arts. Also a dancer and choreographer, she resides, studies, and choreographs in Cambridge, Massachusetts.

A Conversion of Life

Sarah Gottfried

Had I ignored my true calling in this life, I would have become a nun.

There's nothing inferior about such a vocation. It's not the last resort my friends used to joke about when they were frustrated with dating. It takes strength and commitment, solemn perception to the grace of God, and spiritual vulnerability. I've never known a nun I didn't admire or revere, most of them Benedictines. Upon joining their community, they take three vows: stability, obedience, and conversion of life. Each part of the trinity supports the other. The *conversatio* (conversion of life) invites monastics on a journey of daily questioning, constant attention to the ways in which God calls us to move beyond our inherent sinfulness, and to seek God through all interactions, with people and in life.

I am a lesbian who grew up Catholic. The first is nature, the latter nurture. Had I remained fully Catholic I would have been a nun, but because I could not be both gay and Catholic, I embarked on my own journey of being called to a vocation, to pay unwavering attention to the daily challenges in honoring God.

Technically speaking, I am the youngest of eight kids, though my twin brother Nate arrived only thirteen brief minutes before me. My parents both have degrees in social work and worked hard to pay for our Catholic education, preschool through college. My twin brother and I were well-liked, over-involved kids. I was a good Catholic, went to Mass twice a week, sang in the choir, volunteered for everything, and was involved in youth group. I followed all the rituals and waited for the rites to come on cue: reconciliation and First Communion at age seven, confirmation at age sixteen, and finally, eucharistic ministering.

There was one rite I had watched my two older brothers pass through that I wanted for myself: to be an altar server. When I was in fifth grade, the boys in my class met after Mass one day to discuss becoming servers. My brother Nate headed to the sacristy as I held the door for the churchgoers walking to their cars. Because Nate and I had gone to Mass without the rest of our family that day, my mother had armed me with an article from the diocese's own newspaper about how girls could and should start being servers too. She had suggested I show it to the priest to try to convince him to let me join. As I stood holding the door, a jovial woman inquired about why I was there without my brother. I told her he was to be a server, then explained about the article. She grabbed the door from me, gave me a gentle push and told me to "get back there." The befuddled priest gave me a job as crossbearer for all processionals and recessionals. Other girls joined, and eventually we served along with the boys.

I'm not the type of person who hears "no" and thinks, "I'll show them!" I'm usually quiet, sincere, and agreeable. When I'm told that I can't serve God because of the way God made me, my reaction is complete bafflement. Yet, I am empowered by that too. I used to think that if I started with serving, I'd eventually break down the other restricted roles for women within the church. My list of requests for change is long, and I have grown weary.

As I was growing up a "perfect" Catholic, other things were changing. My parents grew apart and eventually divorced shortly after I started serving. They were married for thirty years, and divorce was the first of many tsunamis that rocked my family's Catholicism. I know it was a lonely time for my parents. They

had both been devout Catholics, and the divorce cast a shadow
of shame and embarrassment. My father stopped taking Communion. I lived with my mother, and our church community
responded kindly, more than I probably know. But many didn't
know what to do. People hoped it wouldn't happen to them.
The rules of being good get broken because we are human; the
church's response should be the unconditional love of Jesus.

◆

I never quite transformed out of the tomboy phase like my
mother hoped I would. I think she believed, like many mothers
do, that menarche was to be nature's medicinal blood-letting,
certain to cure me of riding my bike past dusk and challenging the boys to play one more game of baseball. But I couldn't
magically fall in love with the various ways to style my hair or
beg her to let me wear all those pretty dresses. I couldn't will
myself to fall in love with boys either, though I spent many years
thinking I could if I tried harder.

The next Catholic rite I'd need to take was looming. I wanted
to collect all the sacraments and figured it impossible unless my
husband died so that I could then join the monastery. But because
I didn't really want the husband, I thought I should try harder to
want to be a nun. I could have been a nun, wild and curious. I
could have sought safety in the womb of a monastery. It seemed
so wonderful to me to live in community with other women, where
personal strength was galvanized by a commitment to God.

Nate was always more vocal about wanting to be a priest. We
often played church, squeezing and mashing bread and tear-
ing out round pieces, writing petitions in crayon on typewriter
paper and stapling them to construction paper. My brother was
always the priest; no amount of pleading on my part changed
that. He was more stubborn than Rome on that requirement. At
the time I didn't know that his desire to be a priest and mine to
be a nun weren't because of being called; they were a result of
being pushed. Both of us are gay, though being Catholic clouded

our self-realization until college. The Catholic sacraments only present two options: marriage between a man and a woman and holy orders.

Nuns were the gayest role models I could find. I was drawn to what I perceived as their different pronouncement of sexuality. I quickly labeled them as women with subtle and weak femininity, as asexual. I decided that I was that kind of woman too, that I too could void myself of sexuality. I had to decide what asexual looked like. Perhaps it was short hair, clothes that fit or were a little big. Clothes that a woman can move in, that accentuate the shape of a woman's body as either in motion or poised for what's next. Gardening, painting a room, writing on the chalkboard, fixing a broken window. A woman who moves into each moment without hesitation, without wondering if there's a man watching. Now I'd use that description for what is inherently sexy, but at that time I thought I was drawn to those women for other reasons. I certainly didn't want to wear my mother's dresses that inhibited movement or don the scent and skin of a woman luring her male suitors. If that was sexual, then I didn't want it. I didn't want the constant combing of hair or painting of the face to encourage stillness and subordination.

In college, these nuns invited me to pray with them. Sitting in the chapel, I listened as all the sisters recited Scripture, the "he," "man," and "his" excluding them. I got to know more of the nuns. I saw my many mentors praying. A sister I followed across the property line of a military base at a protest forged on with nary a complaint in the cold rain and was arrested. There was a sister who taught me Shakespeare and pointed out every syllable of sexism, and another who taught me how to harvest my voice as a writer and as a person. The nuns I knew stood strong in their convictions, in their love of God and of living in community.

◆

Instead of the nuns of my college years, these days my mentors are lesbians. I see myself in them only slightly more than when I recognized myself in the nuns. I sometimes get confused when talking with them. I look twice to try to remember if it's lesbians or nuns I'm addressing. There is something pastoral about older lesbians—so much so my mind stutters and wants to add a "Sister" before calling their name. Perhaps the similarities are my own invention. There is a need in me to locate where the gay people were throughout my life and why they made the decisions they did.

Coming out is always difficult. There's the uncomfortable squeezing out of what is known and into what is necessary. The chrysalis is both safe and restrictive. As a Catholic, coming out meant leaving behind all I'd known about living a respectable life. I didn't want to cause conflict or hurt my parents who had already known public shame. There still was my own guilt, shame, and grief. My healing began when I found myself following a calling. It involved my reconnection to my love of Jesus, who never left anybody behind.

At the last Palm Sunday Mass I attended, Jesus really did ride into town and save my life. That was five years ago. The bulletin held a job opening for a caregiver at an AIDS home. I was wasting my life filing in "The Dead Room" at a law firm in downtown Minneapolis. I called, had an interview, and started at the homes a few weeks later. At twenty-three with a degree in English literature and no real career ideas, I became a caregiver at an adult foster care for people living with HIV/AIDS. I had spent the year avoiding vocation, falling in and out of love for the first time, and trying to rise from the chaos and bewilderment of coming out and of college. I made one decision that I could accept. I picked myself up, dusted myself off, and decided that the next thing I wanted to learn in my life was how to love unconditionally.

I came to this conclusion after coming to terms with how Catholic I couldn't be if I was a gay woman and refused to be clergy. I had no plan for accomplishing this goal; I had only gotten so far as to declare it. Weeks later, while bringing laundry to the basement of the home where I had been working, I saw a banner on the wall with the name and definition of the home. It read: "Agape Home (Greek for unconditional love)." I felt foolish for not having put the two together before that.

My community includes many coworkers who are gay men and women. That's how these homes started; gay men had families who had disowned them for being gay and for having AIDS. Hospitals didn't want them either. The gays cared for their own and still do. A nearby Catholic Church started one of the homes where I work. The home used to be the priest's rectory. This work is my calling. I get to honor my true self while vowing to constantly seek God, pay attention to and honor God through all people and all things. I wash feet; I care for the sick and learn from all of those who have known isolation and marginalization from their families and communities. Every day is a humbling expression of love and devotion to a God who loves all things. There is much grace and gratitude within each day.

Sometimes residents pass away. On one particularly chilly spring day a memorial service took place. A few weeks before, one of my residents who had died had a proper Catholic burial in his hometown, which honored his family and the faith with which he'd been raised. On this day it was a different kind of honoring, one that could acknowledge who he was, truly. Our presider was a caregiver who used to be a priest. He eloquently spoke about the person we had all loved, about his struggles of faith, about how much he had brought to our lives. Toward the end he sang in Latin and in English, "*Il Paradiso,*" a prayer for someone who has died. Another coworker who is a former nun hummed along with him. It was beautiful and a remarkable tribute. At that moment I felt pride to have been raised Catholic, a feeling I hadn't had since I was in college. I felt like I was exactly where I needed to be and part of me felt like I could finally honor my inherent self—the one whom God made—and my faith.

Sarah Gottfried recently became a licensed massage therapist and works as a caregiver for Clare Housing, a nonprofit that provides housing for people living with HIV/AIDS in Minneapolis, Minnesota.

Saving Religion

Claire Bischoff

It's a crisp, frigid January morning in southern Minnesota, but I'm sweating in the over-heated basement of St. Olaf College's Boe Chapel, listening to a lecture on the minutiae of Mark's gospel. Glancing around the room, I notice a few students have been lulled into slumber by the oppressive classroom conditions and even more stare wistfully out the half-windows, perhaps fantasizing of frolicking in the freshly fallen flakes. We are all here because religion courses are a graduation requirement, but for me, it has become more than that. The academic subject of religion has been wooing me, and I am falling hard for her, eagerly poring over the reading each evening and preparing for the next day's discussion.

On this snowy morning, I am right where I want to be, drinking in biblical theology, hastily jotting down what Professor Hanson is saying as fast as my Catholic-school-trained cursive allows: *Mark begins w/ Jesus' baptism and ends w/ empty tomb = different from other synoptic gospels*. In this moment of utter contentment, something clicks. For the first time, I admit to myself that the science courses that have filled my schedule hold no intrinsic joy for me, that they are simply means to the end of a career in medicine. Like a trendy shirt you talk yourself into purchasing even though you know it is not a flattering cut for your figure, the dream of medicine has been tempting to me.

I am confident I could be reasonably successful and content in medicine, but as I try on the dream one last time, I realize I have to let it go. It will fit others better, and religion is a better fit for me.

In the following weeks, I make it look as if I am taking time with this decision, assembling pro and con lists and asking advice from family and friends. But the reality is that I decided my vocational future in an instant. The heavens did not open, but God spoke to me in the depth of my being, and I knew that pursuing religion was the best choice I could make. I had never felt such gut-level certainty before, and I decided to trust it. While this certainty came as a flash of lightning illuminating the future, as I later reflected on that moment, I had been preparing for it my whole life.

If you listen to the stories my parents tell of my childhood, I was born a would-be academic. My younger sister and I, equipped with our Hello Kitty markers, whiled away afternoons puzzling over worksheets my mother created for us. Around the time I was four or five, my father found me working on basic addition, like $2 + 2 = x$. He tried to stump me but could not. Having impressed him with my addition ability, I decided to debut a new talent, declaring that I could add backward. Intrigued, he asked me to demonstrate. "Four plus two is two," I spouted, rather proud of myself. Furrowing his brow, he requested another example. I replied, "Five plus three is two." A smile broke across his face. "That's great, Claire," he said, "but we haven't taught you that yet. It's called subtraction."

For the girl who discovered subtraction, beginning first grade at Holy Spirit Catholic School promised to be a welcome adventure. However, within a few weeks I was disappointed. We had not progressed beyond addition in math, I already knew how to read, and frankly, I was a bit bored with the whole thing. One day I came home and announced, with all the solemnity a six-year-old can muster, "I'm giving this place until third grade to challenge me or else I'll need to find a new school."

I do not remember this announcement, but my parents assure me it was so. In their estimation, I was not being obnoxious, just the earnest younger self of the college student who would sit in Boe Chapel years later, reveling in the joy that comes with intellectual stimulation. Bemused, they promised that we would find an appropriate alternative if the situation did not improve. In third grade, Sister Kathy conferred upon me the challenge I sought. Under her tutelage, I completed third and fourth grade math so that I could be pushed ahead in that subject the following year.

Generally, I loved school. I worked hard and earned good grades. So I was nervous when my parents summoned me to the kitchen table after parent-teacher conferences my seventh-grade year. Although I had garnered near-perfect marks, the religion teacher was irritated that I rarely participated in class. This perturbed my parents as well, and they were curious why I kept silent when I evidently knew the material. My logic was simple. All the questions the teacher posed could be answered in simple words or phrases: yes, no, Moses, 4 BCE, Jerusalem. If religion only meant spitting back what the textbook said was correct, then it did not seem worthy of more than a minimal amount of attention or effort.

That same year, before a particularly important gymnastics competition, I knelt on my pink bedroom carpet, clasped my hands together on my pink and white gingham bedspread, and prayed. I did not pray for high scores or for my team to win, since I sensed prayer did not work that way. Instead, I called upon God to imbue me with confidence and courage. At the meet, all was going well as I approached the final event, the much dreaded, impossibly narrow balance beam. I silently reiterated my petition. As I mounted the apparatus, my prayer was answered as a most amazing sense of calm enveloped me. I performed to the best of my ability, with nary a wobble, and knew God had been with me.

As eighth grade approached, the preordained time for the sacrament of confirmation, I awaited the opportunity to discuss that radical experience of God's presence. Despite my previous frustration with religion class and memorized answers, I held out hope that we would finally grapple with big questions about life and death, good and evil, God and salvation. So I chose a confirmation name and sponsor, attended the retreats, and otherwise prepared for what the *Catechism of the Catholic Church* calls "the completion of baptismal grace." Much to my dismay, religion class improved little, and the event itself was an utter disappointment. Not only did my mother refuse to let me wear a pretty floral dress like the other girls, deciding instead that a plaid blazer with shoulder pads would be more appropriate for church, I felt absolutely nothing when the bishop anointed me Claire Bridget. While I had not expected leaping flames and the ability to speak in tongues, I had learned that the sacraments mediate God's grace. I had anticipated a heightened sense of God's presence. But that evening, God was nowhere to be found.

My high school religion teachers saved religion for me. Freshman year this salvation came in the form of a simple invitation from Mr. Gleich. We liked him because he offered a kind greeting to everyone who entered his classroom, and we respected him because he allowed students to lead prayer at the beginning of class, even when this meant bowing our heads to REM's "Everybody Hurts," Shel Silverstein's poetry, or Tibetan chanting. Mid-year Mr. Gleich approached me about participating in a day-long service trip to a halfway house and soup kitchen operated by a Catholic parish in downtown Minneapolis. I felt honored that he asked me but nervous about my ability to interact with other students on the trip (would-be academics tend to have difficulty making friends in high school). I said I would think about it, hoping he might forget and save me from a decision. I don't know if Mr. Gleich had a good reason for inviting me or if he simply had trouble filling the roster, but when he renewed his offer, I hesitantly agreed to go along.

As I ladled out corn chowder and conversed with people who did not know where they would sleep that night, my eyes were opened to the fact that not everyone lives a comfortable middle-class existence. The church members who oversaw the kitchen and house demonstrated that being Catholic is not just about attending Mass but also about attending to the needs of others. Their living example of social justice ministry and the church's preferential option for the poor invigorated me because I saw for the first time that Catholic identity encompasses both belief *and* action.

Even now, in moments of excruciating frustration with my faith tradition, when I am certain I cannot in good faith continue to call myself Catholic, I remember the famous people, like Archbishop Romero, and the not-so-famous, like the Sisters of St. Joseph of Carondelet in my hometown, who live the Catholic identity of acting for justice on behalf of the poor, the marginalized, and the oppressed. I love the social justice heritage of the Roman Catholic tradition, and it saves religion for me.

After such an empowering experience with Mr. Gleich, my tenuous salvation was threatened during my sophomore year. In my first trimester Old Testament course, we did nothing more than copy notes from the blackboard and take multiple-choice tests. I could not imagine that the second trimester course, simply titled "Jesus," would be any better. He lived, he died, he rose. What more did we need to know?

Enter Mr. Watkins, a lanky, bearded philosopher-at-heart. He had us pull our desks into a circle, with him seated among us, so we could more readily discuss questions that had no easy answers. From him, we learned that scholars differentiate between the Jesus of history and the Christ of faith, and that Jesus' life, given only the briefest mention in the Apostles' Creed, was the foundation of the social justice ideas with which I had become enamored. In my favorite assignment, we compared the synoptic portrayal of Jesus with Plato's allegory of the cave. Because of my enthusiasm (and, I am sure, my verbosity) in completing this task, Mr. Watkins recommended that I read Marcus Borg's *Jesus: A New Vision* over Easter break.

After break, I eagerly scheduled conversations with Mr. Watkins to discuss the few parts of Borg's book I had understood and to get help interpreting the rest. By exposing me to challenging, scholarly texts about religion and leading stimulating discussions, Mr. Watkins confirmed what I had suspected as a middle school student: that religion required deep thinking, honest questioning, and engaging dialogue. At a time when academics were most important to me, discovering that religion was worthy of scholarly attention was a saving grace.

After two years of requisite religion courses, junior year meant electives. I had heard positive reviews of Prayer and Spirituality and signed up eagerly. Mr. Ruhland, who exuded a spiritual wisdom only enhanced by his long hair and Birkenstocks, expertly led the class. We divided our time between the classroom and the chapel, learning about and engaging in different prayer practices. At the class retreat, we concluded with a prayer service during which Mr. Ruhland named how he saw God in each of his students. Saying he witnessed God in me when I performed my floor routines at gymnastics meets, Mr. Ruhland pinpointed the place in my life where I was most at home with myself and enabled me to glimpse God in this self for the first time. After finals were over, I approached Mr. Ruhland with a fistful of babysitting earnings, asking if I might buy the two books we used in the course: *Prayers for a Planetary Pilgrim* and *Learning to Meditate*, both of which still sit, dog-eared, on my bookshelf.

Practicing and learning about prayer with Mr. Ruhland gave language to what I had only intuitively known as a seventh-grader when I prayed and experienced God's presence: I can have a personal spiritual life, one centered in my relationship with God and not solely coordinated by the all-too-human hierarchy of the Catholic Church.

When I am in direst need of spiritual sustenance, I return to the prayer practices I began cultivating my senior year with

Mr. Ruhland. When I am at the deepest points of self-doubt, I remember that others have seen God in me, that I can see God in myself, and that God continually reveals Godself to me through others. This becomes my salvation. What amazing grace!

It's a crisp, frigid February afternoon in Minneapolis, Minnesota. The phone rings, and I am greeted by the cheery voice of Tom Long, professor at Emory University, offering me admission to their PhD program in religion. I thank him kindly, mention I must discuss things with my husband, and promise an answer within a few days, all the while knowing that I will accept the invitation. Having worked in parish religious education for three years, it is time to continue my love affair with studying religion. I go to Emory as an academic, hoping someday to land my dream job as a religion professor, but I also go as a Catholic laywoman, somehow still attached to an imperfect church that at times drives me crazy. If you asked them, I doubt that any of the fantastic religion teachers I have been fortunate enough to learn from would take credit for the work I do now.

Little do they know. Through their living examples and instruction, I have learned to meet and serve God through my actions, my study, my prayer, and my relationships. My religion teachers saved religion for me, and I now follow in their footsteps, encouraging students to ask new questions of religion, to see it from a different perspective, or to explore why it is such a vital part of many people's lives.

And I continue to save religion for myself by studying, teaching, and writing. Even when I have not been to Mass for six months. Even when I am so wrapped up in myself that I forget to open my eyes to the needs of others. Even then, this vocational path connects me to individuals and communities who take religion seriously, and challenges me to find ways to make religion relevant for students and me.

This is the best way I know how to offer thanksgiving for the salvation I have been offered through the exceptional instruction of faith-filled teachers. Each teacher in her or his way, and all of their disparate voices together, have saved religion for me, both as a vocational calling and as a personal and communal commitment.

Claire Bischoff, coeditor of My Red Couch and Other Stories on Seeking a Feminist Faith *(Pilgrim Press, 2005), is pursuing a PhD in religious education and practical theology at Emory University. After living in Australia for a year, she has returned home to St. Paul, Minnesota, where she is embracing the joys and challenges of being a first-time mother to her son, William.*

My *Pensées*

Rebecca Curtin

As a junior in college I was assigned to read the *Pensées*, a work by seventeenth-century philosopher, theologian, and scientist Blaise Pascal. When Pascal died in 1662, he was in the middle of putting together this final effort—a collection of thoughts and quotes that would ultimately be considered his masterpiece. The disjointed format of the *Pensées* reveals both Pascal's resistance to seventeenth-century rationalism and his moments of religious skepticism. Taken in its entirety, the *Pensées* demonstrates its author's firm conviction and deep faith in God and God's grace. In this text Pascal arrives at few over-arching conclusions, focusing instead on processes of thought, on scientific and spiritual reflection. In my first encounter with Pascal I was struck by how this work could make so much sense while seeming so disjointed. I was moved partly by Pascal's theology, but mostly by the deep conviction of the author and the meditative and complex quality of a work that seems at the surface to be simply Christian apologetics.

My relationship to my Catholic faith also began, in many ways, as an apology. As a young person I believed Catholicism needed a defense. But naturally—like the reflections of Pascal—the relationship I have established since that point with my Catholic faith is much more complex than a simple defense.

When I think of my life as a Catholic and as a woman, so many thoughts and memories rush back as fleeting, breathing moments. It feels unnatural to reform the disjointed quality of my thoughts, questions, and memories (my *pensées*) to clear, linear narrative. Influenced by Pascal's meditative, impressionistic structure in the *Pensées*, I can muse on the great questions I pose to myself in a way that is natural, a way that takes into account the great variety of my encounters with Catholicism. Writing is a meditative practice, a place where I can ask questions without reaching firm conclusions. When I write, I attempt to inherit the formula of Pascal, the joy of Julian of Norwich, the natural wonder of St. Francis. What I have found is that Catholicism is the constant. Despite its various manifestations, its influence in my life is the thread linking all. I imagine these bits of thought to be answers to questions of my own—questions of faith, questions of purpose. I open my mind, release these *pensées*, and let the answers flow in and out of my consciousness.

Memory: Where have I been?

"Your writing is too impressionistic," my professor says, looking up from my paper, the fruit of a year's labor. "You cannot survive in academia being impressionistic."

As a teenager, my faith seemed to me an extension of a fortified and defensive Catholic Church. It was an example of tradition, heritage, and community; a monolithic body made stronger when circumstance required self-defense. I took any attacks on my faith quite personally. And in a religiously conservative public school, in a religiously conservative town, the attacks were frequent: "Catholics are not Christian. They are polytheistic, papist, Mary-worshiping perversions of what Jesus intended." The attacks flew, often and repeatedly in the form of so-called friendly fire. I found myself defending the Catholic Church to my peers and even to people I considered close friends. It was an intense engagement for any young and uncertain woman.

To defend the church, I hardly needed to be intimate with it on a spiritual level. Attorneys for the defense rarely know their clients well. For my defense of Catholicism, I needed a textbook, a historical understanding, and a proud, stubborn heart—all of which I had. What I did not have, I acquired, I studied. I was focused and determined to prove myself, and my church, Christian. Inevitably these debates became competitions of whose religion is more connected to God. Proud and obstinate with history, tradition, and theology at my side, I claimed victory, and Catholics remained monotheistic, normal, and Christian. I became a fighter—St. Michael my hero. I fought for Jesus in the way I believed he fought. He and I fought for identity.

We drive along the Gulf of Mexico, four Harvard Divinity School students in one car—two Catholics, one former Catholic, and one Presbyterian. "I miss being at a Catholic university," I say, my right arm out the window of the passenger side. I spread my fingers. Warm coastal wind dances in the spaces between them.

"What do you miss about it?" Andy looks over at me, taking her eyes off the road for a brief second.

"I don't know." I reply. "It's something—maybe a way of approaching a topic. It makes sense to me. There's something subtly different about a Catholic classroom." I hate it as I say it. I do not want to acknowledge this preference.

Silence. All four of us look out the windows at eighteen-month-old destruction, the remnants of community so quickly changed by one night's storm. Trash litters fields that used to be manicured lawns. Second-floor porches melt into first-floor porches. Many trees barely hold themselves upright, their strongest roots clutching the topsoil. Windows are still boarded up. Ominous chain link fences prevent access to places that were once accessible. We pass a drooping, exhausted, white banner with red letters that read: "Thank you America! Thank you

President Bush! Thank you Governor ——" The Governor's name is cut off. I am struck by the sign's sincerity. Or is it sarcasm? John leans forward from the back seat. "Catholic universities aren't afraid to explore the interconnectedness of subjects."

"Yes," I reply. "Or the interconnectedness of our lives, our experiences, the relationships between people. Community is paramount. Catholic universities create communities that concern themselves with learning *and* with being. And, it was okay for all this to be addressed in the classroom."

"The blending of spiritual and intellectual life, and the acknowledgement of both by a community. That acknowledgment is so important," Rachel adds thoughtfully.

"Acknowledgment is important." I look out the window at the neglected landscape. I see a once vibrant town, on the edge of this country, struggling to find its legs again.

Pain. The world is full of pain. The images of suffering accost our senses, the sounds of hurt ring in ambulance sirens and in a newscaster's composed, pseudohuman voice. Community can help to reconcile this pain. And participation in this community does not drown my voice. I am still myself, although joined by a chorus of others. I cry out in anger, sorrow, and indignation.

At eighteen, I leave California to attend the University of Notre Dame in South Bend, Indiana—a bastion of Catholicism. I withdraw from Catholicism here, in this place where I am more under its influences than I have been at any other period in my life. Surrounded by its sights, its smells, its devotees, its students, its teachers, I seek spirituality in nature, outdoors, in solitude. At Notre Dame I no longer have to fight for Catholicism; it is alive and well. I do not know what to do but distance myself from it. Because it needs no defense, no hero here in this stronghold of American Catholicism, I stop attending Mass regularly. I isolate myself from the spiritual community. I only feel comfortable in Vespers services, in darkness, singing by candlelight.

Bright star! would I were as steadfast as thou art. (Keats 284)

◆

Growth: Who am I?

Me, of-many-names. Me, desperately-attached-to-her-mascara. Me, skipping-Mass. Me, needing-the-ocean. Me, longing-to-be-loved-by-everyone. Me, grumpy. Me, joyful. Me, strong. Me, able-to-do-more-than-people-notice. Me, singing. Me, praying. Me, thinking. Me, loving. Me, living. Me.

We joke about Christianity, my roommate and I, because its hold on us is so deep, its influence so subconscious. We lay on the floor together, laughing, tears streaming down our faces. Abruptly, Mehgan becomes silent. "I hope that I'm not the Antichrist," she says gravely, turning her head toward me. The giggles erupt again, echoing against the high ceiling.

Sometimes harmonies combine to create a body of sound, and this produces pitches higher than musicians intentionally create themselves. In that created space God is most present. God exists in overtones, in the unintentional extension of created space. The subtleties of certain truths are at their most poignant in a song or a poem. I find the most beautiful, engaging, captivating moments in a group happen when we sing together. Our involvement with music, with poetry, allows us to participate in scholastic and religious traditions. The rhythms are ancient, and they link us to universal themes.

> *Medieval theories of meter, in fact, frequently assume that the pleasure man takes in meter is a simulacrum of the pleasure he takes in the principle of order and recurrence in a universe which itself would seem to be will and order incarnate." (Fussell 6)*

> *If I speak in the tongues of mortals and of angels, but do not have love, I am a noisy gong or a clanging cymbal. (1 Corinthians 13:1)*

Winter in Northern Indiana is long and often unkind. One January brings an ice storm. The storm is over, but now ice coats every branch. *Every* branch. Every leaf, too. I think maybe the branch beneath the ice will snap if I try to rip it away. But it is alive underneath. Cold coats it, tries to smother it, but it is alive. The tree will lose entire parts of itself to the ice, arms breaking under the weight, but they will grow back. Frozen water is dangerous, deadly, but water itself is so alive. The ice melts on my glove, soaks through to my fingers. I am chilled, but the wetness means we are coming back to life. The ice seeks the warmth from my body. It wants to live. Today is exceptional. It has death and life, silence and noise. Life is busy shedding the ice, shedding death and danger. The branches groan under the weight and some succumb, crashing to the frozen ground. Sheets of ice cry as they slip from roofs. Now there is the constant murmuring of the resurrected, leaves whispering, drops of water falling gently, meeting the ground and more ice.

We realize that God often exists in the empty spaces. Beth looks up at me and says, laughing, "There was an uncomfortable pause in the conversation, so I was like 'Hey, how about that Holy Spirit?'"

I smile back at her. "There was an empty space, and you filled it. Everyone appreciates that."

> *This movement, she felt, must be the timing of the earth rotating on its axis, traveling its elliptic course about the sun. And this feeling of moving with the earth was somewhat like the feeling of being in the ocean, out in the ocean beyond this rising and falling of the breakers, lying on the moving water, pulsing gently with the swells, and feeling the gentle, inexorable tug of the moon. (L'Engle 57)*

◆

Calling: Where am I going?

Everywhere we travel we create communities for ourselves. We become part of preexisting communities, or we begin new ones. Communities help us bridge the great distances we feel between others and ourselves. What has always struck me about

Catholicism is the way faithfulness must necessarily involve community. My struggle has been how to reconcile my private faith with the public, collective one. No one aspect of my personal Catholic faith can give the complete picture. The words themselves must be understood as community, a communion of separate thoughts that become one when placed together.

And what is my place as a woman in the community of faith? What is my vocation? Where do I belong?

Do not fear darkness. Light emphasizes differences. In the darkness we can be one. Darkness needn't be evil.

> *Fathers and teachers, I ponder, "What is Hell?" I maintain that it is the suffering of being unable to love. (Dostoevsky 301)*

Look within, within. Lose self-consciousness. Throw it away. Leave it behind with the winter chill, in the frostbitten air. Offer it to God, to someone who knows how to handle it. It is too much for you.

> *She stood behind him at his feet, weeping, and began to bathe his feet with her tears and to dry them with her hair. Then she continued kissing his feet and anointing them with the ointment. (Luke 7:38)*

Kissing the feet of another is the ultimate form of humility and love.

The train pulls away from Lourdes, the place where ice melts and where my candle burns, lit from another's flame, on fire with the prayer of a stranger. We rush by water that is the most peculiar color blue that I have ever seen, deep liquid cobalt, colored with greens, perfectly suited to the ocean. The giant Pyrenees rest on this green place like the Rockies over Boulder. But here the ground feels as though it has been exhausted by centuries. Young mountains have the tendency to revitalize a landscape. Planes leave vapor footprints on the sky overhead. I know only where I have been, and not even that for sure. I think how I touched an icicle on the wall of a grotto by a river, and how I was instilled with a cold that is real, hot with life. As the sun goes down, I say good-bye to the mountains. They have become like the clouds—shadows of themselves against a darkening sky.

It cannot be that, as Pascal says, "Nature is corrupt, proved by nature itself" (Pascal 4). I want to acknowledge God's call to us: Take back nature! Care for nature! Love nature! We cannot be separated from nature just as we cannot be separated from our own natures.

> *O Divine Master, grant that I may not so much seek to be consoled as to console; to be understood, as to understand. (Prayer of St. Francis)*

> *You know what that apple Adam ate in the Garden of Eden, referred to in the Bible? Logic. Logic and intellectual stuff. That was all that was in it. So—this is my point—what you have to do is vomit it up if you want to see things as they really are. I mean if you vomit it up, then you won't have any more trouble with blocks of wood and stuff. You won't see everything stopping off all the time. And you'll know what your arm really is if you are interested. (Salinger 180)*

Until two years ago, I had never truly thought about studying religion. I have always been surrounded by it, and it is difficult to study what we know intimately. But I began to feel that I could not study anything else. I want to create, to share, and to learn. Sometimes I feel that if I belonged to another denomination I would be a pastor, shepherding a flock of believers. Can professors be pastoral? Can we minister with our papers and with our lectures, where others minister with their presence and the word of God?

Yes. If the duty of ministry is to enrich the spirit, we can. If the duty of ministry is to lead by example, we can. If the duty of ministry is to be humbled before the great questions of our time and of all times, we can.

What about the duty of professors? Like many aspiring academics, I have a tendency to live in my head. I think how, for me, a retreat to books, to the gathering of knowledge, is a spiritual activity, an escape from a chaotic world. It is a retreat of the spirit to the workings of the mind. I have lived here. I have thrived here. In times of crisis I retreat again and again to my books, points of stability in a changing world. Every time I read the same books they change for me. I learn more and I grow. I cannot now see how even in their changeableness they will remain points of stability. I depend on the way we mold together, the books and me, each encounter full of the bliss of discovery.

But, when I think about this vocation, this call to the life of study, I cannot help but wonder what good are books when my world falls apart? What can they possibly say to make me whole again? How can books and the people who love them minister to others? The books try to give me the answers. I try to listen to them. They are part, but not all of the equation. Can books fill the rift of the broken heart, mend a broken spirit? Can philosophers and scientists, novelists and poets, theologians and academics help heal people? Can they take the place of families? Of course not. But to read and to study, to grapple with the great questions we have all grappled with for centuries, to engage one another in conversation, in true dialogue, highlights the most important aspect of the work an academic can do. To study, to teach, to learn requires attention not only to the work at hand or to the subject to be studied, but also between learner and teacher, between brother and sister, between friends. It demonstrates the *power* that attention to someone can give. This is transformative power. When we engage on this level, that invisible person ceases to be invisible, the one who has been pushed aside may take center stage, the forgotten member of our society may be remembered.

Thus, since all things are both caused or causing, assisted and assisting, mediate and immediate, providing mutual support in a chain linking together naturally and imperceptibly the most

*distant and different things, I consider it as impossible to know
the parts without knowing the whole as to know the whole without knowing the individual parts. (Pascal 64)*

She slides a book across the table to me. I ran to her in tears,
worried that the diagnosis of the ailments in my writing style was
fatal, seeking a second opinion. I notice the book in front of me
is her book, newly published, glossy cover pristine. "Apparently
my publisher likes impressionism" she says. Her eyes sparkle.

*Rebecca Curtin received her Master of Theological Studies from Har-
vard Divinity School in June of 2008. A native of San Diego, California,
and a veteran of the action sports industry, Rebecca hopes to continue
writing and to pursue an academic career in the field of religion and
literature.*

The Artist as Monk
A Reluctant Catholic Novelist's Stay with the Benedictines in Bridgeport

Felicia Schneiderhan

Bridgeport is the near-south side Chicago neighborhood famous for politics and the Irish and the White Sox. It's also the home of the Monastery of the Holy Cross, where a group of Benedictine monks bear witness to God's presence and their ministry in the city. Their mission statement—found on their very modern web site—proclaims: "For centuries, monks have retreated to deserted places, not merely to 'get away' from the hustle and bustle of urban life, but also because the desert is the place of confrontation with evil. Today's desert can be found in the alienation, poverty and noise of the modern city. By God's grace, we witness to the gospel by a life of community, simplicity, prayer and silence."

I retreat to the monastery as a fiction writer, a reporter, a freelancer, a grant-writer, and a writing teacher. I am all about the writing business. But I miss the joy of creation—the very reason I got into this line of work. It feels more and more like work and less like vocation. I fear I am losing my metaphors.

So I come to write and rewrite a novel about a young Catholic postulant in a convent in the mid-1960s, in the midst of Vatican II chaos. This is before my time; this is my mother's story, and the story of many women I have interviewed who left the convent during the 1960s, and some who remained. And over time, I've come to see that writing the book is more than my fascination with the story—it is also my journey to try to make some peace with my Catholic upbringing.

It's the hierarchy I struggle against—the power structures, the hypocrisy of too many leaders abusing their positions. The distance between the clergy and the laity, rather than all of us coming together to love God and one another.

My only obligation here is to attend Mass. I am also invited to the Liturgy of the Hours, which the monks come together to chant seven times each day. I have not been to Mass in a long time—I don't even go with my mother anymore. I have seen too many disconnected priests at the altar, preaching condescending homilies and basking in their power to convert bread and wine into the living Christ. I have known priests personally, in my family, who abused the power and wealth they were given. It's no doubt my own problem to see things so black and white—Catholicism is either all good or all bad; it's hard to separate the religion from my faith. My black-and-white thinking might be the impetus for writing this particular story—to explore faith in a religion I find troubling. There's so much about Catholicism I fight—the history of violence and oppression, the power complexes, the prejudice and hypocrisy—that I struggle to accept any of it. But for some reason I feel compelled to write about it, and to do so at a monastery.

The draw could be the unusual Benedictine tension of hospitality and solitude. None of the monks know why I am here, and they do not ask; they stock the refrigerator in the women's retreat house and set out clean towels; they give me a key and set a place for me at dinner; they do not ask my business, and I do not tell them. I come here to be anonymous so I can write in the city I love.

The retreat house is a three-flat recently acquired by the monastery, across the parking lot from the church. I've taken the room off the kitchen, with the high, firm, double bed. I have my laptop, tea, and quiet—except for the dull roar of city life around me and the wind whipping through the eaves.

I honor the obligation and go to Mass. These are monks—they are humble—I can see them living their lives as they say they do, in poverty, in service. And I feel called to attend Mass, anyway. What pulls me back? The practice? The discipline? The contemplative point of view as a way to approach the world? I feel right at home in this chapel, with the smell of incense and warm dark hues of ritual; and in a retreat house like this, I feel at ease in the lack of stimuli, in the silence and isolation.

I join them for their evening meal, in the dining hall, where three tables are set in a U shape. One monk serves and one monk reads aloud from religious commentary and the other five listen and eat without conversing and without making eye contact. Dinner is good—the monks eat well—but it is such a rushed affair. There's enjoyment, but not prolonged enjoyment, because there's no time—the monks must clean up and return to the chapel for Compline, the evening prayer, at eight o'clock.

The last time I went to Mass—was it a year? maybe more—was a Christmas midnight service with my family. Afterward, I was so disturbed that I stayed up until dawn, tossing and turning in my parents' guestroom, sparring with the discord in my heart. I don't know when my faith in Catholicism died. Sometime in my late teens, when I wanted to rebel against everything I once loved—my parents, my faith, my friends, and my education. But I missed God. I threw him out when I threw out Catholicism, without knowing that God and religion are not the same thing. I missed the intimate relationship I once had with him, but without Catholicism—without the Mass and the rosary and the sign of the cross—I didn't know how to connect with him again.

It was that Christmas morning when I called out to God, and he answered me. He gave me a place where I could meet him, apart from dogma and doctrine. It suddenly occurred to me that the one thing God and I have in common is that we like to create. We are both artists. Suddenly, I had a common ground on which to meet God again.

Sitting in the chapel on my first day on retreat, I think, what if I give in? It seems like I'm Catholic, though I don't believe a lot of it. It seems my mind takes to it, if only because that's the way I was raised and trained as a child, but still, it's a very real part of me. What if I just give in? What if I pursue the study? Because I need something. I miss the spiritual path. I struggle against so much.

A young priest who has just been ordained says the Mass. The last time I visited the monastery he was still a monk, and the youngest among them, and therefore lowest in rank. At meals he would not look at me nor acknowledge me; in my self-absorbed world, I took that to be a sign that he was avoiding me because I was a young woman and tempting, representing the world he was about to give up forever in taking his vows. On this visit, now that he's a priest, he is highest in rank. He still doesn't look at me, but I feel like that's because he has no use for me. And I'm fascinated by the change in dynamic between him and the monks.

His homily is about how we need to preach Christ and Catholicism to people and be ready for the consequences. He begins with Alexander the Great conquering and bringing a Greek culture with him, imposing it on those he conquered. I am hopeful, thinking he is going to say that we need to do the opposite and be respectful of other people's cultures and not inflict our beliefs on them. That perhaps people will be more willing to listen to Christ's message if we don't force it on them. But no, he goes the opposite way: we need to be like Alexander the Great; we need to preach Catholicism and be ready to take the heat.

All my good feelings about the Mass—yes, I can believe in parts of this, I can be a part of this—disappear with that sermon. And I am back to sitting in the pew, silently seething, powerless, voiceless, aching to rebel.

My will is so strong—as strong as the will of my protagonist. Back in my sparse room, she holds her ground against me, unwilling to go in the direction I want her to go. Or maybe she doesn't see where I want her to go. Maybe I should surrender and listen to her because she's going where she needs to be.

By my last morning of the four-day retreat, I am anxious and restless and despondent. I am sick of the monastery. I don't care about my obligation—I am irritated and not going to Mass. I am ready to go home, back to regular life, filled with responsibility and distractions. But I have just a few more hours in this sparse place, so I sit with my sprawling novel, just staring at the words on the screen.

My time hasn't been nearly as productive as I had hoped. I'm rifling through pages and pages, inserting and removing commas, chopping entire paragraphs, adding more pages, even at this last stage, and the last paragraph of chapter one is still not right. Now I fear the early scenes detract from the forward movement, now I'm not sure where anything goes.

I am trying to listen to where my protagonist wants to be. I start in one direction that seems to make sense, and it goes nowhere. I follow her impulses on the page, and they seem completely incongruous with the rest of the book. Is she someone completely different than I imagined? Do I know her at all?

It's painful to be working on this. How can I still be questioning this? Shouldn't I be closer to some kind of end, rather than so far?

The church bells ring for Mass, disrupting the buzzing stillness. And as it did on Christmas morning, it suddenly occurs to me that writing is my meditation—writing is my practice for connecting to God. It is active and solitary, a small study of what God must experience with his work all the time.

I remember my Christmas revelation—my point of connection. God is the master creator, the master artist, and I am the creation. And with all creations, there is the push and pull—sometimes the creator is in charge, sometimes the creation.

Few things are as exhilarating as when you see your creation surpass your expectations and become more than you ever imagined it to be. Few things can be as frustrating as a stubborn creation who resists and won't budge.

As a creator, I have to risk letting the creation be something separate from me. I must give it room to grow in ways I haven't planned, which is what God does with us by giving us free will. As creators, we must have faith that our creation will live—but we must be willing to take the chance that it won't. We never know until we let it live; we are always trying to keep it one step ahead of death.

So much of art, like spiritual practice, is about the ego. It's an expression of self, and yet it is not for myself—it can't be, to be truly good. If I only create for selfish reasons, then my art will never soar. If I do it for selfless reasons, then it transcends me and becomes something greater than me, greater than what I was ever capable of alone. Because art is not just an expression of myself—when it's really good, it's about the human experience, but when I set out to make it about the human experience, I kill it.

I want an audience, to be heard, to be wealthy, to have time and space to practice my art—but beyond all that, what I truly want is the rapture of perfect creation. I want that moment when time and space and everything else falls away, and I become empty of myself, and therefore able to hold more than myself—I become an instrument for true creation, for the divine. In that moment, I think of nothing—I only let the creation pour through me. And I will keep coming back for it. Days of sitting before a stubborn protagonist, stilted metaphors, and clichéd images only breaks me down so that I give up myself, and then God can work through me. I must be frustrated and broken so that something bigger can take over.

Finally, in the last hour at the monastery, I surrender. I stop forcing something to happen. I give up. And something begins to happen on the page. I stop trying to impose my will on her; I begin to see where she's leading me, and I follow. And I can give her words so that she can live.

Is this practice so far from Catholicism? The image of the suffering Christ, and the transcendent Christ, and the need we all have to let go, to be humbled, to pick up our cross and carry it, knowing that we will stumble and fall—knowing that this failure is crucial for us to ask for the strength from our creator to go on.

I come to the monastery to escape the distractions. I come to be with my own kind, monks who are trying to emulate Christ so they can connect with him. As an artist, I am like monks. I live in the world, but I am not of it. Imagination is the habit I wear, the writing my meditation. My work is done alone, but to serve my community. I live my vocation, whether writing a novel or a feature article or a federal cancer grant, to tell a story, to see as many points of view as possible, to give them a voice. I am a servant to society.

I bear witness to multiple points of view, to the power of creation, to hope.

A retreat is about going within, but that's only half the story. I forget the other half every time. At some point I am called back into the world, and I face the same demons. It's what I take back into the world with me that matters.

Six months later, the agent turns down the book, just as so many others have done, with the same general line: *interesting story, beautifully written, but I don't think it's commercially viable*. New friends and family members who express interest and to whom I entrust the manuscript politely read twenty or so pages and turn it back with no explanation for why they cannot go on. I wonder what God expects me to do with this thing, why I bothered to write it in the first place.

I look to other artists and monks; I pick up Thomas Merton's autobiography, *The Seven Storey Mountain*, and find he talks about artists on the very first page:

> My father and mother were captives in that world, knowing they did not belong with it or in it, and yet unable to get away from it. They were in the world and not of it—not because they were saints, but in a different way: because they were artists. The integrity of an artist lifts a man above the level of the world without delivering him from it.

I am disappointed that I did not come to this conclusion first, that my ideas are not original, yet my path to them was authentic—this is the path to knowing God, perhaps, in our own way. We walk where others have walked before, without seeing their tracks, but their tracks make it possible for us to go on. And I am relieved that somebody else understands this plight.

As frustrating as this practice can be, I will pursue this discipline until I cannot write words. I wear the mantle of imagination and bear witness to the unspoken, the unheard voice. Art is my point of connection to God. I cannot abandon it.

Felicia Schneiderhan grew up on the Mississippi River, the daughter of a former nun caught by a fisherman. Her short stories and essays appear in various literary journals, including Slow Trains, Mars Hill Review, Sport Literate, *and elsewhere. As a freelance journalist, she is a frequent contributor to the* Chicago Sun-Times *travel section and* Lake Magazine. *Felicia is currently at work on a memoir,* Life Aboard Mazurka, *about her newlywed year living aboard a boat with her husband Mark in Chicago.*

Spiritual Identity

*Glory be to the Father, to the Son, and to the Holy Spirit,
as it was in the beginning, is now, and ever shall be, world
without end. Amen.*

*When I (Kate) was a kid, I loved the Glory Be. It was such a
short, lovely little prayer. A quick dash amid the long rosaries
with my grandpa. A brief offering before a cross-country running
race. I almost felt guilty when the priest assigned me only three
Glory Be's for my penance. So quickly I was released of my sins
that it seemed almost, well, sinful.*

*But now, when I hear this prayer, I realize that much of the mystery
of Catholic theology is bound up in two sentences—the ever-
lastingness of a hard-to-even-imagine three-headed God. Simply
complex. Like the spiritual identities of young Catholic women.*

The clashes and tensions of Catholicism are what keep Rebecca Lynne Fullan Catholic. Like the shortest Catholic prayer
that captures the immensity of Catholic mystery, she loves Jesus'
human divinity and celebrates the simultaneous concrete and
effervescent nature of the Eucharist. Helena Fleig also savors
the contradictions of her Catholic identity. Not until she started
dating a Zen Buddhist man did she begin peering into the com-
plexities of being Catholic. While she feared she would find an

emptiness in not knowing all the answers, learning about Zen is offering her an appreciation for the "not-knowing" of God and her Catholicism.

I (Kate) am a runner. Apart from formal education and going to Mass, it is the activity I have done for the most consecutive years, the thing I know most intimately. I know the internal struggle before stepping into a seven-degree winter morning, the sanctity of ten miles with only the sounds of my breathing and my shoes, the meditation of rhythm.

As I stride to the door at the end of my daily run, I check my breath and slow my body down. I bend down and untie the key from my shoelace. My body shifts into "hurry up and get ready for the day" mode. This run is ended; go in peace. But, for just a moment, like kneeling at the end of Mass, I pause and am thankful for the morning, for the run, for this ritual. To my unending surprise, it has, again, managed to prepare me for the bumps and twists of the day. Running is quiet space amid the chaos, like my childhood parish used to be. Running has the familiarity I still feel walking into any Catholic Church on a Sunday morning. As I have skidded into my late twenties, I am more and more aware of the way Catholic practice plays out in sometimes funny, sometimes disconcerting, ways. Running and Mass—their movements, their imagination, their words, and smells—are intertwined in how I am spiritual and religious.

Kate Lassiter understands this hold of Catholicism on our spiritual imaginations as she writes, "I want more of a role for women and others seemingly marginal to the church, but I don't even know what that would look like." As young women wonder how we could ever be anything but Catholic, we live in the shadows and on the border of our religious tradition. Young Catholic women live on the edge of an institution that doesn't quite know what to do with them.

Eileen Markey clings to and pushes against this Catholicism. She loves its mystery, its ability to hold faith and reason in tension. She loves its language for the indescribable Divine. But she also has big questions about whether or not she can really raise a son in a tradition whose theology rejects homosexuality and women priests, and promotes what she sees as black-and-white thinking. "My church doesn't want me," she writes. "It's a profoundly lonely feeling." Her faith is, as she describes it, "an awkward postmodern thing."

Sarah Albertini-Bond relates to Eileen's bind. After a lifetime of Catholic school, Sarah graduated from college and felt like she had binged on Catholicism. So she began to eat from the American religions' table of plenty. She savored the delicacies provided by Jews, Muslims, Buddhists, atheists, Wiccans. And then, her appetite refreshed, she found that her Catholic ritual and Catholic life had more flavor than she had ever realized.

Monica S. Hammer's spiritual journey, not altogether unlike Sarah's, started with a childhood Lutheranism, moved to a silent meditation group and participation in Evangelical prayer, then gravitated toward the Virgin Mary, Julian of Norwich, and Hildegard of Bingen. These three women drew her into Catholicism, an RCIA program, and Catholic confirmation. Praying with Mary and Julian and Hildegard is safe and holy for Monica—a Catholic sanctuary for her spiritual expression.

The journeys in these stories are winding, but not without purpose. The women who walk them learn invaluable lessons that root us and challenge us, the twists and turns enlivening our Catholic identities.

Religious Education

Eileen Markey

I should have known I was asking for trouble when I chose Thomas as my confirmation name. Even at seventeen, I thought a sincere faith could withstand rigorous questioning. And I have always been a Catholic with doubts. Now I am a Catholic with doubts and a child. The doubts grow more urgent lately because deciding to raise my child Catholic is, in many ways, deciding whether I would do it all over again myself.

Already I hear a clock ticking like a time bomb. The questions are only a few years away: Why are only men priests? Why does the church say my friend shouldn't have two mothers? If Catholicism is the one true faith, is Ali bad because he doesn't love Jesus? Who says what priest comes to our parish? Why do they have gold chalices when there are poor people?

All right, he's only three, but simpler whys will soon start and this unapologetic feminist, straight-queer, anti-authoritarian mama bristles at the idea of absolute answers. I'll have a hard enough time toeing the party line on bedtime. My husband says his atheism exempts him from negotiating what to do with the boy's religious instruction. He's a fantastic partner and parent in every way, but no help on this matter, saying only "I know this is important to you; I'll support what you decide."

The fact is I have questions of my own.

Why do some bishops advocate for Republicans? Which is worse: abortion, on which the church speaks clearly, or the death penalty, about which they barely speak at all? If these guys are living with grace, why do they seem so defensive? Why do I belong to a religion if I disagree with so much?

Thanks to a Jesuit education, a mix of thirteenth-century mystic Meister Eckhart, the twentieth-century novelist Graham Greene, and a timeless belief in Eucharist, I've managed to remain on the Catholic team. The Jesuits prize intellectual rigor. They cut a steady example as worldly, educated men animated by desire for God. If these guys, who are much smarter and more dedicated than I, can stay with this institution, maybe I should too. Meister Eckhart wrote the most mind-blowing Zen-like sermons on the nature of God and the need to see God without the labels of love, truth, spirit. God is nothing, he argued. God is empty. God is, simply is; it's we humans, with our limited minds, who hang our names and constructions and limitations on God. Graham Greene's heroes are always broken and filled with doubt, but they fumble on. I recognize them. And Eucharist is the greatest story ever. The divine became flesh, and as the central rite of our religion we take part in that flesh. It is, like the Christ from which it flows, the most astounding amalgam of celestial and tangibly corporeal. How does one explain belief in something so absurd? I can't. I just believe.

What's kept me Catholic is an understanding that doubt is what makes faith genuine— that the presence of doubt is what makes the church ring true.

So I stay. I stay even though the men in charge often contradict all the gospels taught me about humility, forgiveness, and compassion. I stay despite the corrosive corruption of a church that fetishizes authority and infantilizes the voice of its people. No bishop has yet been held appropriately accountable for the child sexual abuse scandal. I stay despite the sexism, the homophobia, the Gnostic disrespect for body, the soul-negating fear of argument. I stay even as my allegiance in these culture wars is squarely on the side of secularism. I stay because I believe what I think is the heart of it and because leaving seems like treason.

I believe in Eckhart's ineffable Godhead, not this anthropo-morphic God we can make small enough to fit in the ballot box. I go to Mass because I know I'm just a frail human and we need ritual. I've received communion at an immigrant parish in the Bronx, with Mother Teresa in Calcutta, at the Cathedral of Notre Dame in Paris, in a tiny Gaelic-speaking village in Ireland, and among aid workers and journalists in Phenom Penh, Cambodia. Life in each place and the circumstances that took me there were radically different, but the miracle of Mass was always stable. Despite variations of language, music, and architecture, the church and sacrament were always home. Something happens there that my proudly rational mind can't grasp but that makes my soul soar. This faith of mine is an awkward postmodern thing.

But I can't really hand the kid Camus and Rushdie and say, "Look, honey, there is this howling emptiness. We make our own meaning. Mama believes in the most fantastic bit of the church. And ethno-culturally, we're Catholic and, really, 99 percent of the moral code is excellent, so, off to CCD you go."

The idea of growing up without Catholicism seems like a great void, like the ultimate white bread. No Advent calendars, no sweet moments before the Nativity scene in the front of church, admiring the tableau of baby Jesus in the manger surrounded by lowing cows and the humble donkey, no sugary sheet cake flowers and the hum of relatives at First Communion parties.

Then there is the loyalty issue. My Irish ancestors suffered for their faith. I can hear fifteen generations of Irish people rolling in their graves at the thought of me going across the street to the Anglicans, a church with such similar theology, but a greater respect for the maturity of its members. I can hear those relatives, "So Paddy's granddaughter would rather the Queen of England be the head of her church."

My son has an uncle who does not have a tone for the religious. His family left the church when he was six or seven and he's like a tuning fork that doesn't vibrate. He doesn't have that part in him that allows him to understand the transcendent. To him, religion is just the man behind the curtain in the *Wizard of Oz* and the people who are duped. He sees no holy residue on every blade of grass.

And of all the things we will give this profound, sacred child—from breastfeeding to cuddles to a love of learning—shouldn't a vocabulary for the divine, the means to communicate with the ineffable, membership in a worldwide community be among them?

I can't imagine keeping this faith from him. There is nothing that can take the place of Eucharist. It's sacramental. It's social. It's political.

God became flesh and dwelt among us. I want him to have that. This life is imbued with the divine. God is among us. That's what communion means. Every fragment of human experience, including the corporeal, is experienced too by God.

Catholicism informs every aspect of my life. It's how my marriage moves. It's how I chose my profession as a journalist who tells the stories of people Christ would have sat with: the criminal, homeless, immigrant, and reviled. It's why I smile to people on the street, knowing Christ comes in the face of the stranger. It is why I believe in working for economic justice and not for war. It's why at the depths of my periodic depressions, I know ultimately all is one. Not only is there meaning; it was born into the world, and had a mother.

But being Catholic increasingly makes me feel like I'm on the wrong side of the rational versus sectarian split in this country. There was an article on the front page of the newspaper a few years ago about the church equivocating on evolution. Catholicism's belief in faith and learning had always been a source of pride. When secular friends would warily ask what science I was taught in Catholic school, I would proudly retort that the post-Galileo church wasn't antiscience. We weren't some whack-job Christians. Then I'd remind them that Mendel, the father of genetics, was a monk.

I'm familiar with the line on working for change from within. My Catholic membership card has been taped together with that idea for going on fifteen years now. But Rome doesn't hear the concerns of loyal dissenters. To Rome, we are just unruly Americans seduced by our sex-obsessed and selfish culture. Our usual retort—the church is the people in the pews, not the hierarchy— rings hollow since the people in the pews don't make the rules, count the money, or decide who gets denied communion. In the wake of the failure of true, open response to the child sexual abuse scandal and the election of Pope Benedict XVI, I feel a new sense of outrage, or maybe just resignation. By staying I'm tacitly assenting to how this organization operates. The pope has said he would be satisfied with a church that is smaller, if more pure. There is no room for equivocation or relativism, he's said.

My church doesn't want me.

It is a profoundly lonely feeling.

I love this church and I also can't, in good faith, profess membership in this organization that fosters inequality, refuses to truly repent for wrongdoing, and distrusts the fresh air of argument. I love this faith and I need to practice its central tenets in a community, but I don't want the men in charge to infect my son with their certainty.

So we struggle on. He's three now and says bedtime prayers to an unnamed God, gives thanks for the day, and requests for help in being good and kind. I see the value of religion as an agent of social control—I'm up to my elbows attempting to raise a civilized child. But it also seems unconscionable to fill his open little mind with this Catholic narrative and label it TRUTH. We go to church, but not regularly. I am emotionally exhausted after Mass because it is too often celebrated with small-minded certainty by a priest just out of seminary who sees my presence in the shrinking congregation as assent to increasingly reactionary Vatican dictates. My son goes to synagogue too, where the lesbian parents of a playmate are part of a proudly queer and proudly Jewish community. As he grows he'll join our after-dinner conversations with beloved Jesuit priest friends. He is surrounded by religion. He is surrounded by people whose lives and work as attorneys, activists, social workers, teachers, human rights advocates, and writers are inspired by Catholic social teaching. He will be engaged in a Catholic dialogue.

I give him religion. But I can't give him certainty, because I don't have any to give.

Eileen Markey is a reporter who loves living in a progressive community in the Bronx, New York. She writes about urban public policy, teaches journalism, grows vegetables on the roof of her apartment building, and marvels at the wisdom of her now four-year-old son.

The Religious Buffet

Sarah Albertini-Bond

"Any boys who have made their First Communion and would like to be an altar boy, please see Monsignor Konrad after Mass."

Sitting in the pew of St. Matthias, I had an epiphany: I've just made my First Communion. I can be an altar boy.

It wasn't until after Mass, when my parents and I were standing outside talking with Monsignor Konrad that the reality of the situation became clear. "Sarah, you can't be an altar boy," Monsignor Konrad said.

Undeterred, I stood as straight as I could and announced, "I could be an altar girl, then."

My parents said nothing. I do remember them reaching out to me—as if to brace me for what they knew was coming.

"No, you can't be an altar girl," Monsignor Konrad told me. "There is no such thing as an altar girl."

"But why not?" I asked.

"Because girls aren't allowed to be altar servers."

"That's stupid," I said.

"You might think it's stupid or silly, but that's the way things are, and it's not going to change," he said.

◆

I grew up in a Catholic family. Social events were rooted in religious events—Christmas, Easter, weddings, baptisms, and funerals. At home, my family kept holy water and a statue of St. Francis of Assisi in the front vestibule and St. Joseph guarded the backyard. If something was lost, my grandmother walked around the house praying, "St. Anthony, St. Anthony, something's been lost and must be found." If we couldn't immediately identify a saint for a cause, my mother dragged out her *Book of the Saints* to look one up. My father kept a cross in his armoire and looked at it every time he dressed for the day.

I attended Catholic school from kindergarten through college. I've never had a school year without a theology class. It was always very clear to me that developing my mind was just as important as developing my soul. In grammar school our teachers gave us guilt trips for not doing our homework and for squirming in church. In high school, cliques were as much about wearing the right lipstick as assisting the nuns with Mass. By the time I started college, the fact that my dorm was next to the church seemed perfectly normal to me.

However, by my college graduation, I felt a restlessness in my soul. I kept wondering if this was all there was to my spirituality—my hand dipped into the holy water, I automatically made the sign of the cross, and then sat through an hour-long Mass. Until the next week.

In the years since that conversation with Monsignor Konrad, I learned and relearned that the Catholic Church was an unyielding organization; I had to accept my place, or lack thereof. By the time I hit my early twenties, I realized that my own philosophies about life and faith were no longer the same as those of the Catholic Church. It felt like what I was hearing from my church's hierarchy was that if I wanted to be a "good" Catholic, then I had to do what the church decreed. The Catholic Church seemed to be fulfilling Monsignor Konrad's prophecy—it did not change. Or, worse yet, what little change occurred, I disagreed with.

I signed up for some spiritual counseling and was assigned to a man studying to be a Jesuit. The sessions were long and emotionally draining. For the first time in my life I had to explain my faith rather than serve as a receptacle for tradition. During one of our sessions, I said, "It's like all my life I've only had one thing to eat. It used to taste good, but it's all I've eaten so I don't know anymore. I can't taste what I'm eating—I just fill my mouth with food. I know it's nourishing but it's not fulfilling me. Then I see this big buffet off to the side but I'm being told, 'No, be happy with what food you've been given.'"

My spiritual counselor just about jumped off the couch when he heard me say that. "That's it! You need to go to the buffet. Sarah, go to the big buffet that you see."

I remember sitting in my chair, feeling as bolted down as my spiritual counselor felt freed. "You do realize that my bland meal is a metaphor for Catholicism and the buffet is other religions."

"I know," he said, "and I want you to put down Catholicism and try out the other religions you see." I must have looked disbelieving because he continued. "You need to try the rest of the buffet. But I think in the end you'll come back to Catholicism—you'll find it's the most filling."

I never officially left the Catholic Church. I simply stopped going to Mass and no longer identified as Catholic. Sunday mornings were no longer consumed with making sure that I made it to the holy water in time to make the sign of the cross before the choir director cued the gathering song. In the meantime, I ran right to the religious buffet with little aim. I divided my time between reading about religious beliefs and attending services.

I sat in Jewish temples and listened to rabbis weave the teachings of what I knew as the Old Testament with the teachings of ancient rabbis. Reading what Jewish folks called Hebrew Scriptures put my questions of God into a larger historical context.

I listened to wise men with the souls of poets speak about the beauty of submission to Allah. I danced and sang with abandon during a Christian revival. I learned the difficulty and joy of staying still in silent meditation at a Buddhist center. Talking with Quakers about the meaning of employing religious beliefs for social activism gave me much to think about during their silent meeting. Wiccans I met eloquently linked my feminist philosophies and environmental beliefs with spiritual practices. Atheists happily debated with me whether it was possible to be morally good and not believe in God.

I went far and wide, into any religious house that would have me. I read books and pored over websites about religion. I exhausted religious people with my questions about the meaning of faith and religion.

I never doubted that there was a God. I wished I could have—it would have been far easier for me to deny God and believe that religion was nothing more than a cultural construction. It would have solved things neatly. Then I could have stopped worrying about disobeying dogma because I no longer would have believed in a God or put stock in the Catholic Church's teachings.

But I couldn't. To deny God, to deny his love and power in my life was as difficult as denying myself breathing. Just as surely as I breathed, I knew there was a God; but how best to acknowledge that God?

I didn't think that God cared what name I called him or where I went to celebrate him. What mattered was that I believed.

I loved the history of Judaism. But if I acknowledged that history was a part of my faith, then I believed that Jesus came down from heaven to save me. I believed that Jesus, a Jewish man, walked among other human beings and cared for those less fortunate, and stood up against injustice. In caring for those less fortunate than himself, Jesus died, not for crimes that he committed but for the sins of all, then rose from the dead three days later.

So Jesus pointed me in the direction of Christianity. And the history of Catholicism drew me into staying Catholic. Catholicism endured throughout history for a reason, but I wasn't sure if that was enough of a reason for me to continue believing in it.

I hit a stumbling block. History pointed me to Catholicism. My own philosophies pointed me to a more liberal tradition, like Unitarian Universalism. For a while I tried doing both—one week of Catholicism, one week of Unitarianism. While sounding practical, that arrangement left me more confused. I railed inside against the priests who stood at the pulpit and reduced Catholicism to blind acceptance of dogma and catechism. And then the next week, I felt despair when religion seemed boiled down to a series of logical steps with little passion.

Sitting in the pew of St. Aloysius Gonzaga in Washington, DC, I stared at the altar after Mass. This Jesuit parish seemed as inclusive as I could imagine my Catholic experience to be. Yet, I knew Catholicism was more than this parish. The pope and the rest of the hierarchy reminded me of how very different I was from what the teachings decreed a Catholic should be.

I felt myself becoming more and more frustrated with the limits of the teachings. Finally, I hit my boiling point. I got angry with God, asking him what kind of God he was that he created such division among people. The war I felt in myself paled in comparison to the religious fighting that consumed people across the globe. I fumed, "Who was he to demand that his people tear themselves apart, all so we could worship him?"

My soul was screaming, anguished. Exhausted, I sat in the church, staring up at the altar, mute with sorrow as tears trailed down my face.

Despite my anger, or perhaps because of the pain that it caused me, I experienced a small part of the divine that afternoon in St. Aloysius. I felt the Holy Spirit moving in my soul and with it came a flash of insight. Then I felt peace as I joyfully surrendered to something greater than I am.

I realized that God doesn't demand that we tear ourselves apart—we do that to ourselves. In our attempt to understand he who is greater than all of us, we assign labels and divisions. And in spite of the fighting and the labels, God has faith in us.

Faith isn't a blind adherence to dogma and catechism; it isn't a logical progression through facts and figures. Faith is love, a profound movement in the soul that defies logic. Love is the act of belonging completely to another, complete trust and adoration of one who completes you while you aspire to be better than you were without that person.

I don't agree with the Catholic Church on many social issues. I believe a respect for the Earth, a gift from God, is not tangential to giving thanks to God. I think gender and sexual orientation should have nothing to do with one's calling to lead and celebrate the Mass. I believe that people have the right to decide what is good in their personal lives, who and how they should love, and this in no way weakens their devotion to God.

But there is much to love. I love the history of the Catholic Church because it is an imperfect history; there are many mistakes that were made in the name of God. Yet, the church has learned from its mistakes and endured—a testament to the faith of the many rather than the mistakes of the few. I love the mystery that is incorporated into the faith, that to be a Catholic is not just a purely logical decision. I am humbled as I stand in the shadows of saints, using them as guides to loving God *and* being an imperfect human. I love that part of being a Catholic is not only having faith but also performing good works.

I found the wisdom of using history as a guide from Judaism. I found peace when I finally understood the beauty of submitting oneself to God, just as the Muslims showed me. There was a joy in my soul when I could express myself merrily before my God, as I had at a revival. And I knew that patience was rewarded when I allowed myself to quiet down and open my soul for meditation; for that I thank the Buddhists. My atheist friends were right, God didn't give me the authority on being moral. With God, however, I find a path for me to live an ethical life.

I don't always like and agree with everything I hear at church. And the Catholic Church, as an institution, doesn't always like what I do. But the church and I need each other. Without each other we are incomplete and with each other we inspire the other to do better while reaching out to the other.

I have faith in the Catholic Church, not only for what it is now but also for what I hope it will be. And I believe the church feels much the same about me.

Many, many years after my conversation with Monsignor Konrad, my mother called me on the phone. "Sarah, I have to tell you that something you've always wanted is happening. But I'm sorry, it's too late for you," she told me.

"What is it?" I asked.

"St. Matthias is allowing altar girls," my mother said.

Yes, it is too late for me to be an altar server at St. Matthias. However, unlike what I used to believe, institutions and people can change. It's just a matter of time. And faith.

Sarah Albertini-Bond graduated from Fordham University in 1999 with a degree in English. She currently lives with her husband in Virginia Beach, Virginia, working as a customs compliance analyst and pursuing her writing when not at the office.

Zen and the Art of Catholicism

Helena Fleig

Three summers ago, I finally read a book that had been lying around my parents' house for quite some time, Fr. Robert Kennedy's *Zen Gifts to Christians*. That same summer, somewhat ironically, my fiancé Doug and I began dating. Although my choice of reading was initially driven by intrigue and spare time, I soon found myself turning to *Zen Gifts* as a roadmap for the unfamiliar spiritual ground my relationship with Doug led me into that summer.

Like me, Doug was raised in a nice Catholic family in the suburbs of New York City; but unlike me, he now identifies as Zen Buddhist. As I reflect on my Catholic identity and sense of spiritual grounding, I am ever-more aware of the influence that both Zen Buddhism and our relationship have had on me; of how, over the past three years, my Catholic identity has been shaped, and continues to be shaped, by someone and something that is simultaneously foreign and outside of myself, and uniquely one with who I am.

The summer Doug and I started dating represents a significant turning point in my understanding of Catholicism, myself, and the world around me. As a college student, a sincere, but at times burdensome desire to gain knowledge often stirred me to find answers and achieve a life of prestige and success. My sometimes excessive need to be in control of my life must have had at least some bearing on my relationship with God, as I approached both my academic studies and my religious practice in largely the same manner: with diligence, ambition, and even some anxiety. As I read *Zen Gifts* and started dating Doug, I began reminding myself to "let go," to practice self-emptying, and to give myself to a radical trust in God; and the care I had to give to these little reminders only highlights how novel they were to my spirituality at the time.

I sincerely believe that the new understanding of God that Kennedy introduced to me in *Zen Gifts* helped me to reach a place in my spiritual life where I could forge a deep relationship with Doug. Grounded in the Christian apophatic tradition, Kennedy's book affirms the profound possibility of knowing God through "not-knowing" by recognizing God as mystery, as present even in darkness. In a similar manner, my relationship with Doug embodied the very notion of "not-knowing" in its unfamiliarity, unpredictability, and dependence on trust. In the words of Kennedy, I found a place for myself amid the tensions I sometimes experienced when my worldview met Doug's head on. The conversations that we began to have that summer—often either implicitly or explicitly connected to our Catholic and Buddhist identities—were eye-opening and, at times, difficult. Doug's sensitivity to the faults he found with some of the church's actions sometimes highlighted the flaws and human nature of the church as an institution. In this space I held myself in tension between Doug's often fair observations and my desire to claim a Catholic identity for myself that is empowering and liberating.

My conversations with Doug could have led me to the notion that the church must be either fully right or fully wrong. However, I found myself drawn, instead, to Buddhism's teaching on nonduality, a profound concept that theologians such as Father Richard Rohr have argued can be found in the gospel teachings of Jesus. Whereas dualism seeks to divide reality into static and opposing halves (those who are good versus those who are evil; our bodies versus our spirits), nondualism embraces a more holistic perspective that challenges such neat and clean divisions. Looking at the institutional church from a nondualistic perspective allowed me to see that it has, throughout its long history, made choices from both ends of the spectrum. And recognizing humanity's paradoxical espousal of both sinfulness and grace has helped me forgive the church for its similar lack of perfection. I found hope in the belief that, in the muckiness of these gray areas, the church is still striving to listen, discern, and evolve. My church may sometimes be one of hierarchy and patriarchy, but it is also a church of liberation—one that is of and for the poor. From Buddhism I have learned that the dualism of black and white simply cannot capture all that is the Catholic Church.

At the end of that first summer, Doug decided to recycle some of his belongings by offering them as "mail art" to friends and strangers. One of the items I requested was a drawing of Christ on the crucifix that Doug made when he was a boy, probably before he had even heard of Zen Buddhism. The drawing was done in crayon on graph paper, giving both the cross and Christ's body very precise dimensions, with sharp angles and a boxy silhouette. Colors were carefully chosen, with Crayola-red blood marking the paper.

Years later, when Doug was visiting me in Cambridge, Massachusetts, we spent a cold afternoon at Harvard's FOGG Museum. While there, he decided to make a pencil drawing of a Pieta sculpture that was part of the museum's medieval art collection. Doug concentrated on the details of Mary—the expression on her face and the dramatic folds of her clothing. He drew the outline of where Christ's crucified body rested on Mary's lap, but he chose to leave Christ's figure simply as an empty silhouette. He gave the drawing to me as a gift, and I remember staring at it speechlessly. Literally, it was an empty Christ. Christ as self-emptying.

In my bedroom, I hung both of Doug's drawings on my wall, side-by-side: Christ represented by a young Catholic boy and Christ represented by a Buddhist man. I often meditated on them, feeling as though they somehow represented a growth process that I too was undergoing in my own way. In Doug's drawings, and through my own conversations with a spiritual director, I trusted that I was being led into new levels and experiences of faith. I began to feel that my relationship with Doug and my dialogue with Buddhism was an important part of that growth and that, in God, I could find the strength I needed for that dialogue.

I have a favorite part of *Zen Gifts* in which Kennedy quotes Thomas Merton in a letter to the Polish writer Czeslaw Milosz regarding "the glib clichés that are made about the will of God." Those clichés, Merton complains, "are enough to make anyone lose his faith." He continues, "For my part, I have given up my compulsive need to answer such questions neatly. It is safer and cleaner to remain inarticulate, and does more honor to God" (Kennedy 25).

Over the last three years, I have grown in so many ways. My understanding of God has deepened, my relationship with Doug has grown stronger, and my graduate studies at Harvard Divinity School have enriched me. Though it may be ironic to some, these growth-filled experiences have put me in Thomas Merton's camp, in taking solace in the unanswerable. I have felt pressure, at times, to have the answers to the various questions posed to me. Though my faith has very much deepened and matured, in some ways I feel that I know less now than I did (or *thought* I did) three years ago. Perhaps it is simply a matter of quality versus quantity; for I am confident that what I do know has the potential to shape my life in a profound way.

At the end of our first summer together, Doug embarked on a four-month stay in Turkey. The night before he left, I spent a very special afternoon with his friends and family, enjoying each other's company and soaking up some final precious moments with each other before our lives took us all in separate directions. Doug's mom invited me to stay for dinner, but it was a Sunday, and I had planned to make the forty-minute drive home to attend evening Mass. As I contemplated my options and examined the anxiety that began creeping up about missing Sunday Mass for the first time in my life, I suddenly felt oddly resolved that I would stay for the evening and attend Mass the next morning. I realized that the pull I was feeling to stay with Doug's friends and family was not simply the selfish desire to spend a little extra time with my boyfriend. It came out of a sincere recognition that God was present so fully in that very moment that I simply could not bring myself to leave it.

I remember sitting around Doug's dining-room table that evening, looking into the faces of all who were present: the members of Doug's life-giving and inspiring family, friends from as far away as South America and California and as close as Brooklyn, and even two of Doug's neighbors—twin boys with the same mental disability and sense of humor. The atmosphere was joyful and bustling. Food passed every which way, conversations crossed the table in all directions, and the twins' presence added a lively sense of laughter and gratitude. I had to hold back tears of happiness, as it was there at Doug's family's table—where old and young, "abled" and "disabled," from near and far were seated—that Christ was fully present in each one of us, and in the bread we were breaking. As I attended Mass the next morning, I found myself ever more grateful for the sacrament of the Eucharist. I will never look at the ordinary meal with family and friends as anything less than sacred.

When he tried to speak of the profound mystical contemplation of God—by which divine wisdom is infused into our souls— St. John of the Cross found that only the imagery of darkness could convey such an understanding. Lest we be frightened by this description, St. John assures us that such darkness is necessary in order to purge the soul "of its habitual ignorances and imperfections, natural and spiritual." Darkness "prepares the soul for the union with God through love" (John of the Cross 348).

Whenever I read these words of St. John, I can only hope that whatever darkness I may experience leads me to a more profound union with God as I am challenged to embrace knowing

God through "not-knowing"—a union that, I believe, could only be enhanced by my love of others.

Helena Fleig trained for a career in secondary education in the fields of history and religion while earning her Master of Theological Studies from Harvard Divinity School in 2007. She currently lives in San Francisco and teaches in the religious studies department of a Catholic high school in Belmont, California.

An Unconventional Peace

Monica S. Hammer

I once had a summer job doing market research in downtown Chicago for a cruise ship company. The office was decorated with hula dancers, and the marketing people were chipper, highly enthusiastic people who often reminded me to dress more casually. My responsibilities included developing a strategy to get Midwestern retirees interested in Mississippi riverboat cruises, which actually meant that I did a lot of data entry.

On the way into the city each morning, my mother and I shared the newspaper on the train together. At the station downtown, she would buy juice for me and coffee for herself, walk me to my building, and then move on to her own job. It was a lovely ritual that inspired me to create my own ritual to celebrate paydays. Every other week, I treated myself to a chocolate walnut cookie and a small carton of milk at lunchtime, and sat in the sun by the Chicago River to relish the yummyness of my life.

During payday rituals, I passed a big Catholic church right in the middle of downtown. Homeless women and children congregated on the steps and elicited much more attention from the lunch-goers, myself included, than the homeless men on the street corners. One payday, I impulsively gave my cookie to one of the homeless children. That same day, I decided that I might as well check out the church, since the sanctuary might be just as pleasant a place to rest as the river on this particularly hot summer day.

It was indeed cooler inside. As my eyes adjusted to the darkness, I heard the mutterings of the rosary, and the pleas to Mary sounded foreign to my Lutheran ears. Nevertheless, I relaxed into the smell of incense, headed to the back of the church, and looked at the various statues of Mary. Taking notice of what seemed to be rather quaint and charming kneelers, I decided to try them out. I settled into my weekly contemplation of just how great my life was, and it was then that I sensed a powerful, potent force all around and most especially above me. It pressed down on me like a heavy fog, and I wanted it to infuse me. I found my head bent down almost perpendicular to the floor, and my body filled with a kind of electrical peace.

I was so pleased to realize that I was experiencing grace, a gift that was undeserved and unasked for. Had I been alone, I would have obeyed the incredibly strong urge to lie prostrate on the floor. Instead, I asked God who Mary might be, and for help in getting to know her. My prayer was carefully worded because, in truth, I was hesitant to learn about a woman who, heretically to my Lutheran sensibilities, seemed to receive just as much attention as God. But I was not such a fool as to ignore the possibility of a relationship between the mutterings of the rosary, the women outside the church, the images of Mary, and this mystical experience. I wanted God to know that I was receptive to this beauty and eager for more. I even went so far as to give my carton of milk to another mother and child as I was leaving the church, in hopes of receiving another grace.

Back at college that fall in Minnesota, I thought about how I could pursue similar mystical experiences. I realized I felt a similar peace during long, quiet walks in the arboretum, and I decided to attend student-run Friday-evening Christian meetings. Granted, Friday nights were a supremely uncool time to have a club meeting, and I fretted about missing out on my friends' plans for the evening back at the dorm. But I decided that my reputation and a little bit of fun was a small price to pay for feelings of enlightened bliss and joy that I was beginning to experience with increased frequency. Buoyed by their bright-eyed and bushy-tailed enthusiasm, I sang songs with the Christian kids. And as time went on my mystical experiences began to evolve: I experienced pain in the palm of my hands at times of others' suffering, had vivid dreams about the past and future, and became aware of a spiritual deadness in some people's eyes.

It was confusing to navigate the spiritual world by myself, so I turned to my spiritual mentor for help, an upperclasswoman named Lara who always seemed to be fasting and keeping the Sabbath. Lara began taking me to her warehouse church on Sundays, where people sang, danced, and spoke in tongues. The children had the most fun, running around during the service with flags, tambourines, or whatever pleased them. But I didn't like praying in a warehouse, no matter how spiritually gifted the people. Moreover, my spiritual gifts, as I learned to call them, were different from those of the fundamentalists who were often performing the laying on of hands and spiritual tremblings. So Lara and I began praying back at our college in the church crypt.

One night, as we prayed in that crypt, I felt a flash of cold darkness invade most of my body, my feet and hands cramping into contorted shapes. I felt terrible fear, and had absolutely no idea what to do to stop this hostile takeover of my body. Lara had been praying in tongues, which usually involved her closing her eyes and turning her palms upward, and I don't know when she realized what was going on. But at some point, I remember her placing her hands on the right side of my head, continuing to speak in tongues. I had no idea what she was saying while she prayed over me, but I could feel a wrestling for control inside of me and the darkness slowly pouring back out of the left side of my head. I still didn't have control over my contorted feet and hands as Lara dragged me up the steps to the phone in the foyer to call her pastor for help. He said I should call upon the Trinity myself, which actually hadn't occurred to me. So I did call upon the Father, Son, and Holy Spirit, most especially the Holy Spirit, crying hysterically the whole time.

To this day, I still feel bruised and overly sensitive on the left side of my head, and safer on the right side where Lara placed her hands. I had no idea how to contextualize this trauma, and I felt that Lara had betrayed me by leading me to a spiritual place that was unsafe. I also felt like God let me down. I spoke to Lara's pastor and preachers as far away as Texas to try to gain a sense of understanding about what happened and, more important, to learn how to prevent it from ever happening again. The scariest part was realizing that these pastors, all of them men, didn't seem to know what to tell me.

As the preachers continued to give me spiritual advice, they were also asking questions ("What was the demon's name?") that made me feel more fearful than secure. I retreated into academia, and a Buddhist monk and professor was actually the one who recommended to me women mystics like Hildegard of Bingen and Julian of Norwich, instructing me to look for spiritual guidance from within my own cultural history and gender. In them I found kindred spirits for the first time in my life. Their holistic vision of the earth and the spiritual universe resonated with my innermost self. They also taught me to see Mary as the ultimate feminine mentor and role model, revealing the secrets of giving birth to love. All three women showed me that women experienced God through dreams, angels, and visions.

And in turn, these women chose to respond to God's call: Hildegard composed music, painted, and cultivated medicinal herbs; Julian wrote down her experiences (as the first woman to write a book in English, no less); and Mary gave birth to Jesus. What was I to do with my experience? When a professor invited me to spend the summer in England, I decided to take a pilgrimage to Norwich, following in the footsteps of Julian's contemporary, the mystic Marjorie Kemp. I took the train to a little cell in a little church in the little town of Norwich, where Julian spent her life praying. There was a little altar in her cell with the words, "Thou art enough for me," etched in stone and illuminated by candles. I was inspired to learn that tremendous spiritual riches came from such a simple life. So inspired, in fact, that I thought about converting to Catholicism once I returned to the States.

I was still skeptical of Catholicism from my study of religious history and prejudiced from my upbringing as a coolheaded Scandinavian Lutheran, but my knowledge of Hildegard and Julian and what they taught me about Mary made me feel that I had more in common with these women than with almost anyone else. So in September, I went to the local Catholic Church in my new neighborhood in Southern California and presented myself as someone who was thinking about becoming a Catholic. It just so happened that a Rite of Christian Initiation for Adults (RCIA) class was about to start, and the church drummed up a woman my age named Jenna who could act as my sponsor.

Jenna was an Irish Catholic from Boston, and I thought her age of twenty-eight, her job as a consultant, and her fantastic array of suits were all quite glamorous. Over occasional Sunday brunches and Saturday coffees, she marveled at the complexity of my spiritual path compared to the solidity of her family traditions. Her faith was simple and deep, and I smiled when she told me her stories of family rosaries turning to gold. And I thought of her when I dug up my Polish great-great grandparents' rosaries. I grew up believing that I was to pray directly and only to God—seeking mediation from saints or anyone else was misguided, unnecessary, and even dangerous. But despite my misgivings about praying to Mary as a nondeity, my soul felt cleansed when I first prayed the rosary, and my heart felt like it was blooming.

Every Tuesday, Jenna and I attended classes taught by Father James, a monk from somewhere in the mountains who was entirely too good-looking to be a priest. He grew up the son of an apple farmer from Washington and sometimes betrayed an Eastern Washingtonian accent that was particularly endearing to his congregation. He could not have been more than ten years older than me, and his mental agility was a skill I needed in a priest because my liberal arts training and fear of making any false commitments forced me to question anything that didn't make sense to me. I didn't expect the church to have an algorithm of faith, but I did want to make sure that I could, at the very least, follow the logic of the basics, and learn the reasoning behind the controversial issues. Centuries of Catholic theology usually withstood my inquiries and helped me flesh out questions I hadn't thought to ask.

Father James helped my faith in Catholicism as a religion take root. The Catholic women who showed me the way to their beloved church also led me to anticipate being treated as a strange and unruly outsider, like they themselves were treated. Marjorie Kemp, for example, who inspired me to go on that pilgrimage to Norwich, was considered to be insane. Julian's bloody visions of Jesus were never fully embraced by the church either, and even today people say Hildegard's visions were actually just migraine headaches. As a representative of the establishment, Father James didn't seem to think I was crazy, and that meant a lot to me. He didn't offer advice or sensationalize my experiences like religious male leaders from other denominations. Instead, he listened to me talk about my experiences, acknowledged that I wasn't alone, and validated my faith and God's faith in me.

Father James also allowed me to have and hold my differences in opinion when we came to a crossroads regarding some church doctrine. In fact, he confessed that the church frustrated him at times, as well. When he took the RCIA class to his monastery, Father James told us that he had joined the priesthood so that he could work quietly for God by building and managing the gardens. Instead, the church sent him out to be a parish priest, and he was doing his best to do a good job. Not only that, he also confessed that he believed priests should be allowed to marry and that he was taking steps to voice his opinion within the church's steep ladder of communication.

Women's roles in the church bothered my feminist sensibilities as well, so I looked to Mary, Hildegard, and Julian for guidance. When the church's teachings differed from their own experience, they responded with inexhaustible patience and temperance. And if Father James could sacrifice the idea of marriage in order to submit to the church as a priest, then surely I could be a member of the church that discounted women's ability to lead and love, right? I could work for change from within, right? Sounded simple enough.

And it was, theoretically. In fact, I found the hardest thing about becoming a Catholic was being with other Catholics. One Sunday, I arrived at Mass late and sat at the back of the church, which gave me a great view of the other parishioners. Like most people I saw out at the beach or at the mall in Southern California, the women were blonded to perfection and the men were confident in their wealthy, white, heterosexual way. It took a good fifteen minutes for me to look around and compare diamonds to find my favorite engagement ring. I then wandered off into thoughts about Jenna, struggling with her own adorable romances. As a twenty-eight-year-old single woman, a dreaded age to be single in So Cal years, how much did she hate staring at all these wonderful diamond rings each Tuesday and Sunday? I was thinking about which Jane Austen character she most resembled before realizing, full of remorse, that I had officially spaced out.

I decided to refocus on the actual service by taking the lead from these rich, beautiful people all around me. But then I realized everyone was just like me, except they had diamond rings. None of us were actually paying attention. When I brought my observation up with Father James, he assured me that not all Catholics were like the ones in his church. He suggested that I consider joining a monastery in order to find a community of Catholics that I felt were engaged with God. Nothing more flattering could come from Father James than his belief that I would make a good nun, and it is still on my list of my favorite compliments of all time. But while Father James focused on serving God by serving the church, I considered the church a resource from which to draw in my own quest to know and love God. My real role models were Hildegard, Mary, and Julian, who all lived their lives as women with radical relationships with God. These women, the church, and perhaps even the foil of my Orange County parishioners fostered a shift in my own relationship with God. I learned that loving and knowing God meant working to love those who were most in need.

For this reason, I applied to the Jesuit Volunteer Corps, an organization whose mission includes simple living, social justice, spiritual growth, and community. While trying to do good work during my year of service in North Carolina, I met other Catholics who are faithful to the church, despite the church's unfaithfulness to them. There was the priest who was awfully fond of rainbows and managed to assemble a little queer following in the back corner of the church. And I talked with a nun who told me how difficult it was to swallow the reality that the church would not let her become a priest and how amazing her life is now, as a leader of a women's collective devoted to mysticism.

Just like Julian and Hildegard, there are many Catholics who live on the outskirts of the church, but nevertheless have strong relationships with God. Seven years after my conversion, I still believe that the church can help me live a holy and humble life, but I try to take responsibility for my own relationship with God. These days, I usually choose to attend early morning Mass during the week so that I can pray in peace along with the immigrants and the elderly in my community. And on good days, I can still feel a powerful grace all around me, above me, and in me.

Monica S. Hammer is thirty-one years old and aspires to sing in a Catholic gospel choir.

We All Wear Uniforms

Kate Lassiter

We start with a common educational scene: I am in a classroom. Large windows overlook Twenty-first Avenue. Whiteboard behind the professor. Students have gathered around an oblong seminar table. I hear my voice as it exits my mouth and makes its way into the ears of my colleagues. Sheets of paper with words I wrote lay prone on the table. These words are not my own. I only borrow them from a client who told them to me; I poach upon his story of living and moving and being. The few words that are my own are meant to evoke self-discovery for myself, possibly for others.

In this presentation to my colleagues, my client's story comes to the front, and I want to believe that I fade as we analyze his therapeutic hour with me, his young healer-in-training.

But I am not allowed to recede. My professor of pastoral psychotherapy stops me in the middle. "You're on the border," she says. *"You're on the border,"* she says it again, this time more emphatically, staring straight into my eyes. She says nothing about my "him." She sees through my recession, and, though she knows only pieces, she names my story, not my client's. Clearly. Abruptly. Succinctly. She understands. Borderlands are often shadowlands.

But shadowlands are funny places, filled with moments of past where the sun hits the human body, casting the counterimage.

The shadow is a step ahead, moving forward, as if willed by something outside the body. The body follows the shadow, the shadow not wholly other, but an obfuscation of the self that leads. These are foreshadows: sites of prophetic revelation that only make sense as the story proceeds.

Lately, thoughts of Bishop Ireton High School flood my memory. I have flashbacks: Music practice before Mass in the gym whose metal bleachers creaked and groaned when filled with the eight hundred students. The uniforms—pleated khaki skirt in the summer, plaid wool kilt in the winter, blue oxford shirt, maroon blazer, white socks, lace-up brown or black shoes. The Colonel, a retired Marine who patrolled the hallways, handing out detention slips for breaks in uniform code or for tardiness.

In my recent move across town I found my old notes from one of my high school religion classes. I paged through the notes, reading nuggets of wisdom culled from the Catholic intellectual tradition. "Every existence is a graced existence," and "We are saved as a people, a group, a collective." I know these words. I memorized them for tests. Repetition. This is how we learned. Over and over again, words and images burned into our collective teenage minds.

I remember standing outside the doorway of room G-19 in the basement, memorizing the first and second creation stories in Genesis for Introduction to the Hebrew Bible as a freshman. Over and over, I said to myself, "On your belly you shall crawl and dirt you shall eat all the days of your life." As I looked through these old notes I found the dot matrix printout of Jesuit Gerard Manley Hopkins' poem "As Kingfishers Catch Fire." And though I am standing in front of a filing cabinet alphabetically cataloging my life, I hear Sister Alethaire's voice from miles away, and from more than a decade before, leading the entire Morality 1 class that repeats in tandem with clear, measured beats, "Selves— goes itself; *myself* it speaks and spells, / Crying *What I do is me:*

for that I came." Inherent in group memorization is the intuitive knowledge of timing and rhythm, of cadences. My classmates and I learned it at an early age in the Mass: "We believe in one God, the Father, the Almighty, maker of heaven and earth. . . ."

But the high school memory that continues to resurrect itself most often is this: I lay prostrate before the altar and tabernacle in the school chapel after required confession. A red candle glows above the tabernacle, a constant reminder of Jesus' presence in the Eucharist. I hear Sister Alethaire's voice say to the class, "Prostrate yourselves and remember the goodness of God."

To the floor we go, I go, for this is both a communal and individual act. We kneel, I kneel, gently, but swiftly, so that the back of my kilt doesn't rise too far. My face is down, my forehead resting against the back of my hands folded on top of each other, my legs outstretched, and my tears staining the chapel carpet. "I love you. I love you. I love you," I say, over and over again, not sure if I am reassuring myself of this knowledge, that God indeed loves me, or if it is a cry of lamentation, calling out to God to hear my plea and to answer in kind.

The bell rings. It is 2:08 p.m. The class rises. We girls half-tuck our blue Oxford shirts back into the kilts; boys put on their blazers; Sister Alethaire returns her rosary to the hidden pocket of her habit. In class the next day, we start another novena to St. John Vianney, the Curé of Ars, patron saint of confessors and priests. I wonder if, like the Curé of Ars, I could someday be a divine conduit of healing, grace, and forgiveness.

◆

"You'd be a priest if you could," my ex-seminarian friend Mark says to me on a Sunday in November seven years ago.

"No! Well, maybe. It's complicated. I don't think that's what my calling is, regardless of rules," I answer. I pause, look out the kitchen windows of the volunteer house onto the streets of Southwest Baltimore, the sunlight streaming in, and try to think of how to say it.

Mark gets up from the long table, opens the refrigerator door, and pulls out the cheese and tomato. "Damn, we're out of bread. I guess we can't make grilled cheese and tomato sandwiches." I'm still standing at the window. I still don't know how to say it.

Four years later Mark and I will meet again at a bar on Cleveland's Westside. I will tell him this story and he will say, "I don't remember that night." How is it that this memory haunts me, and not him? How is it that I am still dumbstruck when he asks me the exact same question again?

This past year I was struck by the shape and color of Catholic Triduum services in Nashville, the Vatican of the Protestant South, as I've been told. My Protestant friends do not understand why I do not attend services on Wednesday nights for most of the liturgical year, but spend day after day during Holy Week in large, ornate, stone churches built in replica of cathedrals and naves in Italy, Spain, France. Vivid rose windows and large pillars prescribe how I act and think, how and where I genuflect, how I cross myself with holy water. How do I explain to them that these days are different from every other day, that on these days I am most fully aware that "I am not worthy to receive" as we celebrate, darkness creeping upon us. Yet year after year I make my way to the front of the altar for Communion on Holy Thursday, anticipating mystery in the incense and the chanting of *Pange Lingua* by the faithful. I line up to kiss the feet of Jesus on Good Friday while the choir intones, "Women of Jerusalem, do not cry for me, but for yourselves and your children."

On this Good Friday, the parish placed a crucifix nearly eight feet tall in the central aisle at the Cathedral of the Incarnation. The faithful gathered in the evening, in semidarkness as the sun set through the stained glass storytelling windows. Shadows settled upon us. We yelled in tandem, "Crucify him. Crucify him."

We heard, "And Jesus wept in the garden."

We watched as the priests knelt, and then lay prostrate before the empty tabernacle and the stripped-bare altar. We were a people gathered to mourn, to weep, to pray for healing and hope and redemption. And as the priests and seminarians lay prostrate, I felt my mouth whisper again, "I love you. I love you. I love you," as tears marked their path down my cheek.

◆

Catholic piety runs deep. Catholic girls know the routines. We learn to say the rosary, repeating the Hail Marys while fingering the beads, looking to see which Sorrowful Mystery comes next. We perfect the art of genuflecting in our uniform skirts, the waistband rolled to show more leg. We cup our hands to receive the Eucharist. We memorize pieces of the *Catechism*— sex is for marriage and is ordered toward both procreative and unitive goods. We pray for vocations to the priesthood and the religious life.

But what of Catholic women? What does our piety look like? Outsiders like my professor tell me that we walk on the borderlands within the church.

"You're a Catholic woman," she says. "The institution barely recognizes you."

And I try to respond with a smart answer, "Yes, but we have tactics, ways that we negotiate the given-ness of ecclesial structures. We're institutional people. If we didn't have ecclesial structure, we wouldn't know how to change it."

Catholic women know piety. They know about kneeling at the foot of the cross, laying themselves prostrate before the Divine, and too often are forced to lie prostrate to institutional demands. I ask women friends how they negotiate their feminist sensibilities, and more often their queer sensibilities, with Catholicism. And their stories echo mine. They too have dangerous memories that are paradoxical—sorrowful and joyful, humiliating and empowering, painful and pleasant, confining and liberating.

And their questions are like mine: how is it that a Dominican nun's words from fourteen years ago can resound more clearly in my head than the words of the priest who stands at the pulpit today? Despite homilies that do no justice to the Word, we remember and take part in ritual actions of dangerous memory each Sunday. It is that anamnetic longing for the One who assumes our full humanity for the redemption of female, male, intersex, transgender, and beyond throughout all of salvation history, as patristic father Athanasius said. These fissures allow us to remember what those deemed marginal to the institutional church have learned in the shadows of the Mass and religious education. We are saved as a people. The Church is bigger than the church. Radicals like Dorothy Day and the Berrigan brothers are as much a part of the tradition as the Bishop of Rome. Thank God for that.

Walking in the shadows requires certain qualities: quickness, stealth, transgression. I want more of a role for women and others seemingly marginal to the church, but I don't even know what that would look like. I stay, often staring out the kitchen windows and onto the streets, trying to put into words the sense of both mourning and yearning, all the while filled with memories of empowerment, transgression, absolution, celebration.

On a trip home to the Washington DC area, I moved my body in rhythm with the young and young at heart while the large, imposing outdoor statues at the Hirshhorn Museum cast their shadows on those of us pulsing to the loud music. A friend of a friend of a friend introduced me to Laura. When she heard that I study theology, she shook my hand, pulled me close, and spoke loudly into my ear over the music, telling a story that was her own, but one that I have heard in many iterations: a cradle Catholic who must reconcile church teaching on sexuality with lived experience, and who asks a simple question: "What did God make me to be?"

In these moments, I have no collar, but I offer absolution of a type. I have no magisterial teaching authority, but I profess, nonetheless. Joan of Arc—young, unread, barely able to spell her name, archetypal gay hero for wearing men's clothing and doing men's work—prayed to Catherine of Alexandria, the strong-willed, well-read, female defender of the faith in the early fourth century CE. According to legend, Catherine was beheaded by the Roman authorities who would soon become defenders of the church and state under Constantine, milk flowing from her wounds after the wooden wheel of destruction would not break her. Joan was put on trial by the ecclesial authorities who represented the interests of the church and royals, and died by fire after refusing to recant. Scorned in their day, they were both named martyrs of the church at one time.

I don't wish martyrdom on Laura, but in a tradition with such breadth and depth, fissures abound. It's only a question of timing, of seeing when historical trajectories rub hard against current realities. And while historical recovery and reinterpretation stimulate my intellect, the personal angst I feel persists: I offer priestly duties of pastoral care—guiding, healing, reconciling, and sustaining—with recognition from the academy as an institution.

My struggles with Catholicism—a worldview that has different notions of time and space and belonging and claim—are shaped by a life in the shadow of the nation's capitol, Washington DC, where everything is a serious game of political strategy. My Protestant friends get more worked up over papal statements than I. They do not seem to understand that I don't live in a religious democracy, and so my ways of moving through church, of understanding ecclesial community, are so much larger than what a democratic church polity could account for. In some ways, I have more freedom to act precisely because I do not live in a pure democracy, church or otherwise. The tactics and strategies of politics I observed growing up inside the Beltway will continue to serve me well as a Catholic doing theology professionally. Just as I learned that there are formulaic, ritualized strategies that prescribe the interactions between political parties, I also learned that there are tactics, ways that individuals and grassroots organizations make new visions out of the skeleton of the old. So too do I view my profession and vocation as a deployment of tactics to help create a new world and church by working through the structures that are a given.

Sometimes I do consider leaving the church, but I know I cannot leave behind the richness of the Catholic tradition or the institution in need of reform. But even here I get it only half right: God made me, the Catholic Church claimed me through baptism, Eucharist, and confirmation to know, love, and serve God, and now with the fullness of an adult conscience, years of Catholic school, and degrees in theology, I serve the God who calls for *metanoia* from both individuals and communities. The Catholic Church needs me in her in order to be fully awake to the fullness of creation.

I can walk away, but why? I would yearn for the shadow of the long-standing faith, where what is hidden is that which brings fullness of redemption. I would long for the call of justice in the social teaching that reminds me that I do what I can in the fields, but that the harvest is plenty and laborers are few. And I worry that I would forget a foregone conclusion: I am an ambassador for a God who is, a God who calls for all creation to cry out in joy, regardless of whether I play an official role in the hierarchical church or relish my role as a strategic bricoleur, nimbly welcoming all with the words of St. Francis de Sales, "Do not wish to be anything but what you are, and try to be that perfectly."

My lapsed-Catholic-turned-atheist, queer, organic farmer friend, speaks softly into the phone. "My San Francisco grandma asked me if I went to Mass today," she says. "I told her no. She said that she prayed for me. That she prays to all the saints for me and remembers me and my brothers when she goes to Communion."

My friend pauses and takes a deep breath, memory and words unspoken living in between us, "Do you ever pray for me?"

I pause too, inhale deeply, and fall prostrate on my living-room floor, my phone cradled in my ear while the setting sun filters through the budding tree leaves. "Of course," I answer, feeling far removed from the safety of class with Sister Alethaire, but knowing the answer that will come. "How can I not? I love you. I love you. I love you."

Kate Lassiter is a Theology and Practice Fellow and a PhD candidate in religion, psychology, and culture at Vanderbilt University. Being a good Catholic queer girl, she relishes the surety of dressing in a uniform, searching out icons of saints that she might have tattooed on her body one day, and substituting gender-inclusive language during Mass.

Red Light District

Rebecca Lynne Fullan

My mother held my hand. She pointed at the candle, dangling and encased in red glass, shining out scarlet over the tabernacle's gold.

"You see?" she asked me, squeezing just a little. "When the light's on, that means that Jesus is in there. You can tell by the red light."

I looked. Red was and is my favorite color. I loved it. I loved the code, the mystery, the magic. I loved Jesus, in his beautiful box and elsewhere, too.

But time passes, even when you love like that. Time pushes. I am no longer a child. But I think I am still a Catholic.

I could give it all up; I could. I think this to myself from time to time, often when kneeling with hands folded, saying the appropriate words, looking up at God and feeling a nameless anger that runs like a current through my spine, down and out through my fingers. I could take off this red velvet cloak of a religious identity—though I love red velvet on my skin. I could go for something sort of vague and universal. If we peel back my beliefs like a spiral of orange skin, underneath there will be the aftertaste of a universal divine reality that I find essential—not necessarily this specific Catholic story. I could, oh, I could be something else. Something that would not tell me my desire for a man can be sacramental, but my desire for a woman only disordered. Something that would not say that my body bars me from a high form of God-intimacy, that my not-male hands cannot tease out the divine because they are connected to a body that blooms in round circles and deep channels.

I could. I might. But there is the matter of Jesus. I was struck, at a panel discussion among Catholic thinkers I recently attended, how almost no one mentioned Jesus when they described being Catholic. I expect that he haunts them nonetheless. He haunts me, standing at the center, the crux, of what it means to call myself a Catholic.

Catholicism is, all the textbooks say, a sacramental faith. Sacraments with a capital S (for Catholics with a capital C), and sacramentals with a small s, joining to make life absolutely shot through with holiness. The sacramentals as holy objects conspire with your fingers and your uttered prayers while the Sacraments move you through time with continuity of blessing and divine relationality. And the Sacrament of Sacraments is, of course, the Eucharist. The intake and swallowing and digestion of Jesus, so that Jesus becomes all knit up in your flesh, your cells, in your bones, like the carrots and chicken you had for dinner, but with all that God inside. When I was little, I thought there was actually a secret Word (you know, the one that's in the beginning, the one that Jesus has only to say to heal whomever he desires), and that only priests knew it, and that if I knew it, I could turn anything I pleased into Communion. I imagined presiding over whole Jesus-meals, grinning and announcing at the end that while everyone thought they were having an ordinary pot roast, they were actually communing with the Most High.

After my First Communion I couldn't get off of my knees. I clung to the hand of our family friend Sister Barbara, feeling like some kind of beautiful firework had deigned to go off inside my eight-year-old chest. It wasn't until years later that I heard the whole transubstantiation story, about the ultimate realer-than-reality of what I was consuming. There, with my French braid and white dress, I would have told you, if I could have known the words, that the true presence had taken up residence in this strange, vast collection of elements I was (still am) trying to cobble together into a self.

A fiery priest with an urban flair and a long drab robe first explained the doctrine to me. I was sitting with about a thousand other teens, in a big old revival-style tent meeting we borrowed from the Protestants. He explained if time moved in a line, the sacrifice of Jesus had pierced through that line, stood outside and above it, so that it was always-now, and when we eat his body and drink his blood we touch that always-now. So we are part of it. Made sense to me; my metaphysical imagination has always been in healthy shape. But it was not that priest who showed me what really happened to me on my First Communion, nor was it his cosmological poetry that explained to me why it mattered.

Instead, that mystery was given to me anew by an old, congenial, diocesan type at the same summer gathering two or three years later. I had not lost my ardor, not then, in the blaze and the sweat, but I was perhaps more cautious of the trappings—like an all-female chastity talk and "women's Mass" presided over by male priests, and the catalog of mortal sins on the back of our program booklet, including masturbation and "getting drunk on purpose." So I waited with an ever-so-slightly thicker skin, and this old white-haired fellow got up for our final homily in the final Mass of the retreat. He spoke so gently, his voice like the even ascent up a barely sloping hill. In this drowsy tone, he gave me the secret of my First Communion, my every Communion.

"In a few moments you will come up here and receive Communion," he said, "and when you take it in your hands or on your tongue, the celebrant will say, 'The Body of Christ.' But what if we said, 'You are what you celebrate. This is Who you really are.' What if we said that instead?"

I sat up. I looked around. Were my fellow teenagers and their chaperones going to jump out of their seats and throw the man from the tent for heresy? Were they going to dance and sing, turn their faces up in joy, scream in terror, run away? None of the above, apparently. Everyone was sitting still, wiping their sweaty faces and fanning themselves. This was just a gentle old man. No threat. Not even a very exciting speaker. But there it sat, in our midst like the consecrated host, a piece of ordinary, brilliant, revolutionary truth, God incarnate *and* a simple disc of bread. This is Who you really are.

I could give up being Christian altogether if it weren't for this God-man, perplexing, persistent, bloody-minded, and mysterious, arousing my passion, my questions, my laughter, just when I am ready to throw in the towel instead of nicely wiping someone's feet. In the legend of my life, according to my mother, one day when I was still in a car seat, we were driving around and I started crying, "They killed him." They pulled the car over and asked me what was going on—the him was Jesus.

It's a little awkward, isn't it, to be the kind of child who weeps for Jesus in the car, to grow up and try to explain this without sounding like, you know, some kind of religious nut? I get nervous of such things. But if I'm honest, for me, the fundamental him has always been Jesus. Jesus stands as the exceptional and the everyday—true man yet very God, the kernel of God in any person. Particular, like your best friend's smile, and universal, like recognizing what a smile is. That's what Jesus is. It's hard not to love a both-and, generous, recklessly incarnate kind of God. It's hard, when you actually peer down under all the dust and jitters and outstretched claws, not to love any other human being.

When these ideas get inside you, they burrow in deep, like greedy crows' beaks that search out a kernel to crack. Last year I saw this crazy man on the street, lurching himself along, his face twisted, holding his side, and I was rooted to the spot, trapped between what I needed reality to be and what was actually happening. He pierced the timeline of my morning rush to work with his graceless suffering and I was stymied. I stumbled along on my blue shoes with tiny clicking heels, stopping to turn around from time to time, trying to keep him in my vision. Thinking, *Shit, again, Jesus again, and I too frightened to attend to him.*

Or another time, when it was a young man with a cardboard sign, hunched over his crossed legs, and I stopped, wrapped in a fantasy in which he would be grateful and good-looking. Instead, I got involved in a mumbled argument about whether he would take the box of cereal I was offering without milk. Jesus sometimes comes off as quite irascible. Look at him in the gospels, withering fig trees when they don't provide fruit to his liking, in or out of season. Sure, he makes it a lesson about Godly omnipotence later, when his disciples murmur, but I believe in this tired and pissed-off Jesus, as well as the all-seeing God.

Remember my own body processing his. Remember that simple disc of bread. True God yet very man.

Do I go too far? It's hard to be temperate with Jesus, and I've heard tell he doesn't care for it. I want to be burned. I want to understand. I want to be swept away laughing, like an earthly pleasure, from the center out. And I am not entirely unseduced by a narrative of nails, and blood that falls, of necessity, of design, and of desire, between my open lips. And I am not sure if any of this really matters. Like a goodly few before me, maybe I just get swept up in the weird and wonderful narrative, and mixed in a little religious kink to keep my own interest. But the weirdness of the story makes me think there is something to it—the ridiculous image of people stripping down and throwing on a new life, whole-cloth. There is something intensely beautiful about the disruptiveness of Jesus, the turn-your-life-upside-down, wear-an-instrument-of-torture-'round-your-neck *strangeness* of this seemingly familiar figure. Something that makes me rush out on the water and then suddenly notice there is no ground beneath my feet. *Eat my body, drink my blood. Take up your cross and follow me. Love your enemies.* They become so commonplace we forget the whistle and sting of these words, chafing cheeks as surely as a winter wind.

It's like an optical illusion. Change the way you look at it and the young woman becomes old, the familiar story new and tingling and strange. Chalk it up to Catholic imagination; I do. The Sacraments and the sacramentals, the blessings showered about like sneezes, the veritable army of saints. All saying something, something like *Look*, something like *See*, something like *You were right, you know, it isn't what it seems.* Sometimes it's all a jumble, a whirlwind of stories and cosmology that is mine as fundamentally as the narrative of my own birth, and yet mysterious, full of contradiction and sparks of meaning that trouble me, often productively, like a feather dipped in water and stirred.

When I was young, I walked by a pond with my father, and he told me about the Incarnation.

"Would you do it?" he asked me. "If they said to you before you were born, take on a body, and live in it a little while, and it will all end in your suffering and your death?"

I looked at him. I hesitated. I believed there was always a right answer with him. Sometimes I still do.

"Well . . . no . . ." I said.

He smiled at me. "But something in you said yes, didn't it? Somewhere you said yes."

I stared at him. How did he know? How could he know? It didn't occur to me he had only to look at his own no and yes, that I was not so mysterious and yet, such a mystery. You are what you celebrate. You are what you eat. You are the Body of Christ.

I'm not saying there are bells and whistles every time. I go weeks without Mass, noting the Sundays but not taking the time to hurry down to church, not getting up an hour earlier or leaving an extra hour before my evening commitments. Sometimes the whole procedure makes me irritable, and it would be easiest to let it slip through my fingers. Jesus is bizarre. He can't be predicted, but you surely know if it's him or if it's not. Except for those times when he's strolling along in broad daylight and you think he's just some dreamy, uninformed whack-job hitchhiking to Emmaus. Jesus is not safe—he doesn't even call himself good, just all-encompassing, intimidating things like "the Way," and most of the time he leaves the definition to you and me. I'm peckish for things divine, but eating bread-flesh can get either dull or creepy, depending on which side of the hyphen your brain decides to entertain.

But when the world shatters, as it does with a frequency that pierces right through all my pretty metaphors, or when it comes together with a sudden brilliance, there's a Somebody I'm longing to see. Despite skepticism. Despite dissent. Despite an honest belief that no religious system is better than any other. Because he's crazy like a fox, sparkling like a deity, beautiful like a man. Because he has a hundred stories from just a handful of words in the dust.

Just a few weeks ago I cut my skin on my own perfectionism and ended all torn and ragged over nothing much at all. I lay on the floor when the storm passed over me and I felt him like I hadn't in months of theological reflection. *Oh Christ, you holy bastard, where have you been?* I asked the fluorescent lights above me and the inner dazzle within. When he smiled, I knew that he'd been waiting in his favorite secret hideaway—behind the doors in me that I seal up tight with shame, there in the darkest corridor, the most unfriendly looking room of me.

I could walk away; I could. But there it is nonetheless, and there I fear and hope it will remain. Look. Can you see it? Here in this chest, in this body, in my skin: that red light. Flickering. Burning. Oh, Jesus Christ. You sweet disruption. You forcible sacrament. And I for you, lit up, despite everything. This Catholic girl, all grown.

Rebecca Lynne Fullan holds a Master of Theological Studies from Harvard Divinity School and an AB degree in Comparative Literature from Bryn Mawr College. She has been a Catholic all her life, and a young woman for the more recent portion.

Conclusion

We believe in one God, the Father, the Almighty,
maker of heaven and earth, of all that is seen and unseen.

We believe in one Lord, Jesus Christ,
the only Son of God, eternally begotten of the Father,
God from God, Light from Light, true God from true God,
begotten, not made, one in Being with the Father.
Through him all things were made.
For us men and for our salvation, he came down from heaven:
by the power of the Holy Spirit he was born of the Virgin Mary,
and became man.
For our sake he was crucified under Pontius Pilate; he suffered,
died, and was buried.
On the third day he rose again in fulfillment of the Scriptures;
he ascended into heaven and is seated at the right hand of the
Father.
He will come again in glory to judge the living and the dead,
and his kingdom will have no end.

We believe in the Holy Spirit, the Lord, the giver of life,
who proceeds from the Father and the Son.
With the Father and the Son he is worshiped and glorified.
He has spoken through the Prophets.
We believe in one holy catholic and apostolic Church.
We acknowledge one baptism for the forgiveness of sins.
We look for the resurrection of the dead, and the life of the
world to come. Amen.

Sometime during my early twenties, I (Jen) started thinking about what we're really saying in the Nicene Creed. It concerned me that most of Jesus' earthly life is left out of the prayer and the language we use for him and for God is androcentric. So I started praying about it and, for a while, I did not proclaim it with the rest of the congregation during Mass. Slowly, I started saying the prayer alongside the rest of my community, speaking a version of the Creed that God put on my heart to say. "We believe in one God, the Creator Almighty, maker of heaven and earth . . . We believe in our brother, Jesus Christ . . . For us and for our salvation . . . he was born of the Virgin Mary and became flesh . . . he ascended into heaven and is seated at the right hand of the Creator . . . With the Creator and the Son, she is worshiped and glorified. She has spoken through the prophets. . . ." Sometimes I used to get nervous and would step just enough away from my cantor microphone to be sure that no one would hear me. I still get nervous at the parish where my brothers and sister and I grew up, as though someone is going to hear me and get offended at my inclusive language. No one seems to notice, though. So I keep reflecting on it and saying the prayer as I believe God calls me to say it. Maybe I'm not so much nervous as I am hopeful that someone will hear me praying and we'll get to have a conversation about what comes before "Amen."

I (Kate) remember the first time I read Joan Chittister's In Search of Belief. *I was on the annual silent retreat with JVC: East. Oh, how I dreaded those three Ignatian days, dreaded the challenge of silence from the first day I learned about it months before. With a resigned heart, I wandered around the retreat center in New Jersey and stumbled onto Chittister's book—she takes the entire Apostles' Creed apart and rewrites it according to what it means to her, intertwining her Benedictine way of life, her Catholicism, and her love of the natural world with her earnest ability to see God in all living things. I swallowed up the book with an energy for the Creed I had become unsure I would ever be able to muster for most things Catholic. At the end of the weekend, we celebrated Mass. As my mouth formed the words of the Nicene profession of faith, I realized I could edit the Nicene Creed just as Chittister did with the Apostles' Creed. I shifted the gendered language, emphasized the role of the Holy Spirit, and imagined a way to live the creedal belief that the church—human—is holy. For the first time in a long time, I felt ownership and participation in what made up my Catholic identity. In one weekend, a Benedictine sister redeemed my Catholicism.*

With that same spirit—a spirit that encourages dialogue, creativity, and renewal—we offer this collection. These women's stories paint a vivid picture of Catholic identity. Amid the diversity of their perspectives, we've watched five salient themes emerge.

For many of these young women, Catholic identity is rooted in growing up Catholic. Something about Catholic rituals and the Catholic way of thinking and expressing faith seeps into our bones and grabs hold of our religious senses. Like previous generations of Catholic women, our identities are indebted to Hoge's so-called "Catholic glue." That glue often sticks because these women attend Mass and participate in parish life. But Catholic glue is also—and equally—bound up in models of faith like Dorothy Day, finding sacraments in daily life, the tenets of Catholic social teaching, dreams of an institutional church that embraces its LGBTQ community and expresses sincerity about being Catholic. This Catholic glue underlies many of these women's Catholic experiences.

The first of the five themes we've watched emerge from these memoirs is that having strong Catholic role models, often women, sustains our Catholicism. Our moms, our academic mentors, saints like Julian of Norwich and Hildegard of Bingen— these women inspire our Catholic identity. And like Kate Barch Heaton and Emily Jendzejec, several women in this collection aspire to emulate Dorothy Day's radical commitment to the poor. Importantly, we share this respect for Catholic role models with previous generations of Catholics who introduced us to *The Lives of the Saints* and urged us to echo Mary's "yes" to God. Learning to follow the examples of other "gutsy Catholics" appears to be quite intergenerational.

Second, for many of these authors, Catholicism teaches us that holiness is not only in churches or in formal prayer gatherings; it is also in working with the poor, exploring nature, meditating in a quiet room. An appreciation of the many sites of holiness pervades our Catholicism and our lives. In our search to connect with the spiritual, we turn toward the tradition, to contemplative practices, to the lives of saints, to Merton and Mary. As it turns out, these experiences bind us to the Catholic community. We learn the stories of the Catholic Worker movement and involve ourselves in efforts like it—in year-long service commitments like Johanna Hatch, Deborah Heimel, and Monica Hammer, and in smaller, everyday ways, like Kate Barch Heaton's humble dinner invitation and Rebecca Lynne Fullan's efforts at sharing her abundance with those she meets on the street.

Appreciating the natural world is an important point of connection to God for our generation. Whether it's lying in the snow making snow angels like Sister Julie or spending time, as Kate Lucas did, on retreat in the mountains, these encounters with nature facilitate a relationship with God, allow us to marvel at "God's grandeur," to borrow from Gerard Manley Hopkins. And there is something Catholic in these experiences—ritual, awe at the divine, a sense of community.

As we read through these memoirs over and over, we eventually were surprised to see a thread of embodied sacramentality emerge from several women's experiences of Catholicism. Helena Fleig and Nelle Carty literally experienced Eucharist at family dinner tables, and Eileen Campbell found her Catholic identity coursing through her veins, enmeshed in her bones. Rebecca Lynne Fullan digested the host at Mass, awed that it becomes a part of her body just like her chicken and carrots. And Kerry Egan's eucharistic understanding of breastfeeding suggests the profundity of Catholic mystery in women's lives. The physicality of this Catholicism is incredible—and it makes us pause in wonder at the depth of Catholic identity. It seems

Dorothy Day's sage wisdom is true, "Women think with their whole bodies" (Day 270–76).

Third, many of us are committed to integrating spiritual practice and social action into our Catholic identities. We encounter God in Haitian orphanages like Meagan Yogi, in women's shelters where Johanna Hatch came to know both service and God, in a welcoming multicultural Mass with Tefi Ma'ake, and at the gates of Fort Benning, Georgia, where women like Jen Owens and thousands of other Catholics prayed with their whole hearts and spirits, with their hands and feet. Our attempts to be faith-filled activists are part of what fills out our Catholic identities—in fact, often keeps us Catholic.

These stories allay Tom Rausch's concern that uncritical and nominally Catholic involvement in service and social justice work threatens to collapse our sense of things religious into ethics. On the contrary, for these women, this interplay between faith and action is part of what makes the Catholic glue stick. This work strengthens our Catholic identity and actually seems to help us persist amid the difficult theological questions regarding race, gender, socioeconomic standing, and sexuality that permeate this collection. Work with and for others, accompanied by careful reflection and the use of the spiritual imagination, enlivens what it means to be Catholic.

Fourth, many women in this collection push against the church's stances on sex and sexuality. Increasingly, sociological data suggests that young Catholics refuse to accept the church's attitude toward homosexuality. Both Hoge and Rausch point out that young adult Catholics have "little patience with what they see as the official church's negative attitude toward sexuality; that is, issuing black-and-white condemnations rather than articulate positive values" (Rausch 7). This sentiment rings true for several of the women in this collection. Eileen Campbell supports Bishop Kevin Dowling's insistence that in Africa, condoms can actually contribute to a culture of life, preventing the transmission of death through HIV/AIDS. Margaret Scanlon is concerned that there isn't stronger emphasis on the condemnation of the

violence of rape or more widespread dialogue on the circumstances surrounding abortion.

For Kate Henley Averett, the church's teachings on sexuality
cause her a double pain of exclusion: living with the knowledge
that she cannot be ordained and that the church would not bless
her wedding to a woman. Rebecca Lynne Fullan also knows this
intimately, frustrated that her "desire for a man can be sacramental, but [her] desire for a woman only disordered." Eileen
Markey worries about what to tell her son when he returns from
CCD with questions about his friend with two moms. Sarah
Gottfried struggles to reconcile the church's attitude toward
her homosexuality with her Catholic identity while, in contrast,
Deborah Heimel found her Catholic JVC community unquestion-
ingly supportive of her sexual orientation.

Rausch also observes that his students "feel that homosexu-
als have the right to express their love physically and do not
see recognizing gay marriages as undermining the institution
of marriage. The refusal to support even domestic partnership
seems nothing more than prejudice to them" (7). Like Rausch's
students, these women challenge the church to support a more
fluid understanding of sexuality that embraces the love that can
develop between partners of the same gender.

Finally, the tension between the church as it is and the church
as it could be is central to several of our Catholic experiences. We
dream of a more widespread commitment to service and justice
work, women priests, and more inclusive rules in the church.
When we started this project, we didn't plan to edit a book on
church reform. But, as it turns out, several of the women who
sent us their memoirs are calling for it.

The Hoge study observed that one of the identifying marks
of post–Vatican II Catholicism is a shift from thinking about Catholicism as a "church of obligation and obedience" to a "church
of choice." This means that, increasingly, young Catholics across
the country are making choices within and about Catholic identity. And for a smaller number of young adult Catholics, the Hoge
study observed, "Catholic identity is derived from a knowledge of

the faith wherein the individual claims the authority to interpret doctrine and autonomy to offer doctrinally grounded reasons in favor of change" (226). These are the women in this collection. Certainly, these women are only a small portion of the wider young adult Catholic population—this is a group of women with access to higher education that takes seriously the theological questions of our twenties and thirties, and many have studied theology in seminary and university. Several authors fit our description of conscientized Catholics: we daily construct our Catholic identities, amid grappling with dismissal of women's ordination and concerns about the church's attitude toward the LGBTQ community. Drawing on our experiences in light of what we know of the tradition, we come to our own conclusions about how to be Catholic women.

We began this project unsure of what we would find, only convinced that we must not be the only young women who want to talk about being Catholic and women and under thirty-six. As we culled through the pages of these stories, we saw a diverse collection emerge—funny stories of growing up with a uniquely Catholic blueprint, compelling accounts of women putting our faith into action, thoughtful reflections about being a woman and Catholic, engaging tales of vocational discernment, insightful memoirs about spiritual identity. We come away inspired. And filled with hope.

In the beginning, *we were two eager young Catholic women,
fumbling our way through div school at Harvard—
new to New England, new to each other.*

On the first day, *we discovered our mutual admiration for
and inspiration in
Paulo Freire, bell hooks, and other radical teachers in a class
called Education for Liberation.
Amid musings on being women with Catholic stories in higher
education,*

*we spent hours chatting, until the streetlamp near the corner
of Eliot and Park
no longer shared its light. We became friends; and it was good.*

On the second day, *we became a group of five young Catholic
women.
Unique among our mostly Protestant pals, we traded anecdotes—
our adventures through Catholic girlhood, our attempts to
practice social justice,
and our love for Dorothy Day and Thomas Merton—
over kidney bean curry in the house on Eliot.
There were Catholic dinners in Harvard Square,
Buddhist meditation in the house on Broadway,
the proclamation of The Vagina Monologues in Andover Chapel,
lots of laughter, and many cups of tea. We built community;
and it was good.*

On the third day, *we traipsed down to Dorchester for a taste
of Spirituality in the Pub. Disappointed, we wondered what
would happen if
we invited women of our generation to craft essays about their
Catholicism.
As we meandered toward the train, we speculated, "What
would they say?
How would they say it?" We talked excitedly; and it was good.*

On the fourth day, *we tested the waters.
We asked anyone who would listen what they thought about
publishing a collection of memoirs by young women about
their experiences in Catholicism and Catholic identity.
Stories likes these, indeed, have yet to be published collectively.
With a resounding thumbs up, we launched in; and it was good.*

On the fifth day, *we praised the wonders of email communication and no-fee blogs. From Andover-Harvard's basement
computer lab, we spread the word in twenty-first-century fashion.
Far and wide, apparently, the message was received.
The inbox bopping steadily, we were off; and it was good.*

On the sixth day, *we revised, edited, and worked with other young Catholic women to hone their pieces. Recognizing the hard work yet to come,*
we were energized by the positive response.
We're beginning to hear one another into speech; and it is good.

On the seventh day, *we do not hope for rest.*
Our vision of this project is to expand the sounds and types of voices that speak for Catholicism. We acknowledge the Catholic imprint that marks our ways of being in the world, and we claim our place as members of a community that carries our shared tradition.
We're continuing the story; and it'll be good.

(www.fromthepewsintheback.com)

Afterword

Growing Pains
*Honoring Thy Mothers
and Challenging Them Too*

Donna Freitas

It is almost eerie to recall a conversation I had almost two years ago with Jessica Coblentz, now a recent college graduate and author of "To Share a Meal with Jesus." I met with her at the request of a colleague—one of her undergraduate professors—and was immediately floored by her stunning intelligence, bright conversation, emotional investment and stake in the Catholic tradition both as a young woman and as a college student. She expressed interest in a career as a theologian, and I wanted to convince her to start now—that she not only shouldn't but didn't need to wait until she received her master's degree or a PhD.

"People don't realize you exist," I told her. "That's why it's important that you write your story, that you do begin doing theology right away. It doesn't matter how young you are; there is an audience for your voice and an authority that comes from the very fact that you *are* young and a woman."

I've had many similar conversations with other Catholics like Jessica, advising them not to let anyone convince them they haven't yet earned the right to speak on matters of faith. We each have a certain amount of authority that grows from a basic commitment to a tradition, but most important for young women like Jessica, we have authority because we are representatives of a new generation—a generation that my own research shows is, for the most part, misunderstood, since more often than not, Catholic youth have been written off by their elders. So many theologians and sociologists of religion have shaken their heads in dismay at the way younger generations of Catholics have navigated and practiced this tradition—or *not* practiced it, rejecting certain teachings or Mass attendance on Sundays—concluding that young Catholics are Catholic only nominally so, and tend to be apathetic at best.

Apathy has never been the right word, however. Anyone who has talked to young Catholics at length knows that most of us *are* passionate about their faith—even if that passion takes the form of anger.

And, having read the memoirs in this book, you, the reader, already know that young Catholic women like these contributors to Jen and Kate's volume are anything *but* apathetic about their faith. Together, these memoirists are a bold statement that sends cracks racing through the widely accepted theory that the young and the Catholic have simply abandoned ship.

Perhaps, as Jen and Kate ponder in their introduction, theologians and Catholics overall have just been looking in the wrong places when they ask, with dismay, "Where do young Catholics go after they graduate from Catholic colleges?"—the same question that led Jen and Kate to launch this project as both a challenge and response, to say: *Look! We are here!*

Even more important, Jen and Kate ask some of *the* most significant questions to consider when thinking about the nature and place of the next generation of Catholics and, most of all, the young women among them: "Why, [Jen and Kate] wanted to know, is Mass attendance *the* trademark of Catholic identity?

Why not include a commitment to social justice or service work?" These same inquiries are integral in my own research and the challenges I've mounted to the widely accepted belief that apathy reigns among younger generations, a conclusion rooted in studies like Dean R. Hoge's *Young Adult Catholics: Religion in the Culture of Choice* and Christian Smith's *Soul Searching.*

The essays in this book not only fly in the face of these scholars' findings but also ask older generations of Catholics—theologians and scholars especially—to widen their scope of *where* one shows one's commitment to Catholicism. The diversity of these memoirs helps us to relocate and reconfigure the many possible ways a person can express her Catholic identity, can *be a young Catholic woman.* If read with open minds, these stories will expand the scope of the tradition and the wellsprings of theology.

So, in consideration of the above, I could not think of a better title for this book—*From the Pews in the Back.* It asks its audience to acknowledge not only that a younger generation, and young women in particular, have been "sitting here"—so to speak—participating in the Catholic tradition all along, right under everyone's noses, but also that young women in particular feel that we've been *hidden*, overlooked, even alienated by older generations so quick to make assumptions about their so-called absence and silence.

On the topic of feminism and this next generation's—my generation's—unique adoption and expression of it in our own identities, practices, work, and stories, I agree with Mary Ann Hinsdale that yes, this volume is useful for "anyone who works with young Catholic women or who just wants to understand where they are coming from," as she writes in the foreword.

But I challenge my fellow colleagues with PhD's, especially my mother generation of Catholic feminist theologians, not only to acknowledge but also to lift up these voices—each one so personal, yearning, eloquent, and significant, and that together signal the diversity and new questions of the next generation of Catholic feminist theologians—as equal authorities with whom to engage in conversation, *regardless of credentials.* I urge my mother feminists to treat these young women as what they truly are: the fulfillment for which scholars like Elizabeth Johnson, Sandra Schneiders, Carol Christ, Ada María Isasi-Díaz, and Lisa Cahill, among others, fought so hard. These are the women who used patriarchy, who played the game and worked their way into an oppressive system to clear space not only for their own voices but also for the young women who came after—that *we* might inherit a legacy where we could play the game *less* and apologize *less* for our gender, our theology, our stories. Or maybe, *maybe* even offer us a legacy where we wouldn't have to apologize *at all* for our different methods, for our leveling the hierarchies inherent to ivory tower, patriarchal theology, so that class, education, status, and other oppressive structures would be dismantled as a result of the groundbreaking work of our mother feminists.

So without apology, I stand by these memoirs as next genera-tion Catholic feminist theology itself, as *scholarship*, the precise kind of theological conversation, the *fulfillment* that feminist theologians have worked so hard to make possible over recent decades. The young women in this volume are as much my peers and the peers of theologians in departments at universities and colleges across the country as they are the peers of all women in the pews.

If you haven't already, then walk right in and have a seat in the back with them. Their young, smart voices and stories await you.

Donna Freitas is assistant professor of religion at Boston University. She is author of Sex and the Soul: Juggling Sexuality, Romance, and Religion on America's College Campuses *and* The Possibilities of Sainthood.